Ideology, Curriculum, and the New Sociology of Education

Ideology, Curriculum, and the New Sociology of Education

Revisiting the Work of Michael Apple

Edited by
Lois Weis, Cameron McCarthy, and Greg Dimitriadis

Routledge
Taylor & Francis Group
New York   London

Routledge is an imprint of the
Taylor & Francis Group, an informa business

Published in 2006 by
Routledge
Taylor & Francis Group
270 Madison Avenue
New York, NY 10016

Published in Great Britain by
Routledge
Taylor & Francis Group
2 Park Square
Milton Park, Abingdon
Oxon OX14 4RN

© 2006 by Taylor & Francis Group, LLC
Routledge is an imprint of Taylor & Francis Group

Printed in the United States of America on acid-free paper
10 9 8 7 6 5 4 3 2 1

International Standard Book Number-10: 0-415-95155-0 (Hardcover) 0-415-95156-9 (Softcover)
International Standard Book Number-13: 978-0-415-95155-5 (Hardcover) 978-0-415-95156-2 (Softcover)
Library of Congress Card Number 2005027550

Library of Congress Cataloging-in-Publication Data

Weis, Lois.
 Ideology, curriculum, and the new sociology of education : revisiting the work of Michael Apple / Lois Weis, Cameron McCarthy, and Greg Dimitriadis.
     p. cm.
 Includes bibliographical references and index.
 ISBN 0-415-95155-0 (hb : alk. paper) -- ISBN 0-415-95156-9 (pb : alk. paper)
 1. Educational sociology--United States. 2. Education--Social aspects--United States. 3. Curriculum evaluation--United States. I. McCarthy, Cameron. II. Dimitriadis, Greg, 1969- III. Title.

LB2802.S36H83 2006
371.2009794'985--dc22   2005027550

Taylor & Francis Group
is the Academic Division of Informa plc.

Visit the Taylor & Francis Web site at
http://www.taylorandfrancis.com

and the Routledge Web site at
http://www.routledge-ny.com

CONTENTS

PREFACE

GEOFF WHITTY

One of the most stimulating periods of my academic career was the time I spent as a visiting professor at the University of Wisconsin–Madison in the fall of 1979, just after the first publication of *Ideology and Curriculum* (1979/2004).

That was a time in which the work of Michael W. Apple was relatively unknown in the United Kingdom, although Michael had visited us during the 1970s and made contact with the likes of Basil Bernstein, Michael Young, Roger Dale, and myself. Michael Young and I had also published one of Michael's papers in our book *Society, State and Schooling* (Young & Whitty, 1977). Partly as a result of this, his work was initially taken up among British sociologists of education rather than in curriculum studies and other fields of educational studies.

Shortly after I returned to the United Kingdom, I was invited to write a review of the first paperback edition of *Ideology and Curriculum* for the *British Journal of Educational Studies* (BJES), house journal of the then Standing Conference on Educational Studies. It was the first review I had ever been asked to write for that journal, which was at the time a very traditional journal of the educational studies establishment. I suspect *Ideology and Curriculum* was a book that puzzled the editors of *BJES* and that they approached me on the grounds that my work was also outside the mainstream and that I might just be able to make sense of this odd book from the United States.

In 2004, of course, many people would see me, as Director of London University's Institute of Education, as the very embodiment of the educational establishment in the United Kingdom—and there is even a sense in which, much as he would hate to admit it, Michael Apple is himself part of the educational establishment in the United States and beyond.

Ironically, back in the 1970s, we both wrote about Raymond Williams' concept of the "selective tradition." Although we largely applied it to the analysis of the school curriculum and school reform, it could also have been applied to the curriculum of educational studies itself. At that time, our own work was not part of the dominant culture of that field. It was still relatively marginalized in our own contexts. Indeed, that sense of being outsiders was part of the common bond that drew Michael and me together. We published for obscure leftist publishing houses and in radical journals. I remember Michael being allocated small rooms at conferences like the American Educational Research Association (AERA) with such great attendance that people had to listen from the corridor.

Now all that has changed and our work has been brought into the mainstream. Some people might even take the view that it has become part of the selective tradition of contemporary educational studies through a process of "incorporation," another key concept in Raymond Williams' work used extensively by Michael in *Ideology and Curriculum*. To Williams, this involved meanings being reinterpreted or being put into forms that supported or at least did not contradict other elements within the effective dominant culture. I shall return to this issue later.

When I first reviewed *Ideology and Curriculum*, I located it, oversimplistically, in a growing "critical" tradition in U.S. curriculum studies, linking it to the work of other "critical" scholars, as different as Jean Anyon and Henry Giroux, to a degree that, at least with hindsight, was only partially justified. I also linked it, with rather more justification, to the sort of neo-Marxist social and cultural theory that had informed the so-called "new sociology of education" in the United Kingdom, starting with Michael Young's *Knowledge and Control* (Young, 1971) and the subsequent work that Michael Young and I did together (Whitty & Young, 1976; Young & Whitty, 1977).

In my review, I suggested, as I did in extensive discussions at Madison in that fall of 1979, that *Ideology and Curriculum* did not adequately address some real difficulties in Michael's project. For example, linking the political economy of Bowles and Gintis with the cultural analysis of Bourdieu was not as straightforward as Michael suggested. I also suggested that his reading of Marxism was somewhat functionalist, producing a view of educational reality that, in stressing the ubiquity of domination, sometimes obscured the existence of contradiction and conflict. It was what I called a "complex correspondence" thesis.

Resistance and contestation were too little in evidence in the book, though I was already able to point to their growing importance in the new work that he had been developing during my time at Madison. As I had said during our long conversations, he needed to say rather more about potential sites of contestation and the nature of counter hegemonic practice.

Michael's subsequent books have become increasingly theoretically and politically sophisticated, although I know that some postmodernists, for example, would argue that he has annexed—or incorporated—their ideas in ways "that support or at least do not contradict other elements" in his original approach. Similarly, the increasing emphasis on race and gender issues has not always sat easily with the class analysis of the earlier work, although Michael has now made a serious attempt to confront the difficulties entailed.

Like me, Michael has also been attacked by neo-Leninists for misunderstanding Lenin and Gramsci and thereby having an inadequate approach to political strategy. Ramin Farahmandpur (2004), Michael's latest Leninist critic, raises some important issues of strategy, just as David Reynolds—now ironically an education advisor to New Labour in Britain—did in relation to my own work in the 1980s (Reynolds & Sullivan, 1980). Michael and I have discussed at length and written about some of these issues, which go well beyond the remit of *Ideology and Curriculum*, in a coauthored piece—indeed, our only co-authored piece—on "structuring the post-modern in educational policy" (Apple & Whitty, 1999, p. 67). Our 25-year interchange on these matters continues to this day.

An area on which I suspect Michael and I differ somewhat is on the role of empirical research in critical scholarship. Back in 1979, as I pointed out in the review, most neo-Marxist accounts of schooling in Britain were unduly abstract. Classroom research was unfortunately left to the symbolic interactionists and ethnomethodologists. I therefore said approvingly that Michael's book made an attempt to illustrate the theory with empirical data drawn from, for example, an ethnography of a kindergarten classroom, content analyses of science and social studies curricula, and historical studies of curriculum reform. Much of this was due, as Michael generously acknowledged in the preface to the third edition, to the contribution made to *Ideology and Curriculum* by Nancy King and Barry Franklin.

Reading my review again now, I think the situation has changed somewhat. Critical work in the United Kingdom has become more empirically grounded, for example, through the work of my colleague Stephen Ball and his various collaborators. Meanwhile, the U.S work is not exactly more abstract, but arguably rather less empirically grounded. When I wrote for the back cover of the new edition of *Ideology and Curriculum*, that it "remains one of the most compelling and insightful accounts of how ideology actually works in and through the overt and hidden curriculum of schooling and school reform," I meant it as a compliment. Yet I can see that it might also be taken as reference to the relative lack of similarly compelling empirically grounded work in the United States since then. This may, in turn, say something about the relative priorities of educational research in our two countries, an indication that critical work in the United States has not been fully incorporated, at least in funding terms.

That perhaps takes us back to the extent to which Michael's own work has, or has not, been incorporated into the mainstream. There is clearly a sense in which it has. He has been honored by AERA. *Ideology and Curriculum* is identified by its publishers as a "classic" text, and it is widely cited in literature miles away, both literally and metaphorically, from the particular political context that generated it. For the back of the book, I also wrote that the discussion of the politics of the school curriculum is now much more common than it was 25 years ago. That is in no small part due to the impact of the book and of Michael's subsequent ones. I guess there are some on the Right who might claim that, far from having been incorporated, he has helped to "colonize" educational studies for the Left.

For a variety of reasons, the broader political context has, of course, changed significantly since 1979. Although, in some contexts, hegemony is maintained via the forms of supposed technical neutrality discussed in chapter 6 of *Ideology and Curriculum*, there are other contexts where the Right itself has been increasingly keen to politicize schooling. Within those wider struggles, Michael himself clearly remains profoundly *un*incorporated into contemporary dominant views of education. But, while many of his critics have been content to limit their struggles to the academy, Michael has taken the issues into a much broader arena and thereby entered onto the ground of his opponents. He himself points out in the third edition of *Ideology and Curriculum* that authors know they have made an impact when their opponents feel compelled to respond. He therefore thanks conservative writers at the Fordham Foundation and at the *Wall Street Journal* for their vitriolic comments on the new material included in this edition. That reaction is, in part, an eloquent answer to my concerns in that review of 25 years ago that the first edition told us too little about how to move beyond academic critique.

REFERENCES

Apple, M. (1979/2004). *Ideology and curriculum* (3rd ed.). New York: Routledge.

Apple, M., & Whitty, G. (1999). Structuring the postmodern in education policy. In D. Hill, P. McLaren, M. Cole, & G. Rikowski (Eds.), *Postmodernism in educational theory* (pp. 67-87). London: Tufnell Press.

Farahmandpur, R. (2004). Essay review: A Marxist critique of Michael Apple's neo-Marxist approach to educational reform. *Journal for Critical Education Policy Studies, 2*(1). Retrieved 11/29/05 from http://www.jceps.com/?pageID=article&articleID=24.

Reynolds, D., & Sullivan, M. (1980). Towards a new socialist sociology of education. In L. Barton, R. Meighan, & S. Walker (Eds.), *Schooling, ideology and the curriculum* (pp. 169-195). Lewes: Falmer Press.

Whitty, G., & Young, M. (Eds.). (1976). *Explorations in the politics of school knowledge.* Driffield: Nafferton Books.

Young, M. (Ed.). (1971). *Knowledge and control.* London: Collier-Macmillan.

Young, M., & Whitty, G. (Eds.). (1977). *Society, state and schooling.* Lewes: Falmer Press.

INTRODUCTION

Ideology, Curriculum, and the New Sociology of Education

GREG DIMITRIADIS, LOIS WEIS, AND CAMERON MCCARTHY

For more than three decades now, Michael Apple has sought to uncover and articulate the connections among knowledge, teaching, and power in education. Beginning with *Ideology and Curriculum* (1979), Apple moved to understand the relationships between and among the economy, political, and cultural power in society on the one hand, "and the ways in which education is thought about, organized, and evaluated" on the other (1979/2004, p. vii). Tracking dynamics that linked the organization of school knowledge to the constitutive production of social difference schematically advanced by Basil Bernstein and the new sociology of education scholars in Britain, he was the first to lay out this broad theoretical and intellectual project in the United States. Michael Apple's "puzzle" invited researchers to delve into the many aspects of the articulated problem. What stands out in Apple's scholarship is not only his own careful and serious attention to linkages between education and power (his commitment to integrating methodologically theory, practice, and policy), but the work of scores of students, broadly construed, who pursued one or more aspects of this intellectual project.

A corpus of critical knowledge both in and outside the United States has evolved over the past 30 years, and this corpus can be traced in large part to Apple's initial and continuing formulation of the problem. Such work stands as great testimony to Michael Apple, not in the sense that individuals clone him, but that a wide array of scholars have moved, in their own way, to analyze and theorize inequity, power, privilege, and deprivation within and beneath structural circumstance. Apple's framework both encouraged and demanded continuing analyses of public and private institutions, groups and lives, across race, ethnicity, social class, gender, and sexual orientation as lodged in relation to key social and economic structures.

Michael Apple's influence, then, has certainly been through his own ongoing work, but just as importantly, in the work spawned in response to the template that he initially laid out. Rather than closing down discussion, his evolving framework is generative and ventilated. And, it invites intense and extensive research, conversation, and social activism with regard to the economy, culture, schools, politics, representations, and political movements. To Michael's enduring credit, it is not so tightly woven that new evidence cannot enter; on the contrary, new evidence enters all the time, as the world—every aspect of it—changes around us.

THE "NEW" SOCIOLOGY OF EDUCATION

In this respect, Apple's own intellectual journey is instructive. Along with a handful of others (most notably, Jean Anyon), Apple was one of the first scholars in the United States to import the neo-Marxist theories of education that rose to prominence in England in the early 1970s. Often associated with "the new sociology of education," scholars like Geoff Whitty, Basil Bernstein, Pierre Bourdieu in France, Michael Young, and others were interested in how the stratification of school knowledge worked to disenfranchise working-class youth.

The move was profound. As Whitty (1985) makes clear, mainstream sociologists of the time often assumed the most important question was that of "access" to educative institutions—what blocked it or what might encourage it. The underlying assumption here was that additional schooling would ameliorate the seeming handicaps of a working-class upbringing. When more critical approaches to schooling did emerge, they too did not focus on the particularities associated with classroom knowledge or activity. Often quantitative in nature, schools in such studies were treated as one part of large-scale macrolevel forces and pressures that served to sort youth by social class. Traditionally, then, both mainstream and critical sociologists tended to treat schools as "black boxes" (or "empty boxes" as Apple would note correcting for the kind of loose, racial overtones of this term).

In sharp distinction, the so-called new sociology of education explored the ways in which the organization of school curriculum and knowledge itself (the "official" curriculum) worked to sort students. This work focused both on the content and the form of knowledge. By focusing on school curriculum and knowledge, these scholars offered a way to explain how social reproduction was enacted at the everyday level of school practice. In opening up such a discussion, they also offered teachers and others a space for intervention in these processes. The "new sociologists of education" specified and concretized processes of social reproduction that seemed so large and unwieldy as to be completely beyond the control of individual invested actors.

This work contested then (and now) largely prevalent notions that knowledge is "above" politics, that it is, quite simply, disinterested. Beginning with the idea that knowledge itself is intensely political, this work moved in several directions at once. Perhaps the first, most influential summing up of the movement was Michael Young's collection *Knowledge and Control: New Directions in the Sociology of Education* (1971), which contained contributions from Pierre Bourdieu, Basil Bernstein, and Nell Keddie, among others. Here, Young discusses the ways particular kinds of knowledge are validated in the academy—knowledge that is "pure," "general," and "academic." In contrast, knowledge that is "applied," "specific," and "vocational" is marginalized. This distinction is an arbitrary one, though it serves to keep particular elite groups in control of the official school curriculum. Such distinctions are not "natural"; they are, as Young, Apple, and others often argue, arbitrary and a function of power.

No one was clearer as to the arbitrary nature of school life than Pierre Bourdieu and his coauthor Jean-Claude Passeron. In their classic *Reproduction in Education, Society, and Culture* (1977), the authors discuss school knowledge and authority as effecting a kind of "symbolic violence" on marginalized youth. For Bourdieu and Passeron, this pedagogic authority allows for "the imposition and inculcation of a cultural arbitrary by an arbitrary mode of imposition and inculcation (education)" (p. 6). This arbitrary exercise of power, according to the authors, allowed and simultaneously encouraged the reproduction of the given social, cultural, and economic order—a "reproduction of the power relations which put that dominant power into the dominant position" (p. 10).

These authors—and there are others—highlighted the intensely political nature of the knowledge legitimization processes, both in the academy and at the secondary school level. Knowledge is not above or outside of the social realm here. It is a site of intense struggle and contestation. In addition to describing this exercise of power, such work also had transformative impulses. These authors were interested in forging more equitable school systems, particularly for working-class youth. (Coming out of the largely British context, social class was advanced as the most important and relevant node of oppression here.) Key here was the elaborate language of pedagogy and codes developed by sociologist Basil Bernstein. For Bernstein, the degree of "boundary maintenance" between different kinds of knowledge was a function of power. Bernstein was interested in how teachers and students were able to "frame" curricular knowledge in pedagogical settings, particularly in whether students and teachers could freely rearticulate these boundaries. Throughout his career, Bernstein was interested in finding ways "to prevent the wastage of working-class educational potential" (quoted in Sadovnik, 2001, p. 8). For Bernstein and other sociologists of knowledge, this meant asking whether working-class students could introduce their own experiences and knowledge into school life and curricula.

This work, in sum, looked at the complex interrelationship between the stratification of knowledge and social stratification. New sociology of education proponents methodologically participated in the linguistic turn in the social sciences, as Claude Levi-Strauss and Roland Barthes had done in structural anthropology and in literary theory and popular culture analysis respectively, turning attention, then, to the underlying grammar of schooling and school knowledge. These scholars redirected the focus of the evaluation of schooling, here, from treating schools as monolithic and abstract arms of material reproduction to emergent spaces of possibility where change could happen through transformation of the dominant commonsense that informed the organization of school knowledge. Above all else, this work marked "knowledge" itself as a site of power—a site where it could both be exercised and interrupted.

MICHAEL APPLE AND THE INTERROGATION OF "NEUTRALITY" IN SCHOOL LIFE

Michael Apple was one of the first scholars to bring a similar neo-Marxist perspective to issues of the curriculum in the United States. Beginning with the publication of the magisterial *Ideology and Curriculum* (1979), Apple's successive volumes have all had enormous and wide-ranging impact. This includes, especially, the authored texts *Education and Power* (1982), *Official Knowledge: Democratic Education in a Conservative Age* (1993), *Cultural Power and Education* (1996), *Educating the "Right" Way: Markets, Standards, God, and Inequality*

(2001), and *The State and the Politics of Knowledge* (2004). Yet it was his first volume, *Ideology and Curriculum*, that remains perhaps his defining text. Here, he challenges scholars to focus research on three specific areas of school life.

To begin with, he offers powerful strategies for understanding the ways in which curricular knowledge (both the form and content of what Apple and Weis later call the commodified culture in school) is part of a "selective tradition" that serves ideologically to buttress and naturalize structurally based social and economic inequalities. Apple's nuanced investigation of what he came to call "official knowledge" is one of his most enduring and well-known contributions to the field of education. As Apple argues in this early volume, "the language of learning tends to be apolitical and ahistorical, thus hiding the complex nexus of political and economic power and resources that lies behind a considerable amount of curriculum organization and selection" (1979, p. 28). He continues, noting that "schools do not merely 'process' people, [they also] 'process' knowledge. They enhance and give legitimacy to particular types of cultural resources, which are related to unequal economic forms" (p. 34). Here, we see Apple lay out a set of issues he would become perhaps best known for in decades to come. In particular, Apple would again and again point out how teaching particular forms of "official knowledge"—particularly as ensconced in textbooks—works in the interests of powerful groups.

Second, Apple highlights the ways in which the day-to-day regularities of schools—what he and others refer to as the "hidden curriculum"—contribute to the reproduction of ideologies that support existing structurally based inequalities. This impression of regularity and neutrality is sustained and maintained by notions that schools are "above politics," that they remain outside the purview of individual, invested actors, and groups. That these everyday practices tend to be invisible or unmarked only underscores their power to reinforce a structural–functional view of schools. He writes, "The perspective found in schools leans heavily upon how all elements of a society, from the postal worker to the fire fighter in first grade to the partial institutions in civics courses in high school, are linked to each other in a functional relationship, each contributing to the ongoing maintenance of society." This kind of stasis demands that schools abolish all social and political conflict. He continues, "Internal dissention and conflict are viewed as inherently antithetical to the functioning of the social order. Consensus is once more a pronounced feature" (1979, p. 87). In all its various manifestations and permutations, schools are part of a larger social organism that always works toward a broad-based consensus that smoothes over points of conflict. The effect is to allow particular ideologies serving the interests of particular social groups to circulate in unmarked ways.

Third, Apple underscores the ways in which teachers and university researchers, as creators and bearers of intellectual property, both create and employ seemingly "neutral" categories, labels, and knowledge about schools and students (e.g., "slow learners" or "underachievers") so as to maintain the existing distribution of power and wealth in the broader society. Apple writes of the "linguistic tools we employ to talk about 'students' in schools," noting, "much of our language, while seemingly neutral, is not neutral in its impact nor is it unbiased in regard to existing institutions of schooling." Indeed, "much of educational research serves and justifies already existing technical, cultural, and economic control systems that accept the distribution of power in American society as given" (1979, p. 122). This point is particularly important. As above, the seeming neutrality of such labels offers the veneer of scientific validity. In advocating for a critical approach to education, Apple highlights and contests the ways particular issues get "framed" as problems. In so doing, he opens a space to rethink and reconceptualize the very terrain upon which "normalcy" is constructed.

In sum, Apple has worked steadily throughout his career to challenge the idea that schools are neutral institutions. In particular, he has highlighted how the appearance of neutrality often, paradoxically, works to reproduce extant social, cultural, and economic arrangements. In summing up the contours of this initial project, Apple writes:

> The study of the interconnections between ideology and curriculum and between ideology and educational argumentation has important implications for the curriculum field and for educational theory and policy in general. For, as I shall argue throughout this volume, we need to examine critically not just "how a student acquires more knowledge" (the dominant question in our efficiency minded field), but "why and how particular aspects of the collective culture are presented in school as objective, factual knowledge." How concretely may official knowledge represent ideological configuration of the dominant interests in a society? How do schools legitimate these limited and partial standards of knowledge as unquestioned truths? (1979, p. 14)

NEW DIRECTIONS

The social and cultural context here has been something of a "moving target." We thus add to this list two additional areas for research that emerged directly in relation to the broad intellectual project initially laid out by Apple. First, we highlight the ways in which teachers and students contest taken-for-granted meanings "naturally" distributed through schools, thus promoting emancipatory educational practices both inside and outside of formal educational institutions. Although this has meant support for more traditional kinds of political activity (e.g., the support for teacher's unions in the United States and Korea), it has also included an ethic of accessibility in Michael Apple's writing. This ethic is evidenced especially in popular pedagogical books such as *Democratic Schools* (1995) (coedited with Jim Beane). Published by the Association of Supervision and Curriculum Development (ASCD), this book was an effort to disseminate more broadly Apple's ideas to those "on the ground" and has reportedly sold over 100,000 copies. Although Apple has drawn largely on U.S. examples here, he has increasingly worked with more international traditions and movements—most notably, the rise of Citizen Schools in Porto Alegre, Brazil.

Second, and finally, we underscore the ways in which the economy as well as struggles linked to racial formation, social class formation, and gender formation are investigated and theorized both as projects in and of themselves, as well as in relation to schools. Although Apple urges scholars to explore the links between education and power, such forms of power as linked to broader economic, ideological, and social structures have changed markedly over time, space, and place. In particular, Apple's work evidences an ongoing effort to hold on to the "gritty materialities" of economic inequality, while acknowledging the constitutive power of race and gender. Apple's recent attention to what he calls "conservative modernization" and its coarticulation and mobilization of four distinct groups and their agendas (i.e., neoliberals, neoconservatives, authoritarian populists, and the new managerial middle class) is perhaps most instructive in this regard. We see here an effort to locate this "moment in time" in all its complexity—the changing flow of economic resources as well as the mobilization of new minority and majority identities.

Chapters in this volume pick up and develop these particular pieces, as they contribute to his larger project. In large measure, the power of the "puzzle" laid out by Apple lies in its inherent flexibility. Although Apple's work is largely concerned with questions of knowledge systems and the relationship between symbolic and economic systems, both these symbolic and economic systems have radically changed over the past 25 years.

We highlight two such changes. First, recent large-scale developments are wholly transforming social and cultural life outside and inside schools around the world. These developments have been brought about by globalization and new electronic media, changing conceptions of self and "other," and new explanatory discourses. Key here is the broad set of processes that has come to be known as "globalization," or the intensified and accelerated movement of people, images, ideas, technologies, and economic and cultural capital across national boundaries. Driven forward by the engines of modern capital reorganization and the resulting changed interests, needs, and desires of ordinary people everywhere, globalization is sweeping all corners of the contemporary world. These processes are rapidly shrinking the distance between hitherto far-flung parts of the world, deepening the implication of the local in the global and the global in the local. Although in the past century popular media, such as television, film, newspapers, radio, and popular music, had already expanded the range of information, images, and identities available to people, the power of globalization, electronic mediation, and computerization has exploded the pace of this process.

Second, the economic landscape has inextricably shifted over the past two decades. By way of example, what was referred to as deindustrialization by American economists in the 1980s is now understood to be a fundamental shift in the global economy, one that represents a radical break with past practice. As Robert Reich (1991), clearly one of America's most brilliant and original labor economists, describes it:

> [A]ll Americans used to be in roughly the same economic boat. Most rose or fell together as the corporations in which they were employed, the industries comprising such corporations and the national economy as a whole became more productive—or languished. But national borders no longer define our economic fates. We are now in different boats, one sinking rapidly, one sinking more slowly, the third rising steadily. (p. 208)

As Reich describes it, that boat holding routine production workers is sinking most rapidly, as the old corporate core is being replaced by "global webs that earn their largest profits from clever problem-solving—identifying and brokering. As the cost of transporting things and of communicating information about them continues to drop, profit margins on high-volume, standardized production are thinning because there are few barriers to entry. Modern factories and state-of-the-art machinery can be installed almost anywhere on the globe" (p. 209).

Although Reich talks specifically about the U.S. economy, writers in Britain and elsewhere comment similarly, although the particular ways in which the class structure is both being realigned and simultaneously is realigning itself undoubtedly differ by context. Walkerdine, Lucey, and Melody (2001), for instance, argue:

> We are confronted with huge changes in the global labour market, changes that have caused the British economy to become dominated by the service sector, the technology and communications industries, and a huge and powerful financial sector. ... Many of the new manufacturing industries are not even British owned and products are assembled in different places, with capital, production processes, and workers now being much more mobile. (p. 1)

It is worth pointing out here that the worldwide shift in the economy affects not only first-wave industrialized nations such as the United States, Britain, Canada, Australia, Germany, and France. Realignment in the global economy has profound implications for nations, such as Singapore, China, Thailand, Mexico, India, among others, that are now sites of either finance or product assembly processes, spurring widespread change in schooling, identity formation, and cultural production more generally.

In many respects, Apple's earliest work was written against a backdrop where the links between schools, the economy, and identity were more certain than they are today. Yet, given its dynamism, his project has never been more valuable for researchers, critics, and activists attempting to understand and simultaneously contest this new terrain. In many respects, Michael Apple's project was never more valuable.

ORGANIZATION OF THIS BOOK

Chapters in this volume reflect and simultaneously push a broad range of ways in which Apple's legacy has registered across the field of education. Section One, "Revisiting the New Sociology of Education," draws together work that most explicitly asks "what happened" to the project laid out by Apple in the late 1970s.

Madeleine Arnot opens this section, stressing the continuing and abiding importance of the project laid out by Apple and others in the 1970s. She does so in two distinct ways. First, Arnot underscores the importance of Apple's early radical Marxist critiques of liberalism. This gesture was critically important for reintroducing a Marxist tradition of work on schools particularly in the U.S. context. Second, Arnot discusses the legacy of this work for the study of gender and schooling. Although Apple helped to introduce an important distinction between the study of the "formal" and "hidden" curricula, Arnot sees the latter having more abiding influences for feminism. More specifically, Arnot argues that Apple's notion of the "hidden curriculum" encouraged feminists to look beyond visible "texts" toward the invisible power of gender reproduction. Arnot reads these concerns through contemporary work on gender and poststructuralism while arguing for a return to the specificities of work on classroom life.

In chapter 2, Jean Anyon looks back on a series of classic studies she conducted around the time Apple's first volumes appeared. Tracing the ways in which knowledge is distributed to students differentially positioned in the class structure, Anyon argued in these earlier studies that working-class youth were being prepared for arbitrary and demeaning work, while students at what she calls the "executive elite" school were learning to make rules and to control the lives and labor of others. In this chapter, Anyon situates her earlier work within and against the trajectory of work in the "sociology of school knowledge," while simultaneously asking how the social, cultural, and material context has changed over the past twenty-five years. Echoing points about the economy raised in our introduction, Anyon sees the bifurcation of social class lines becoming increasingly pronounced.

Finally, Carlos Torres in this section revisits the contours of Apple's career—specifically his work on ideology, curriculum, and social reproduction. He posits several provocative claims with respect to the landscape now facing critical educators. First, he argues that schools are becoming increasingly heated sites of social contestation, particularly around new legislative pressures such as those generated by No Child Left Behind legislation. Second, he posits that logics of administrative and mechanical control have become increasingly pronounced since the 1970s, thus necessitating new forms of intellectual and political work "on the ground." Third, Torres discusses the ways in which mass mediated images have profoundly replaced the role and importance of school knowledge. Finally, he underscores the massive and often paradoxical social, cultural, and material effects of globalization. Like many authors in this volume, Torres argues that Apple's work provides critical insights for understanding and acting on these pressures.

Chapters in Section Two, "Contemporary Theoretical Challenges," focus more closely on Apple's work in relation to concerns expressed

evolution of school cur. + the concept of gender theory enables a critical analysis of knowledge
that resulted through edu. inst
in forms of poststructuralism and postmodernism, including the work of Michel Foucault. Yoshiko Nozaki's chapter opens the section by asking important questions around power and the curriculum. Nozaki interrogates the notion of ideology, calling it at once enabling and constraining, while looking toward the complexities of poststructural work. In particular, Nozaki explores the work of French philosopher Michel Foucault and his treatment of knowledge and power, as well as the standpoint theory of R. W. Connell. For Nozaki, it is critical to recoup some of the conceptual and political clarity of ideology, while remaining skeptical about all truth claims. She offers the useful metaphor of "riding tensions critically" for developing and implementing curricular change.

resistance more of a focus within current understandings of curriculum theory. Ch 5 looks at the ways
Dennis Carlson's chapter looks at the ways in which the administrative logics discussed by Apple in *Ideology and Curriculum* have become increasingly pronounced and ever more pressing. According to Carlson, No Child Left Behind has increased the general deskilling of teachers with its managerial discourse reaching something of a crescendo. Contesting an easy language of "progress," Carlson looks (as does Nozaki) toward both the limits and possibilities of conceptual frameworks that stress "ideology" and the relative certainties and clarities implied. Moving from Apple through the work of Guattari, Carlson argues for what he calls a "poststructural Marxism"—an approach that allows us to map disparate and dispersed connections between economic forces and other sets of power relations. *"war of underachievement"*

Closing this section, Allan Luke's chapter explores the deskilling of teachers, revisiting some of Apple's important work on the topic. For Luke, the increasing pressures toward standardized curricular and high-stakes testing have created what he calls the construction of teacher as "commodity fetishist." The increasing stress on the administrative and technical aspects of teaching as "craft" or "profession" does not mesh well with the new economic and policy realities of our moment. Rather, Luke argues for a more cosmopolitan notion of what it means to be a teacher. This means "deterritorializing" teachers, enabling them to move between the local and the global so as to engage with complex flows of knowledge, technologies, populations, and ideologies.

Chapters in Section Three, "On Spaces of Possibility," pick up on the political possibilities—both local and global—inherent in Apple's work. Michelle Fine opens this section by exploring recent youth-run research projects on race and schooling. Drawing on Apple's analysis of Porto Alegre "Citizen Schools" and his quest for what he calls "thick democracy"—true decision-making control of workers over matters including politics, economics, gender relations, and so forth—Fine highlights the ways in which youth creative activities and critical agency can work to explore "cracks" in edifices that often seem insurmountable. These youth bear witness, tell counterstories, and develop research that fundamentally challenge dominant voices, thereby serving as a fitting testament to Apple's legacy around possibilities for social action and change.

Andrew Gitlin's chapter argues for what he calls "educational poetics." Against the backdrop of Apple's work on knowledge, politics, and change, Gitlin highlights the complex production of "commonsense" and the "oughts," that often emerge from such commonsense—notions of what is possible and impossible for educators. In developing his approach to poetics, Gitlin looks to the "relative autonomy" of critical agendas, to the kind of imagination and creativity necessary to contest traditional approaches to knowledge production. The goal here is to "(re)imagine the everyday world" in ways that have important political potential.

In closing the section, Luís Armando Gandin explores Michael Apple's work from within the Brazilian context. Reconstructing the social, political, and intellectual landscape of Brazil from the 1970s through today, Gandin highlights the specific persona and intellectual connections Apple has forged with Brazilian progressive educators and students. He discusses the ways in which Michael Apple lent both his name and personal support to movements like that in Porto Alegre for "Citizen Schools" and its development of a critical curriculum. For Gandin, Apple provides a model for the development of sophisticated theory connected to ongoing political investment and action.

CONCLUSION

As the contributors to this volume all maintain, the fundamental shaping importance and originality of contribution of Michael Apple's critical scholarship to the field of education cannot be denied. Beginning with his path-breaking research collected and published in the germinal volume *Ideology and Curriculum*, Apple redirected critical attention to the operation of cultural and ideological mechanisms within the interior order of schooling and curriculum organization and out again to the contested and conflicted world deeply stratified and striated by the dynamic relations and structuring principles of race, class, and gender. The role that education played in modern life was not, as mainstreamers had maintained, an ennobling one, bringing enlightenment and opportunity to more and more members of the downtrodden classes in society. The project of educational expansion in the post–World War II years in fact generated inequality in both its official order, as well as the informal world of schooling in which differential social relations are produced and contested. Methodologically, Michael Apple approached these complex issues in an original manner and with a distinctive voice, offering a sophisticated blend of Marxist philosophy, phenomenology political economy, and cultural and linguistic analysis to better surmise the hidden relations in the political, economic, and cultural fields of schooling. What follows from the contributors to this volume is both a tribute to Michael Apple's yeoman intellectual service to the vitalization and vivification of critical scholarship in the educational field, as well as an unceasing debate with and an extension of the pivotal terms and research objects that define the corpus of Apple's scholarship.

REFERENCES

Apple, M. (1979/2004). *Ideology and curriculum* (3rd ed.). New York: Routledge.

Apple, M. (1982). *Education and power.* New York: Routledge.

Apple, M. (1993). *Official knowledge: Democratic education in a conservative age.* New York: Routledge.

Apple, M. (1996). *Cultural power and education.* New York: Routledge.

Apple, M. (2001). *Educating the "right" way: Markets, standards, God, and inequality.* New York: Routledge.

Apple, M. (2004). *The state and the politics of knowledge.* New York: Routledge.

Apple, M., & Beane, J. (Eds.). (1995). *Democratic schools.* Alexandria, VA: Association for Supervision and Curriculum Development.

Bourdieu, P., & Passeron, J. (1977). *Reproduction in education, society, and culture.* Thousand Oaks, CA: Sage.

Reich, R. (1991). *The work of nations: Preparing ourselves for 21st century capitalism.* New York: Alfred A. Knopf.

Sadovnik, A. (2001). Basil Bernstein (1924–2000). *Prospects: The Quarterly Review of Comparative Education, 31*(4), 687–303.

Walkerdine, V., Lucey, H., & Melody, J. (2001). *Growing up girl: Psychosocial explorations of gender and class.* New York: New York University Press.

Whitty, G. (1985). *Sociology and school knowledge.* London: Methuen.

Young, M. (1971). *Knowledge and control: New directions in the sociology of education.* London: Macmillan.

I

Revisiting the New Sociology of Education

1

RETRIEVING THE IDEOLOGICAL PAST

Critical Sociology, Gender Theory, and the School Curriculum

MADELEINE ARNOT

[handwritten: compare to Best Academy — identity is constructed within an edu. context.]

It is always salutary to be reminded of the past. Retrieving the past *[handwritten: curriculum that understands the progressive identities of females.]* involves engaging critically with the present project. Although this can be positive in the sense of seeing how far we have come, it *[handwritten: individuals not others']* can also be a moment where we see either where we lost our way or where we might even have gone wrong. Revisiting *Ideology and Curriculum* (Apple, 2004) is one such moment. The task asks us to *[handwritten: argument is fundamental in understanding +]* reinterpret the past through the lens of the present and vice versa. In this case, it begs the question, what happened to sociology of the curriculum? *[handwritten: early analysis reveal how gender diff are normalized, girls as other. particular demains of knowledge can be found to construct girls as the other and silence their voices. Thus, Arnot's]*

Sociology of the curriculum as a form of critical theory was a project of the 1970s that engaged teachers and teacher educators in a critical analysis of the structuring of knowledge in ways that were sure to disrupt their commonsense understandings not just of the curriculum in which they were engaged in teaching but also the rationale behind their practice. As such, sociology of education could be said to be a form of political consciousness, as Freire (1972) would have it, a form of conscientization of a generation of teachers. Further, it sought to fundamentally overturn conventional government thinking about the role of knowledge in alleviating social inequalities in education. Post–

World War II curriculists (or curriculum planners) invested considerable energy into the reform of the knowledge diet offered to children, at times making it more relevant to pupils' everyday lives, at other times, imposing behavioral objectives and assessments in ways that pinned down the processes of knowledge transmission. In the 1970s, technicist models of change that viewed "curriculum as fact" offered the possibility of mechanically shifting the distribution of education to a wider group of pupils. At the same time progressive reformers were aiming to make the curriculum more child-centered. The 1970s was a decade of curriculum when reformers inside and outside the school system attempted to reveal what really went on in what was known as "its secret garden."

Critical sociologists joined this political fray by offering a range of deeper critiques of curricular knowledge and its forms of transmission/acquisition in school classrooms. Central to this debate was the tension between social phenomenology and neo-Marxist sociological theory, the former offering a view of the micro-negotiations of meanings and the construction of knowledge through practice, the latter exploring the macro-contextualization of such constructions and the political constraints on such possibilities of meaning making. In this political conflagration, sociologists of education drew into their fold the various theoretical and metatheoretical discourses developed particularly in France, Germany, the United Kingdom, and the United States. It was a time when the writings of Habermas, Merleau Ponty, and Mead were contrasted with those of Marx, Althusser, Gramsci, and Freire, just to name a few.

The extraordinary aspect of this decade of curriculum research, which lingered into the early 1980s, was the fact that teachers provided one of the key audiences and rationale for critical theorizing. In the United Kingdom this focus made particular sense since, in the period up until 1988, responsibility for the school curriculum and its teaching had been devolved to the teaching profession, and teachers who were represented as experts in curriculum delivery to the diverse needs of local school communities. In the United Kingdom teacher unionism was strong and vocal and a number of government agencies worked with the profession to design new curriculum initiatives in the name of egalitarian redistributive principles. At the same time, the examination system remained in control of the forms of knowledge that were transmitted and assessed. They promoted the sanctity of subject knowledge boundaries and "sacred" forms of high-status knowledge (Bernstein, 1990). Social control therefore was maintained by a heady mixture of hierarchically stratified knowledge, high-status knowledge for the elite, and new experiments in integrated knowledge forms for the working class (Bernstein, 1977). Thus while teachers might have appreciated the freedoms associated with discretion in terms of choice of syllabus and pedagogic mode, their agency was nevertheless located within a deeply undemocratic modernist educational project.

In the spaces created by social democratic consensus around education—that education was a good thing and that teachers needed to find new ways of helping working-class pupils engage with success in the educational system—sociologists found both their voice and their audience. The publication of seminal texts, such as Young's (1971) *Knowledge and Control*, Bernstein's (1977) *Class, Codes and Control: Towards a Theory of Educational Transmissions*, and Williams's (1965) *The Long Revolution*, fired the imagination of a generation of sociologists, such as Michael Apple (as well as me, a postgraduate at the time). The connections between teachers and sociologists could be strengthened by the latter's interest in debates about the forms of educational knowledge taught through schooling. In a major shift from earlier concerns with the contribution of families and communities to social mobility and stratification, critical social theorists started to look inside the school, keen now to consider not why working-class pupils failed but why schools had failed them. By the early 1970s, social theorists had started to think critically about the significance of the school curriculum, its structuring powers, its ideological messages, and its framing of classroom interaction, school ethos, and pupil participation. Teachers, their audience, were encouraged to think behind "taken for granted" professional knowledge. But more than that, they were encouraged to become aware of the possibilities of their professional agency in the name of political goals of equality, justice, and democracy.

The historical conjuncture when *Ideology and Curriculum* was published was therefore a time when, for a short period, teachers, sociologists, and curriculum planners were locked in debate about the role of schooling in society. The question Michael Apple, like others at that time, addressed was whether it was feasible to assume that the forms of high-status knowledge associated with the school curriculum and the organizational forms associated with its transmission could be taken for granted. Could they be assumed to be working, especially when it was clear that the legacy of social class inequalities had not been reduced by the educational reforms introduced by postwar reconstruction? Surely in an age when civil rights were matters of such concern, teachers could be expected to engage critically with the forms of knowledge they were being asked to teach by the state. Surely teachers had a role in this reformist age, of becoming agents for progressive change (Young, 1998, p. 42). They could become "insider" reformers in the school and, in hindsight, remain just within government policy circles. In retrospect, of course, it was unfortunate that critical theorists neglected "other powerful intermediary activity, advisors, administrators … who might have provided links between classroom teachers and wider political forces (p. 175). In retrospect, too, the processes of critical engagement with school knowledge might have benefited from far more support from parents, who were later mobilized by the Right in the name of standards and excellence.

Social critiques of the curriculum were inherently dangerous critiques since they were directly focused on social power and the very means by which that power was made legitimate. They raised questions about the very core of the educational project, a modernist project that was to stratify and sift the next generation of young people in ways that would give the illusion of democracy. The school system, despite its undemocratic nature, had become the symbol of the modernist progressive project. It had employed, as many of us were aware by the end of the 1970s, many different techniques to mask its hierarchical structure, its sifting and sorting functions, and its relationships with an explicitly inegalitarian economic formation. There was no strategy that was more successful, as critical theorists such as Bowles and Gintis, Apple, and Giroux recognized in the context of the United States, than liberal ideology and its technologies of neutrality. The postwar theme of redistribution, that of equality of opportunity, masked the intrinsic social stratification and its associated moral order.

It is important, therefore, to locate *Ideology and Curriculum* within the context in which the liberal ideology of schooling framed curriculum practice. When, in 1976, Roger Dale, Geoff Esland, and I[1] first introduced Michael Apple's curriculum theorizing into the United Kingdom (in our edited collection, *Schooling and Capitalism*), it was in the context of a sustained critique of the liberal ideology of schooling. All the writers in the collection were acutely aware of the powerful infrastructure of liberal ideology that represented schooling as contributing to social progressive change, providing personnel to "push back the frontiers of technical knowledge and to consolidate these advances and bring them into our everyday lives" (p. 1). Education was represented as addressing and redressing social inequalities in the unfair distribution of life chances by the equalization of educational opportunity. Central to this project was the view that the education and culture it produced and transmitted were understood to be independent and autonomous features of society. We argued in our introduction that:

Educational policies are directed towards the production of both knowledge and knowledgeable individuals through the sponsoring of academic research and curriculum reform. The idealism within the liberal tradition presents both culture and schooling and politically neutral forces for social change. (Dale et al., 1976, p. 2)

We wrote that the refusal to allow "material concerns to infiltrate the world of thought underlies the traditional British segregation of theoretical and practice, of abstract and technical knowledge" (p. 5). Through such institutionalized separations, the distinction between manual and mental work was replicated. Different educational agencies contributed to this project in an extraordinary division of labor, separating knowledge reproduction (families and schools) from production (universities and elite expert knowledge). This divorce of the world of ideas from material concerns was institutionalized through academic disciplinary discourses. Social scientists, particularly educationalists, reinforced the relationship between culture and its external material base by ignoring the social construction of knowledge and by neglecting to contextualize such knowledge within the political and economic order in which it had meaning. Such disciplines also built their own histories on the assumption of their own autonomy from materiality. "Physically distinct departments and exclusive forms of analysis inhibit both the unification of cultural forms and the identification of common features" (p. 5). In the educational world, this division of what Marx called the "base and superstructure" was symbolized by the separation of analyses of the content of cultural forms (literary analysis, the history of school subjects) from the transmission of culture through pedagogy (Williams, 1976). The implication of this division was that those involved in knowledge production were represented as isolated and privatized actors, alienated from their product and from the social context in which they created knowledge.

This alienation of cultural goods from their producers, which in today's postmodern world appears so extraordinarily naive and distorting, played a key role within the liberal modernist project. It invested knowledge and, by implication, the agency for its reproduction with an "impeccable neutrality" (p. 5).

Seen as objective, apolitical and internally governed, the selection, modification and transmission of a cultural heritage, through the curriculum and pedagogical practice of education, is assigned more often than not a total autonomy from the society of which it is part. Academic freedom, teacher autonomy, the denial of censorship and bias are all called in to support the view of a world in which the free flow of ideas is beyond ideological control. (Dale et al., 1976, p. 5)

Michael Apple's book *Ideology and Curriculum* is symbolic of the critique of this liberal framework. The text and the tradition it created around the politics of education, culture, knowledge, and power were highly significant in that they represented a powerful alternative educational framework that took as its task the deconstruction and exposure of such alleged neutralities and their consequences particularly for the marginalized, disadvantaged, and dispossessed. *Ideology and Curriculum* broke open the liberal illusionary world of U.S. curriculum construction, revealing not just the political machinery involved in curriculum control but the deeply undemocratic interventions of the U.S. economy into the school system. Positioning himself at the center of this radical thinking, Apple took no hostages. He systematically exposed the injustices of a school system that claimed to address social disadvantage while privileging the advantaged. The task he set for himself in the mid-1970s, therefore, was no small task. It involved critical expose but, like others in that period, he also sent out a clarion call to teachers to engage in a political project of social transformation. In that sense, *Ideology and Curriculum* was a book of its time. It reflected frustration and pessimism but also optimism and reforming zeal.

Apple's theoretical framework in *Ideology and Curriculum* was its most significant and enduring aspect. Today that aspect of his work could well be dismissed as all too modernist in tone and in ambition. However, the significance of Apple's introduction of a reconstructed Marxist scholarship into U.S. educational debates cannot be underestimated. It was that "ideological project" that framed two more decades of productive research on the invisible, often inexplicit, ideological framing of schooling and led to so many outstanding scholarly studies that drew strength from his engagement with such radical traditions.[2]

Apple was aware that Marxist scholarship had had an effect in the 1930s in the United States but the "fear laden past of American society" (Apple, 1976a, p. 177) refused acceptance of this scholarly tradition. Drawing on the continental and particularly British Marxist intellectual traditions, Apple argued for a reconstructed Marxist scholarship that would be freed from dogmatism and determinism. A reconstructed approach offered the possibility of breaking the atrophy associated with the individualism, the "atomistic and strict empiricist frame of mind," and the strong utilitarian frame of mind associated with commonsense thought in America. The effects of these elements in Western industrialized culture had been to eschew a "critically oriented notion of the necessity of a plurality of ways of looking at the world" (p. 177)—presumably not just in the social sciences but also within the school curriculum itself. The tendency was to separate value from fact. Marxist scholarship, in contrast, saw both social and intellectual categories are themselves valuative in nature, reflecting ideological commitments. The power of a reconstructed Marxist scholarship was therefore its commitment to see objects relationally. The challenge of this perspective for curriculum studies, "curriculists," and teachers was to understand the historical roots of the curriculum (thus acknowledging that the curriculum is in continual motion), its institutionalized forms of reification and its materially grounded patterns of thought. Although not necessarily obvious, these contextualizing factors gave the curriculum its primary meaning and represented an important research goal to critical social theorists—that of uncovering the interdependences between knowledge and its socioeconomic context.

This example of political analysis, however, also had "liberatory" ambitions. In our introduction to *Schooling and Capitalism*, we argued that such research:

> [A]ims at illuminating the tendencies for unwanted and often unconscious domination, alienation, and repression within certain existing cultural, political, educational and economic institutions. Second, through exploring the negative effects and contradictions of much that unquestionably goes on in these institutions, it seeks to "promote conscious emancipatory activity." (Dale et al., 1976, p. 177)

There can be no doubt as to the political intentions of *Ideology and Curriculum*. This book clearly established Apple's fundamental belief in the purposes of educational research. The rationale was to contribute, as far as possible and within the limits of a constrained educational system, to the political emancipation initially of the working classes, but later also of women, minority groups, black communities, and the dispossessed. Apple made explicit his understanding that democratic change was integral to his academic project:

> Researchers need to affiliate with concrete groups and classes of people who are struggling with the political and economic issues of the lack of responsiveness of so many institutions in advanced industrial societies. This means that their research

problems arise from the needs of these classes and groups not from the dominant institutions of our society. Thus, advocacy research, based on an affiliation with the least advantaged must prevail. ... Intellectually, this means linking oneself to traditions—neo-Marxist, "revisionist," in my own case, a repoliticized critical theory—that see one of their primary tasks to be illumination of the ways our basic modes of professional operation have an ethical and political impact far beyond what we believe we are doing. Only by making such critical awareness a constitutive part of our own activity can we make our research a material force in the struggle for creating and recreating institutions that respond to more than the needs of a technical and economic elite. Perhaps, then, the real question for each of us must be "Where do I stand?" Answers to this one will not be easy, but perhaps even asking it would be a good beginning. (Apple, 1976b, p. 121)

Apple's concept of advocacy research was unusually explicit in his writing. In the context of the 1970s, it was entirely appropriate for an academic educationalist to declare publicly that: "To be just and equal, schools must contribute to the advantage of the *least* advantaged. ... Education ... must play a part with other economic and social institutions in redistributing cultural and economic capital more justly" (Apple, 1976b, p. 121). However, the notion of agency (whether for academics or teachers or indeed pupils) was problematic from the beginning. Apple was all too aware of the contradictions of a rather deterministic neo-Marxist tradition and the liberatory politics he espoused—a theme that shaped his work for the next 30 years. This tension was expressed even in his earliest work in his concern for trying to hold on to the notion that both teachers and pupils have agency, they can make meaning, while at the same time their very consciousness is shaped through the ideological work of schooling. In the late 1970s, this tension expressed itself in his tentative linking between phenomenological description of social processes and neo-Marxist interpretations of education as domination.

Phenomenological description and analysis of social processes, while important to be sure, incline us to forget that there *are* objective institutions and structures "out there," that have power, that can control our lives and our very perceptions. By focusing on how everyday social interaction sustains peoples' identities and their institutions, [they] can draw attention away from the fact that individual interaction and conception is constrained by material reality.

> One does not throw out social phenomenology here. … One combines it with a more critical social interpretation that looks at the negotiation of identities and meanings in specific institutions like schools as taking place within a context that often determines the parameters of what is negotiable or meaningful. This context does not merely reside at the level of consciousness; it is the nexus of economic and political institutions, a nexus which defines what schools should be about, that determines these parameters. (Apple, 1977, quoted in Whitty, 1977, p. 54)

Central to the critical project was an engagement with contemporary social beliefs and policies. In the case of *Ideology and Curriculum*, Apple saw the rhetorical and political function of technocratic instrumentalist models of education. In an analysis that was prescient, given the emphasis today on scientific/technical approaches by neoliberalism, Apple unravels both the mechanisms and implications of this approach. The language of behavioral objectives, he argued, suggested that education could be understood and reformed through scientific procedures. Such models and objectives tended "to cause its users and the other publics involved to ignore certain possible fundamental problems with schools as institutions … systems management also acts to generate and channel political sentiments supportive of the existing modes of access to knowledge and power" (Apple, 1972, quoted in Dale, 1977, p. 74). As Dale (1977) pointed out, the curriculum was expected to bring about the same behavior in all students. At that time, homogenization through the curriculum seemed desirable even if it was not achieved. It suggests that the curriculum subject matter can be perfected and, as a result, any failure can be blamed on the student. This leads to an "implicit freezing" of students' different attributes and interests and assumes that all students coming to the curriculum have equal chances of learning it. Behavioral objectives also imply that there is only one meaning, that it can be achieved. Students, as a result, have little opportunity to make their own meanings.

Apple's prescience in relation to neoliberal curriculum was exceptional. He had tapped very early on the political power of technocratic instrumentalist curriculum planning and its reproductive powers. Here he is talking about the social reproductive function of behavioral objectives associated with curricular knowledge:

The process-product style of reasoning ... evident in the call for behavioral objectives is quite functional to a society that requires a large proportion of its workers to engage in often boring assembly line or in personally unimportant white collar work. By learning how to work for others' preordained goals using others' preselected behaviors, students also learn to function in an increasingly bureaucratized society in which the adult roles one is to play are already embedded in the social fabric. ... Curriculists, by internalizing and using an orientation that lends itself to such preordination, cannot but contribute to the maintenance of a political and economic order that creates and maintains these roles and the meaning already distributed with them. (Apple, 1972, p. 117, quoted in Dale, 1977, p. 75)

Where Apple's text differed from that of other leading critical social theorists such as Bernstein (1977), Bourdieu and Passeron (1977), and Bowles and Gintis (1976) was that where they had emphasized structural and ideological aspects of the educational system of transmission, Apple highlighted the power of the ideological content of the curriculum, the significance of the culture and ethos of the hidden curriculum, and the political and legitimist functions of curriculum studies and curriculum planners.[3] And once the curriculum became the lens through which relations of power could be tapped, there was no reason not to develop a range of different interpretations about whose power was transmitted and reproduced through schooling.

GENDER, IDEOLOGY, AND THE CURRICULUM

One would tend to think the overt curriculum would be easier to research since it was visible, accessible, and organized. Syllabus, textbooks, examination papers, guidance for teachers, professional subjects' networks and newsletters, and resource centers were potentially the subject of research. However, in reality, once the so-called hidden curriculum was represented as a social construction, it attracted far greater interest among critical theorists on both sides of the Atlantic. Although Michael Apple had paved the way, along with leading educationalists such as Jean Anyon (1979, 1981),[4] for an ideological critique of the ways in which the world was represented or "misrecognized" through school subject matter, few critical theorists followed suit. Even the ground-breaking work of Linda McNeil (1986) on curriculum in use did not lead to a critical deconstruction of the relationship between teachers and texts (see also Apple, 1986). Of far greater interest in the United Kingdom was the deconstruction of the hidden curriculum of schooling through ethnographic and youth cultural research. The impact of Willis's (1977) *Learning to Labour* and that of Angela McRobbie (1978) on working-class boys and girls respectively would shift researchers' attention to the concept of identity, culture, and agency.[5] Unfortunately, this is not the place to narrate the developments in the field in any chronological way. Suffice it to say that Apple himself quickly recognized the need to offer more "complex" reproduction theory that did not just claim ideological intervention and distortion in favor of the wealthy in society, but rather addressed the complexity and contradictory conditions found in schools: "no assemblage of ideological practices and meanings and no set of social and economic arrangements can be totally monolithic" (Apple, 1982, p. 8, quoted in Arnot and Whitty, 1982, p. 95).

Apple recognized that one of the complexities of social relations that framed curriculum knowledge and responses to it was that of gender (cf. introduction in *Ideology and Curriculum*). Apple points to his own change of thinking in line with gender theorists:

> Students in most schools and in urban centers in particular are presented with a view that serves to legitimate the existing order since change, conflict and men and women as creators as well as receivers of values and institutions are systematically neglected. (Apple, 2003, p. 95)

Feminist academics in the early 1980s urged male critical theorists to recognize the relationship between patriarchy and capitalism, between male power and that of the corporate/economic elite. Notably, Dale Spender (1987) called for investigations of what she called the "patriarchal paradigm of education." Patriarchal power relations had, she argued, shaped every aspect of schooling." Schools were seen as "boys' schools with girls in them"—the structure of the school, with its hierarchical and authoritarian ethos, its aggressive pedagogic and assessment modes, its competitive individualism, its privileging of male forms of knowledge and experience, had encouraged a superior male status and achievement." In her seminal text *Men's Studies Modified*, Spender (1981) contributed substantially to the ideological analysis of the academic disciplines and the reconstruction effort she called upon women academics to undertake—a project that some would say is still ongoing within the context of women's studies and gender studies.

During the 1980s, the growth of feminist curriculum analysis in the United Kingdom was substantial, although often largely descriptive, small scale, and not nearly as sophisticated as critical sociologists might have liked (see Arnot, 2002) Drawing less on the complex theories of structure and agency, most feminist studies of the curriculum were political more than analytic. Much of the work was located within the liberal sex role socialization rather than neo-Marxist scholarship. The research searched out sex stereotypes in the content of children's reading schemes, curriculum subject material (such as science, math, history, English), television programs, and popular cultural forms (such as comics, children's literature, magazines, and so forth). The methodology was more likely to involve qualitative and quantitative content analysis than an ideological deconstruction such as that expected by *Ideology and Curriculum*.

[with the growth in fem curr. analysis,

Using this analysis, teachers in the United Kingdom developed a range of subject-specialist networks, wrote newsletters, and engaged in action research. They developed new curricular materials using gender-blind material or alternatively girl-friendly approaches. Some teachers defined their work within anti-sexist paradigms and sought to engage students in critical reflection about conventional gender attitudes and roles in society (Weiler, 1988). In the relatively safe space of the school, girls could explore femininity and find ways of breaking out of traditional molds (Arnot, David, & Weiner, 1999).

In 1980, in my contribution to a book similarly titled *Schooling, Ideology and the Curriculum* (Barton, Meighan, & Walker, 1980), I tried to capture the significance of some of this research for the social class and gender ideological analyses of the curriculum (MacDonald, 1980) The range of research then available on gender representations in the school curriculum suggested that these representations were more complex than previously assumed. Not only were there different definitions of masculinity and femininity (plural gender identities), but they also were recontextualized in different ways in different genres, for different audiences in time and space (MacDonald, 1980). Gender relations were dualisms that had to be worked on and through by individuals. Using a Gramscian perspective, I argued that the messages of the curriculum represented an attempt, not always successful, to win the consent from each new generation to the structure and nature of gender relations in society. "Not that capital has succeeded in creating classed and sexed subjects, suitably adjusted to the rigours of work in the home and workplace but rather that no day goes by without it trying" (p. 46). I concluded that relations between the sexes were arbitrary and transmitted in complex ways through habitus (cf. Bourdieu & Passeron, 1977) and forms of embodiment (MacDonald, 1980). The ideologically framed messages of the school, therefore, were only a small part in the whole story.

⌈Increasingly feminist attention was focused on the discursive construction of the subject (male and female learners) within the classroom and school. The knowledge transmitted through schooling about gender relations was not the only discursive framing of students and teachers, as Walkerdine (1990) so pointedly described in her study of sex, power, and pedagogy in infant classrooms. The discursive constructions of gender, social class, ethnicity, sexuality, and disability were simultaneous and not often commensurate. _(equal, proportionate)_ Engagement with these discursive constructions, which accounted for the multiple messages the school and its structures and pupils responded to in complex ways, could not be assumed to be captured by resistance theory. Young people were positioned by these discursive frameworks but also active in positioning themselves, working and reworking their identities in relation with others.⌋Agency was no longer the uninvited guest; it now became central to the curriculum project. This time, however, it was not phenomenology or symbolic interactionism that described this "work" of individuals, it was theories of identity, subjectivity, and engagement/disengagement, and even Freudian notions of abjection and rejection that came into play. The hidden curriculum was represented, therefore, as a form of governmentality and surveillance of pupil citizens. _hidden curr - look beyond visible acts towards the invisible power of gender reprod_

Drawing on Foucauldian notions, the micropolitics and microtechnologies of power and "governmentality," feminist poststructuralist analysis of curricular knowledge offers an exploration of how power works through knowledge. One of the great shifts in thinking about the forms of educational knowledge was Walkerdine's exceptional analysis of mathematical knowledge. Her work explored the deepest recesses of mathematics, the forms of rationality and performance associated with becoming a mathematician and indeed a brilliant mathematician—a position seemingly not available to girls or women. This deconstruction of the inner framing of knowledge and its enlightenment assumptions resonated with the work in the United States, for example, of Belenky, Clinchy, Goldberger, and Tarule (1986), who argued that there could be different male and female approaches to knowledge, and the forms of connectedness associated with "women's ways of knowing" would need to be supported by a different curricular approach. Women were understood to value relational knowledge rather than strongly classified and bounded knowledge forms—a view that was given considerable impetus by Gilligan's (1982) classic study, _In a Different Voice._

Although it is impossible here to provide a systematic or coherent overview of these breakthroughs in the study of educational knowledge, it is important to note the contribution of such feminist theorizing around the curriculum. Feminists propelled the analysis of educational knowledge into the realm of epistemology and ontology, considering the extent to which women had different epistemological standpoints, regardless of whether there were specific female-situated knowledge and methodologies for the generation of knowledge (see for example, Sandra Harding's [1987] classic *Feminism and Methodology* and *The Feminist Standpoint Theory Reader* [2004]).

However, despite its concerns with power, knowledge, and discipline and its interest in the construction of the gendered subject positions in the school, in the United Kingdom poststructuralism has led to far less research on what teachers are actually teaching. Paradoxically, at the same time, the school curriculum was undergoing major restructuring, not least by the extensive neoliberal and neoconservative agendas. The former privileged market-oriented learning, flexibility and the development of communication skills addressing, it seemed, the Left critique of the irrelevance of school knowledge and exploiting the Left's call for the need to reduce social class differences through more modern educational curricula. This almost "schizoid" combination (Bernstein, 1990) of egalitarian rhetoric and neoliberal structures helped sustained social inequality, as did the neoconservative curriculum reforms that returned the school system to a tightly controlled rather dated conventional menu of subject specialisms. Although Apple (1986) engaged with these changing forms of knowledge in the United States, very little attention was paid in the United Kingdom to the content of national curriculum subjects or its use in classrooms. Times had changed and teachers were no longer the audience of critical social theorizing. The autonomy of teachers had declined and the state intervened to establish a performance pedagogy (Bernstein, 1990) whose structures of assessment and monitoring were more important than the content. Critical sociologists concerned about gender, ethnicity, race, sexuality, and social class had not, it seems, anticipated the reintroduction of such instrumentalist and behaviorist educational agendas. The increasingly individualized and competitive learning processes have taken the wind out of the sails of curriculum theory. The classroom lost its power as the site for critical intervention and advocacy research, teachers were now tightly regulated and under surveillance, their conditions of service such that they have little prospect of engaging either themselves or their students in curriculum critique. The pacing of knowledge established by the government took over the time in which teachers and the professional subject networks might fruitfully reflect on the messages transmitted through the curriculum.

Nevertheless, there now appears to be the beginnings of an invigorated curriculum debate. Poststructuralist theory, especially Foucauldian discourse analysis, potentially offers the possibility of exploring in greater depth and with more sophistication the ways in which the subject is constituted within curriculum subjects (Dillabough & Arnot, 2001), and increasingly it is being used effectively as a methodology for the analysis of policy texts (e.g., Maclure, 2003). Performative notions of gender also direct attention to the ways in which masculinity and femininity can be performed within specialized subject discourses. Doing math is for example a way of "doing gender" (Walkerdine, 1988, 1989). Exclusionary discourses within particular domains of knowledge can also be found to construct girls or boys as the "other" and silence their voices. Carrie Paechter's (1998, 2000) work is one of the few examples of how such an analytic approach can explore the construction of gender through school subjects. Interestingly, she focuses on the more marginal subjects of physical education and design and technology education. Her analysis reveals how gender differences are normalized, with girls positioned as "Other." Recently she has explored the gendering of male and female bodies through different types of physical education and sport. Such poststructuralist analysis shows how critical curriculum research can reveal normative and gendered notions of the learner within particular knowledge forms and can therefore contribute to the larger debates about equity and learning.

Finally, it is important not to bypass one of the major critical strands of feminist research that focuses on pedagogy. Although not often concentrating on the triadic relations between teacher, text, and learner in the ways recommended by Apple, nevertheless its contribution to the nature of critical theory/pedagogy has been substantial. Writers such as Sandra Acker, Kathleen Casey, Jo-Anne Dillabough, Frances Gore, Madeleine Grumet, Patti Lather, Nel Noddings, and Kathleen Weiler have made major contributions to our understanding of teachers' work through their exploration of the gendering of pedagogy, teacher identity, and critical and feminist pedagogies. This strand of thinking initially explored the nature of female and feminist pedagogy especially in relation to women's studies—since then it has encouraged a history of the culture of women teachers.[6]

CONCLUSIONS: A LOST AGENDA?

The project outlined by Apple in *Ideology and Curriculum* was followed by a series of other major contributions offering his analysis of the politics of education, and in that sense we have a far better understanding now about the role of the state and the politics of engagement especially in relation to neoliberal agendas and social movements linked to moral regeneration and globalization. In 1977, Apple recognized that the women's movement had a particular politics. He observed that the movement had appropriated liberal notions of rights in order to be treated as "full functioning citizens" in the home and workplace and in the state. His later work explored, to a greater extent, the struggle over issues of gender, race, and class, especially the ways in which people were shaped by such conflicts (Apple, 1982). However, he admitted that such multiple politics were difficult to engage.

It is unfortunate that the impact of these social movements and the politics of late modernity on the school curriculum are not more fully developed, particularly in the United Kingdom. As we have seen the feminist analysis of the school curriculum was replaced largely by studies of identity. Where Bernstein had argued for a theory of transmission and acquisition in which the structuring of educational knowledge was critical, critical sociology appears to have disconnected political discourses about education from the institutionalization of different forms of knowledge. Bernstein's (2000) final work pointed to the importance of analyzing the ways in which different types of knowledge structures and discourses are employed within education and their social class consequences.

Rob Moore and Michael Young have recently returned to the fray with their critique of both the early versions of sociology of knowledge and poststructuralist approaches, particularly those that celebrate relativism. Although the curricular tradition represented by Apple and the ensuing work was powerfully critical, its relativism, they argue, has left sociology of education peculiarly ill-equipped to meet the curriculum challenge posed by debates about the implication of globalization and the massification of postcompulsory education of the past decade (Moore & Young, 2001, p. 446). Postmodernism, for example, reduces knowledge to experience, thus denying the possibilities of categories that transcend experience.

> If all knowledge is reduced to the conditions of its production, it is denied any intrinsic autonomy either as a social institution in its own right or in terms of the application of independent truth criteria that might be applied to curriculum debates. (Moore & Young, 2001, p. 452)

These authors argue against relativism associated with progressive curriculum, reductionism which sees the curriculum as the result of conflicts between social groups, and against standpoint epistemology of the sort represented by feminism, which denies, Moore (2000) argues, the fact that knowledge can "transcend" its social conditions. The organization of knowledge, he argues, is more than a reflection of social differentiation and stratification (p. 33). Critical realism contrasts with sociology of knowledge and standpoint epistemologies by perceiving that there is no necessary relationship between the fact that knowledge is social and society is stratified. By making a distinction between the social construction of knowledge (a form of idealism) and the social production of knowledge (a form of materialism), it can offer non-reductive understandings of the social logic of knowledge (Moore, 2005). Sociological studies of the curriculum are encouraged, therefore, to focus on the role of specialist communities, networks and codes of practice, the balancing of social exclusion and cognitive interests, the autonomous elements of the curriculum, and the experience of learners in decisions about the curriculum (Moore & Young, 2001, p. 458). Critical realism, Moore suggests, in effect encourages us to question again what it means "to be critical" in the context of a sociology of knowledge.

Ideology and Curriculum represented the beginning of this long investigative tradition into the politics of knowledge. Although that tradition has faltered at times, it has also grown. There are signs, especially with the celebration of twenty-five years since its publication, that a critical analysis of knowledge—especially that which is transmitted through educational institutions—will return to center stage.

NOTES

1. My surname was then MacDonald.
2. The work of Lois Weis, Leslie Roman, Cameron McCartney, Joel Taxel, Linda McNeil to name but a few.
3. See MacDonald, 1977a and 1977b for an overview of theories of cultural reproduction.
4. See also Taxel, 1978-1979, 1980.
5. For a discussion of Willis's influence on sociology of education, see Arnot, 2004.
6. Drawing on some of the early feminist work, Michael Apple (1986) addressed the issue of teaching as women's work in *Teachers and Texts*.

REFERENCES

Anyon, J. (1979). Ideology and the United States history textbooks. *Harvard Education Review, 49*(3), 361–386.

Anyon, J. (1981). Social class and school knowledge. *Curriculum Inquiry, 11*(1), 3–42.

Apple, M. (1975). The adequacy of system management procedures in education. In R. Smith (Ed.), *Regaining educational leadership* (p. 116). New York: John Wiley.

Apple, M. (1976a). Commonsense categories and curriculum thought. In R. Dale, G. Esland, & M. MacDonald (Eds.), *Schooling and capitalism: A sociological reader.* (pp. 174-184). London: Routledge and Kegan Paul.

Apple, M. (1976b). Politics and research in E202. *Schooling and Society*, Unit 20. Milton Keynes: Open University Press.

Apple, M. (1977). Power and school knowledge. *Review of Education, 3*(1), 26–49.

Apple, M. (2003). *Ideology and curriculum.* (3rd ed.) (Originally published 1977) New York: RoutledgeFalmer.

Apple, M. (1982). *Education and power.* London: Routledge and Kegan Paul.

Apple, M. (1986). *Teachers and texts; A political economy of class and gender relations in education.* New York: Routledge.

Arnot, M. (2002). *Reproducing gender? Selected essays on feminist politics and educational theory.* London: RoutledgeFalmer.

Arnot, M. (2004). Working class masculinities, schooling and social justice: Reconsidering the sociological significance of Paul Willis' "Learning to Labour." In G. Dimitriadis & N. Dolby (Eds.), *Learning to labour in new times* (pp. 17–40). New York: Routledge.

Arnot, M., David, M., & Weiner, G. (1999). *Closing the gender gap.* Cambridge: Polity Press

Arnot, M., & Whitty, G. (1982). From reproduction to transformation; recent radical perspectives on the curriculum from the USA. *British Journal of Sociology of Education, 3*(1), 93–103.

Barton, L., Meighan, R., & Walker, S. (Eds.). (1980). *Schooling, ideology and the curriculum.* Basingstoke: Falmer Press.

Belenky, M. F., Clinchy, B. M., Goldberger, N. R., & Tarule, J. M. (1986). *Women's way of knowing.* New York: Basic Books.

Bernstein, B. (1977). *Class, codes and control: Towards a theory of educational transmissions.* Vol. 3. London: Routledge and Kegan Paul.

Bernstein, B. (1990). *The Structuring of Pedagogic Discourse.* New York: Routledge.

Bernstein, B. (2000). *Pedagogy, symbolic control and identity.* London: Rowman and Littlefield.

Bourdieu, P., & Passeron, J. (1977). *Cultural reproduction* (R. Nice, Trans.). London: Sage.

Bowles, S., & Gintis, H. (1976). *Schooling in capitalist America*. London: Routledge and Kegan Paul.

Dale, R. (1977). *The politics of curriculum reform*, E202. Unit 17. Milton Keynes: Open University Press.

Dale, R., Esland, G., & MacDonald, M. (Eds.). (1976). *Schooling and capitalism: A sociological reader*. London: Routledge and Kegan Paul.

Dillabough, J., & Arnot, M. (2001). Feminist sociology of education: Dynamics, debates and directions. In J. Demaine (Ed.), *Sociology of education today* (pp. 30–47). London: Palgrave.

Freire, P. (1972). *Pedagogy of the oppressed*. Harmondsworth: Penguin Books.

Gilligan, C. (1982). *In a different voice*. Cambridge, MA: Harvard University Press.

Harding, S. (Ed.). (1987). *Feminism and methodology: Social science issues*. Bloomington: Indiana University Press.

Harding, S. (Ed.). (2004). *The feminist standpoint theory reader: Intellectual and political controversies*. New York: Routledge.

MacDonald, M. (1977a). *Culture, class and the curriculum, 2002*. Unit 16. Milton Keynes: Open University Press.

MacDonald, M. (1977b). *The curriculum and cultural reproduction*, E202. Unit 18/9. Milton Keynes: Open University Press.

MacDonald, M. (1980). Schooling and the reproduction of class and gender relations. In L. Barton, R. Meighan, & S. Walker (Eds.), *Schooling, ideology and the curriculum* (pp. 29-49). Basingstoke: Falmer Press.

Maclure, M. (2003). *Discourse in educational and social research*. Buckingham: Open University Press.

McNeil, L. (1986). *Contradictions of control: School structure and school knowledge*. New York: Routledge and Kegan Paul.

McRobbie, A. (1978). Working class girls and the culture of femininity. In Women's Studies Group (Eds.), *Women take issue: Aspects of women's subordination* (pp. 96-108). London: CCCS/Hutchinson.

Moore, R. (2000). For knowledge: tradition, progressivism and progress in education—reconstructing the curriculum debate. *Cambridge Journal of Education, 30*, 17–36.

Moore, R. (2005). Going critical: The problem of problematising knowledge in educational studies. *n*. Manuscript submitted for publication.

Moore, R., & Young, M. (2001). Knowledge and the curriculum in sociology: Towards a reconceptualisation. *British Journal of Sociology of Education, 22*, 445–460.

Paechter, C. (1998). *Educating the other: Gender, power and schooling*. London: Falmer Press.

Paechter, C. (2000). *Changing school subjects: Power, gender and the curriculum*. Buckingham: Open University Press.

Spender, D. (Ed.). (1981). *Men's studies modified: The impact of feminism on the academic disciplines*. Oxford: Pergamon.

Spender, D. (1987). Education: The patriarchal paradigm and the response to feminism. In M. Arnot & G. Weiner (Eds.), *Gender and the politics of schooling* (pp. 143-154). London: Hutchinson

Taxel, J. (1978–1979). Justice and cultural conflict: Racism, sexism and instructional materials. *Interchange, 9*(1), 56–84.

Taxel, J. (1980). *The depiction of the American Revolution in children's fiction: A study in the sociology of school knowledge*. Doctoral dissertation, University of Wisconsin–Madison.

Walkerdine, V. (1988). *Mastery of reason: Cognitive development and the production of rationality*. London: Routledge.

Walkerdine, V. (1989). *Counting girls out*. London: Virago.

Walkderine, V. (1990). *Schoolgirl fictions*. London: Verso

Weiler, K. (1988). *Women teaching for change: Gender, class and power*. South Hadley, MA: Bergin and Garvey.

Whitty, G. (1977). *Knowledge, ideology and the curriculum*. E202, Black III. Milton Keynes: Open University Press.

Williams, R. (1965). *The long revolution*. Harmondsworth: Penguin.

Williams, R. (1977). *Base and superstructure*. In R. Dale, G. Esland, & M. MacDonald (Eds.), *Schooling and capitalism: A sociological reader*. London: Routledge and Kegan Paul.

Willis, P. (1977). *Learning to labour: How working class kids get working class jobs*. Farnborough: Saxon House.

Young, M. (Ed.). (1971). *Knowledge and control: New directions for the sociology of education*. London: Collier-Macmillan.

Young, M. (1998). *The curriculum of the future: From the new sociology of education to a critical theory of learning*. London: Routledge Falmer.

2

SOCIAL CLASS, SCHOOL KNOWLEDGE, AND THE HIDDEN CURRICULUM

Retheorizing Reproduction

JEAN ANYON

Whether schooling in the United States promotes a meritocratic distribution of income in democratic capitalist societies like our own, or primarily reproduces an unequal distribution of economic life chances has been at the center of educational debates since the late 1970s. The question has been a concern underlying most of Mike Apple's scholarship. I situate this problematic—and the chapter—in Apple's work, and in some of my own research on the social and economic roles of education. I want to retheorize the findings of my 1980s study of social class, school knowledge, and the hidden curriculum of work. I will argue that changes in the U.S. economy since that time require that we rethink the hypothesis that schooling reproduces social class position. In an era when economic growth no longer increases middle-income opportunities, but rather creates a plethora of low- and a relative few high-income jobs, an unequal distribution of knowledge and work dispositions in school could be said not merely to reproduce social inequality, but to exacerbate it by supporting a bifurcation of incomes and class structure.

EARLY SCHOLARSHIP

With the 1976 publication of Bowles and Gintis's *Schooling in Capitalist America* and Apple's *Ideology and Curriculum* in 1979, educational scholarship in the United States began what would be a decades-long concern with "social reproduction"—which European and British scholars were also beginning to theorize (Bourdieu & Passeron, 1977; Dale, Esland, Fergusson, & MacDonald, 1981; Williams, 1977; Willis, 1977; Young & Whitty, 1977).

Apple's *Ideology and Curriculum* introduced U.S. educators to concepts utilized by these and other authors from abroad and promoted discussions in the United States of the educational implications of analytical notions such as hegemony, ideology, and cultural capital.

In *Education and Power* (1982), Apple helped us to think more critically about existing theories of social reproduction. Later, Apple's *Teachers and Texts* (1988) introduced us to uses of political economy in educational investigations. Apple's *Official Knowledge* (1993) described the devastating effects on curriculum and pedagogy of the politically conservative project, and *Cultural Politics and Education* (1996) encouraged us to apply our progressive critique to an ascendance of politically conservative ideas. In all these analyses, an overarching goal of Apple's work was to expose and reduce the reproductive effects of schooling and increase the liberatory possibilities of education.

As a young scholar, I reviewed *Ideology and Curriculum* in 1980. I described Apple's work as suggesting that "Schools ... were an active agency of social legitimation and indoctrination; and an important task was to assess the contribution of curriculum, and of every day discourse and educational experience, to this process of cultural domination and control" (1980a, p. 283). I quote here from his text:

> [A] basic act [of educators and researchers] involves making the curriculum forms found in schools problematic so that their latent ideological content can be uncovered. Questions about the selective tradition [in school curriculum] such as the following need to be taken quite seriously. Whose knowledge is it? Who selected it? Why is it organized and taught this way? To this particular group? The mere act of asking these questions is not sufficient, however. One is guided, as well, by attempting to link these investigations to competing conceptions of social and economic power and ideologies. In this way, one can begin to get a more concrete appraisal of the linkages between economic

and political power and the knowledge made available (and not made available) to students. (quoted in Anyon, 1980b, p. 7)

The study that I reprise in this chapter took those questions seriously and tested them empirically. It provided a rare (if not the only) empirical investigation of the reproduction hypothesis. This early research on schooling in different social class contexts yielded important observable phenomena that can be tested and theorized today.

EARLY STUDY OF SOCIAL CLASS AND SCHOOLING

Reproduction theorists had argued that schools were no longer a great "equalizer," but rather played a central role in reproducing social class status by distributing educational knowledge that leads to power and status (e.g., legal, medical, managerial) to students from higher social class backgrounds and lower level more "practical" knowledge (vocational, clerical) to working-class students. Also alleged as influential in the reproductive capacity of schooling was educator predisposition to reward students in different social classes for behaviors that corresponded to personality traits rewarded in different occupational strata—working-class students for docility and obedience, the managerial classes for initiative and personal assertiveness, for example. Bowles and Gintis, Apple, and others argued these correspondence theories on an abstract level, and I decided to investigate the propositions in K–12 educational settings.

Such an assessment entailed onsite research in schools and classrooms in differing social class contexts. I was able to locate two districts very close to each other in New Jersey: a small, old industrial city where I studied two working-class schools and a middle-class school, and a nearby suburb with wealthy and upper middle-class schools. All but a few students in the five schools were Caucasian.

I did not carry out an ethnography in the sense dominant then, or now, in the mainstream methodological literature—where the perspectives of those we study are of paramount interpretive importance. I wanted to test the correspondence theory by observing practice. I used my data gathering over the multiple sites to compare and contrast what I was seeing, in order to apply, critique, and extend the theory that I thought was explanatory when I began. (A variant of this approach has since been proposed and fully articulated by sociologist Michael Burawoy [1991], and anthropologist George Marcus [1998].)

The research questions I asked were: What potential relationships to the system of ownership of symbolic and physical capital, to authority and control in society and work, and to their own productive activity are being developed in children in each school? What economically relevant knowledge, skills, and predispositions are being transmitted in each classroom, and for what future relationship to the system of production are they appropriate? My concern was to reflect on the deeper social meaning, the wider theoretical significance, of what happens in each social setting (Anyon, 1980b, 1981).

My personal history had included attendance at both middle-class and affluent public K–12 schools and an elite university; I carried out my student teaching in a wealthy private school, and then taught elementary grades in inner cities for seven years. These experiences seemed to me to conform to the hypotheses put forth by the reproduction theorists, and so I had a sense that I would find real differences when I began my research.

What I did not expect was how clearly the patterns of difference would stand out—and how overly simplistic the social reproduction theorists (as well as my own memories and assumptions) had been.

I discovered that the schools I studied did seem to distribute knowledge differentially to the social classes. This section provides a brief summary of the differences I identified among the schools, focusing here on work tasks and school knowledge. (I leave unmentioned here the contradictions in and between the schools and classrooms which, I argued then, could be the bedrock of future social transformation.)

In the two working-class settings, school work typically involved rote behavior, following steps whose reasoning was not explained. Work rarely involved decision making or choice. This experience over the years of schooling could constitute preparation for adult labor that is mechanical and routine and thus presented a reproductive attribute of school experience for working-class students.

In the middle-class school, work typically involved getting the right answer to questions posed by teachers and textbooks. If one accumulated enough correct answers, one obtained a good grade. Students were to follow the directions to get right answers, but the directions sometimes called for figuring and a bit of decision making. I argued that this environment was appropriate preparation for future office work in bureaucracies. The predominate tone of activity and interaction in the middle-class school was one of patriotism and student "possibility." Students and teachers spoke and acted as if students who worked hard and accumulated enough good grades would be rewarded by college and good jobs.

In the affluent professional school, work was often creative activity carried out independently. The students were continually asked to make sense of their experience—to "think," to develop and express their own ideas and interpretations, and to apply analytical concepts in creative linguistic and artistic ways. The method of control teachers employed was primarily through empathetic negotiation with students.

The children in this affluent professional school were learning large amounts of high-status symbolic capital (e.g., artistic, intellectual, linguistic, scientific knowledge and skill). Their schooling was developing in them a relation to their work that was creative and relatively autonomous and appropriate development for later professional, high-paying occupations as "symbolic analysts."

In the executive elite school, work and knowledge were highly academic, intellectual, and rigorous. Students were not encouraged to use personal creativity to make sense of the world, but rather to follow rules of good thought, rationality, and reasoning. In many cases, knowledge involved understanding the internal structure of systems: the logic by which systems of numbers, words, or ideas are arranged and may be rearranged. There was a practice and a sense around school tasks that the rationality of logic and mathematics is the model of correct and ethical thinking. In this school as well, the curriculum and curriculum-in-use delivered high-status cultural capital to its students.

The information the children were provided about U.S. society was heavily analytical: this was the only school in which the textbooks and the class conversations I observed involved discussions of economic classes, U.S. inequality, labor unions, and the ideological role of religion in social systems. Whereas working-class students received little or no patriotic rhetoric, middle-class students were offered a pluralistic view of society as open and full of potential, and affluent professional kids were exhorted to develop to their fullest creative potential, while the executive elite students were provided a more honest view of a society that sometimes involved stark honesty. The executive elite children could be seen to be developing a consciousness of themselves as a social class that could, and should, act in its own interest.

Although not recapitulated here, the study also suggested that there were class conflicts in educational knowledge and work. There was class conflict in the struggle to impose the knowledge of powerful groups on the working class and in student resistance to this class-based curriculum, class conflict in the contradictions within and between school knowledge and its economic and personal values, and in attempts to impose liberal public attitudes on children of the affluent. Thus, I argued in 1980 that rather than being simply reproductive, as Bowles and Gintis (for example) had theorized, schools also demonstrated contradictions that had the potential for nonreproductive effects.

As I have argued at length more recently (Anyon, 2005), contradictions in schools—and the economy—that highlight injustice also illuminate possibilities for educator activism. Contradictions provide the bricks and mortar with which concerned educators can build resistance, contestation, and organized movements for change. Without such activist work, however, the differential distribution of high-status knowledge and work dispositions—if it can be shown to continue today—has consequences even more pronounced than we envisioned in 1980.

THEORIZING SOCIAL REPRODUCTION

The U.S. economy has become substantially more unequal since my 1980 study of social class and schooling. The reasons are well known:

> The growth in inequality has been fed by the erosion of workers' gains in manufacturing (the loss of unions), the high incidence of layoffs and plant closings, and the general shift to a service economy, which entails a much larger share of low-wage jobs than in the case with a strong manufacturing-based economy. (Sassen, 2001, p. 205)

One significant consequence of these changes is rarely acknowledged, however: economic inequality in the United States has taken the form of an increased polarization of incomes, with fewer income opportunities in the middle (p. 205).

During the past quarter century, international finance and information technology—and the professional legal, technical, design, accounting, and marketing services that support them—have become the leading economic sectors in terms of profit and reach. These sectors have generated a sharp increase in high-income jobs that require high-status cultural capital: symbolic, conceptual, creative work, involving systems analysis, the development of new financial products, and global planning (Sassen, 2001, p. 286). Although these sectors are responsible for most profit production in the United States and the vast majority of "good jobs," which require symbolic work, the percentage of the labor force involved in such work is only about 20%–80% of U.S. employees remain hourly wage workers (Reich, 1992; Sassen, 2001).

The advanced economic sectors produce not only high-income jobs, but many low-wage jobs as well. Businesses that spring up to service complexes of wealthy firms in cities, and high-income employees and their families in suburbs, pay very low wages—photocopy stores, food delivery, landscaping and lawn care, clothes cleaners, home maintenance, health care, retail stores—are all staffed by workers most of whom earn low wages. This, in tandem with the rise of service jobs in other areas of the economy, has produced a situation in which middle-class opportunities are less available, and the solid incomes they provide more difficult to obtain (Sassen, 2001).

The bifurcation of U.S. occupations into low and high wages is not a malfunction of the economy. Rather, this polarization of opportunity is a function of the way the economy operates now, part of economic growth. We have moved from a strong manufacturing economy in the three decades following World War II, when economic growth created a strong middle class, to an economy whose growth produces a class structure of rich and poor (Sassen, 2001). This is not to argue that the middle class has disappeared, but that economic growth now does not contribute to a larger middle class. Rather, it contributes to larger and larger percentages of jobs offering extremely high and extremely low income.

Since the high paying jobs are, more than ever before, based on the use of high-status cultural capital (the appropriation and manipulation of concepts, symbols, and abstract systems), it becomes important to ask what roles education—and a differential distribution of such capital in schools—might play in the reproduction of social class at this historic moment.

I should also note that the return to educational credentialing has changed since 1980. The wage advantage of a high school diploma has plummeted, and the return to college graduation has risen barely at all since then. In fact, for people of color and white working-class women, racial and gender discrimination may eradicate most of the wage gains from a college diploma (Lafer, 2002). There have been more college graduates than there are (decently paying) jobs for them; in fact, many college-educated people now work in low-wage jobs, and one in ten lives in poverty (Anyon, 2005). The service economy has lowered the overall wage of most jobs, and in an oversupplied market, employers ratchet up educational credential demands, using college graduation as an indicator that potential employees will have high school reading, writing, and mathematical skill (Lafer, 2002; Murnane & Levy, 1996).

Because of this, a distribution of knowledge and work disposition among the social classes, like that demonstrated in my early research, becomes an ever more powerful source of inequality and constricture of opportunity—as it provides conceptual, analytical knowledge to the affluent, but not to the rest. Unlike the past, when high-status cultural capital was rarely necessary for manufacturing and other jobs that paid decent (middle-income) wages, such knowledge and work skills have become prerequisites for the "good jobs."

An important consequence is that, unlike in earlier times, when education could have a "leveling" effect, by providing middle-class opportunities and incomes for working-class and middle-class students—who did not possess high-status knowledge—education today can actually exacerbate and foster a polarization of opportunity and income because those without cultural capital typically have low-wage work awaiting them.

As Pierre Bourdieu reminds us (Bourdieu & Passeron, 1977), working-class and middle-class parents and families typically do not have the high-status cultural capital that academic and economic success requires. When such capital is not provided by the education system, there is little if any other source of its acquisition. That is, if middle- and low-income students do not receive cultural capital in school, they are not likely to have the opportunity to learn it elsewhere. The type of knowledge and work dispositions distributed by education becomes, then, an increasingly powerful wedge separating rich and poor. School knowledge, without activist intervention for substantial reform, will not merely reproduce inequality, it will produce class polarization.

REFERENCES

Anyon, J. (1980a). Education and personal political development: The contribution of theory. *Journal of Curriculum Theorizing, 2*(2), 280–283.

Anyon, J. (1980b). Social class and the hidden curriculum of work. *Journal of Education, 162*(1), 7–92.

Anyon, J. (1981). Social class and school knowledge. *Curriculum Inquiry 11*(1), 3–40.

Anyon, J. (2005). *Radical possibilities: Public policy, urban education, and a new social movement.* New York: Routledge.

Apple, M. (1979). *Ideology and curriculum.* New York: Routledge.

Apple, M. (1982). *Education and power.* New York: Routledge.

Apple, M. (1988). *Teachers and texts: A political economy of class and gender relations in education.* New York: Routledge.

Apple, M. (1993). *Official knowledge: Democratic education in a conservative age.* New York: Routledge.

Apple, M. (1996). *Cultural politics and education.* New York: Teachers College Press.

Bourdieu, P., & Passeron, J. C. (1977). *Reproduction in education, society, and culture.* Beverly Hills, CA: Sage.

Bowles, S., & Gintis, H. (1976). *Schooling in capitalist America: Educational reform and the contradictions of economic life.* New York: Basic Books.

Burawoy, M. (1991). *Ethnography unbound: Power and resistance in the modern metropolis.* Berkeley, CA: University of California Press.

Dale, R., Esland, G., Fergusson, R., & MacDonald, M. (1981). *Schooling and the state,* Vol. 1. *Schooling and the national interest.* Sussex, Eng.: Falmer and the Open University.

Lafer, G. (2002). *The job training charade.* Ithaca, NY: Cornell University Press.

Marcus, G. (1998). *Ethnography through thick and thin.* Princeton, NJ: Princeton University Press.

Murnane, R., & Levy, F. (1996). *Teaching the new basic skills: Principles for educating children to thrive in a changing economy.* New York: Free Press.

Reich, R. (1992). *The work of nations: Preparing ourselves for 21st century capitalism.* New York: Vintage.

Sassen, S. (2001). *The global city: New York, London, Tokyo* (2nd ed.). Princeton, NJ: Princeton University Press.

Williams, R. (1977). *Marxism and literature.* New York: Oxford University Press.

Willis, P. (1977). *Learning to labor: How working-class kids get working-class jobs.* New York: Columbia University Press.

Young, M. F. D., & Whitty, G. (1977). *Society, state and schooling: Readings on the possibilities for radical education.* London: Taylor and Francis.

3

SCHOOLING, POWER, AND THE
EXILE OF THE SOUL

CARLOS ALBERTO TORRES

PERSONAL INTRODUCTION

[T]he increasing, predominantly class-based gap between the vital women's movement and feminist theorizing in academy has led in part to a kind of careerist academic feminism whereby the boundaries of the academy stand in for the entire world and feminism becomes a way to advance academic careers rather than call for fundamental and collective social and economic transformation." (Chandra Talpade Mohanty)[1]

When I arrived at Stanford University in June 1980 to begin my Ph.D. coursework, I did not understand nor could I read a word of English. I still remember the face of the admissions officer in immigration. After looking at Stanford's paperwork documenting that I had received a full fellowship for a Ph.D. in education he realized that I was totally illiterate in the English language and thus unable to communicate with him!

After taking a summer course, I started my program in October. Because of my training in political philosophy, sociological theory, and political science in Argentina and Mexico, I had solid theoretical knowledge and had already published several books in Spanish and Portuguese. Yet given the barriers of the language, I was unable to read the new developments in the political economy of education published in English, and particularly, the theoretical developments in educational theory in the United States. Once I could read English, one of the first theoretical pieces that caught my attention was Michael Apple's *Education and Power*. I continued to read his work until I decided, with Raymond Morrow, to interview Michael Apple about his views on education and power.[2] Since that interview fifteen years ago, I learned to appreciate the private as well as the public persona of Michael Apple, and I continued to learn from him, having explored in depth some of his most intimate perceptions and personal struggles in my conversations collected in *Education, Power, and Personal Biography*.[3]

This chapter is written in honor of one of the most prominent cultural critics and critical educators of the United States. The epigraph from Mohanty serves an important purpose. Mohanty's perspective applies not only to feminism but virtually to any school of thought, paradigmatic tradition, "intellectual cottage industry," clique, or perspective in the social sciences that has become part (even if only a marginal part) of the academic canon. In following the career of Michael Apple, particularly once I got to know him, it has been refreshing to realize that his passion is the pursuit of social transformation of hierarchical capitalist societies and the transformation of power and hegemony in education, not the advancement of his own academic career.

As a former printer and union activist, Apple does not consider the confines of academy the "whole world" as Mohanty chastises some academics. Apple's work calls for fundamental and collective social and economic transformation. It is his relentless work in analyzing the connections between education and power in the areas of curriculum and educational policy and leadership and his peculiar ability to link theory and practice through research and activism that have brought him to such a prominent place in the realm of critical studies in education, a position that has virtually no match in the context of the United States.[4] Yet, as it is clear throughout this book, his contributions are not restricted to critique and utopia in U.S. education but have reached the four corners of the globe, making Apple a global public intellectual in the best of the neo-Gramscian tradition.[5] There is no question that among his many contributions, *Ideology and Curriculum* stands out as emblematic, a landmark book. In this chapter I will analyze some of the key themes of Apple's lifework.

In his preface to the 25th anniversary edition of his *Ideology and Curriculum*, Michael Apple argues that for more than three decades he has tried to unveil the complex connections among knowledge, teaching, and power in education. *Ideology and Curriculum* was his first book addressing this complex subject, and many more books were to follow. In his research agenda initiated by *Ideology and Curriculum*, Apple discusses what is, in my opinion, the soul of a political sociology of education in the context of the struggle for democracy and the broken promises of public education in the United States and elsewhere.

This chapter is an attempt to capture the emotional, analytical, and normative implications of what *Ideology and Curriculum* taught us. Yet, in my conclusion, I will also focus on the key question that Apple himself poses in his new preface to the third edition: "what has changed and what has stayed the same in the years since the first and second edition of this book."[6] I will analyze this question in the context of new developments in the study of globalization and education, considering the perennial concerns of the scholarship of class, race, gender, and the state.

IDEOLOGY, CURRICULUM, AND THE ARROGANCE OF POWER

If, for the established powers, democracy is deliberate delusion, then politics is the industry and the art of emasculating the truth. (Carlos Alberto Torres)[7]

Power corrupts, and absolute power corrupts absolutely, as stated by Lord Acton in what could be considered one of the founding notions of a libertarian philosophy, always suspecting raw power and the exercise of power tout court. Yet, one may want to imagine different expressions of power—from the exercise of power in the context of the liberal Enlightenment, to the contemporary exercise of power in the context of historically ignorant and narrow-minded neoconservative and neoliberal technocracies.

The brilliant insights of the Enlightenment, even with all its failings (e.g., its Eurocentrism, its male-centrism, the list is rather long), were attempts, albeit limited, to exercise the power of reason to improve the human condition and subjugate the forces of nature. The reasoning is that by moving away from the fanaticism of religion or esoteric practices and seeking empirical proof for scientific arguments there is room created for the social democratic planning of a society, as Karl

Mannheim (1893–1947) so clearly analyzed in his classic work *Ideology and Utopia*.

After Machiavelli, the founding father of modern political science, there is no question that power and interest intersect continuously in human affairs, and therefore, the exercise of power is always a struggle about conflicts of interest, ideology, and hegemony. Thus, not surprisingly, as *Ideology and Curriculum* so insightfully demonstrated twenty-five years ago, education is a site of contestation.

The apparent ignorance of this fact by neoconservative and neoliberal technocracies has a different meaning. Technocrats of any political sign resort to political expedience (to solve the social problems and policy dilemmas) and seek to build hegemony (to preserve the integrity of the capitalist system).[8] Technocrats rely on a very specific intellectual source: they draw on a notion of knowledge as instrumental rationality rather than substantive rationality.[9] They have a distinctive notion of the "good society": they rely on the theology of the supremacy of the market in the allocation of resources and the Darwinian premises of the survival of the fittest.

Traditional liberal educators, on the contrary, believe that education contributes to economic development and the welfare of society in several ways, and that education and labor markets should be somewhat coordinated. In the traditional liberal perspective associated with modernization theories, education contributes to economic development in several ways: (1) by raising the productivity of the newly educated; (2) by raising the productivity of individuals working with educated people; (3) by expanding the flow of general knowledge to individuals (e.g., instruction in health care and nutrition), thus reducing the cost of transmitting useful information; (4) by acting as a device for selecting the more able individuals and thereby enhancing their occupational mobility; and (5) by strengthening economic incentives, that is, the tendency for people to respond positively to a rise in the rate of reward for their efforts.[10]

The New Left provided theoretical notions that challenged both optimistic perspectives of liberal modernization theories, but also provided a theoretical background to challenge the positions of conservatives and neoconservatives. There is no question that theoretically, Apple locates his work in critical dialogue with theories of social reproduction. These theories, presented with a historical nuance, are well represented in *Ideology and Curriculum*.[11] I argue here that social reproduction theories constitute one of the founding premises of critical theories of education with all its variations.[12] Therefore, it should not be surprising to realize how much Apple relied on some of the insights and findings of social reproduction theories, particularly in his earlier work.

By focusing on the notion of social reproduction and its implications for education, *Ideology and Curriculum* was one of the first books that, even with its Althusian overtones, offered a systematic appraisal of education from a critical perspective.[13] I offer here a systematic presentation of some of the key reproduction theses presented in *Ideology and Curriculum*. Although this is my personal rendition of some of the key premises of social reproduction theories as presented in several critical perspectives, they are not idiosyncratic but remain largely a framework, perhaps better viewed as a list from which many scholars, unions, social movements, and community organizations have structured their critical discourses in education.

I acknowledge Apple's early warning, following the insights of Raymond Williams, that "There is a danger of reducing all social inquiry to a search for the macroeconomic basis of the reproduction of inequality and hence to dismiss any microinstitutional analysis of symbols and interaction. This would be a grave error."[14]

Thesis 1

Schooling justifies and reproduces inequalities in capitalist societies. A number of elements intervene to produce this outcome, including school tracking, racist behavior, elite networking, disciplinary sanctions, lack of relevance of subject matter for people's lives, inefficient resource allocation, and lack of efficacy of schooling as measured in high dropout and repetition rates or irrelevant *pro forma* learning. In "Ideology and Practice in Schooling" Apple is very clear about what schools do. They assist in capital accumulation, political legitimization, and production. While he offers this synthesis, he also offers a nuanced understanding that these functions do not exhaust what schools do: "Accumulation, legitimation, and production represent structural pressures on schools, not foregone conclusions."[15]

Thesis 2

Schooling reproduces authoritarian, classist, racist, homophobic, and patriarchal relationships in capitalist societies. This is the result of the authoritarianism of administrators and school bureaucrats and is compounded by the authoritarianism of parents, politicians, and the authoritarianism of knowledge production, distribution, exchange, and consumption once it is defined as "official knowledge."[16]

Thesis 3

Schooling and knowledge are unable to counteract the commodification of social relationships because the capitalist culture creates nothing by a culture of consumption. Not surprisingly, then, the molecular biologist Richard Lewontin argues that "the knowledge required for political rationality, once available to the masses, is now in the possession of a specialized educated elite, a situation that creates a series of tensions and contradictions in the operation of representative democracy."[17]

Thesis 4

In some instances, schooling is viewed as a "babysitting service" for children and youth, allowing parents freedom from care of them for the few hours they are at a learning site. Schools resemble boarding warehouses more than learning places despite the barrage of cognitive tests that, in my opinion, have yet to prove they are a true measure of actual knowledge and learning. Schools have lost their edge as state instruments acting in *locus parenti* helping children and youth to become morally socialized and cultivated in the disciplines of the spirit and the body. In short, a most meaningful cultural creation of the 19th century and modernism may have become totally irrelevant in the 21st century, despite Gramsci's incisive thesis that "Every time the question of language surfaces, in one way or another, it means ... to reorganize the cultural hegemony."[18]

I am aware that these theses—as presented—overemphasize some of the processes, routines, codes, and practices that take place in educational settings. Theories of social reproduction and resistance continue to inform the analysis of critical sociologies of education. The next section discusses what has changed since the publication of Apple's *Ideology and Curriculum*. I will be quite selective in my analysis, focusing on items that seem particularly relevant for this conversation. Needless to say, in what follows I hope to be more provocative than evocative.

WHAT REMAINED THE SAME AND WHAT HAS CHANGED SINCE THE PUBLICATION OF *IDEOLOGY AND CURRICULUM?*

Education as Social Reproduction

[T]he exercise of imperialist domination demands cultural oppression and the attempt at direct or indirect liquidation of what is essential in the subject people's culture. But the people is able to create and develop a liberation movement only because it keeps its culture alive despite permanent and organized oppression of its cultural life. (Amilcar Cabral)[19]

Radical democratic scholars and practitioners have come to the conclusion, after decades of struggling, that education and schooling are not the means to bring about a social revolution in contemporary societies. As Durkheim has reminded us time and time again, schooling systems, as they always were, are conservative in nature. Yet a number of contemporary factors contribute to underscore this situation. In the 1990s, we have observed a slowdown in the activism of social movements. That led many to argue that after the fall of socialism, capitalism seems to have triumphed all over the world (for example, Fukuyama's highly controversial theory of the end of ideology). With the triumph of capitalism, individualism as a philosophy of life seem to have triumphed because with the decline in the welfare state, most forms of organized solidarity have also been damaged, perhaps beyond repair. With the destruction of organized solidarity, competition, not collaboration, has emerged as the key goal in educational institutions and civil society.

However, today one may dispute whether there is really a slow down of resistance showing an even more proactive role for social movements and community organizations. There is a large and well-documented experience of resistance and challenges to top-down globalization models,[20] what some people have aptly termed the "globalization discontents." Many new initiatives show innovative approaches to social and political struggles.[21] The uproar about the neoliberal educational reforms like the No Child Left Behind Act and its implications is another indication of the extent that educational settings are sites of contestation and struggle despite the dynamics of social reproduction.[22] Therefore, allowing educational settings to be controlled by the neoconservatives and neoliberals, by leaving school settings or by falling into a kind of moral nihilism of broken promises and broken spirits, has proven to be disastrous for political struggle.

Hence, a basic normative and political premise is that if schools and other places of education are sites of contestation and struggle, progressive, radical, and democratic educators and activists should continue struggling, no matter what the odds are. In my opinion, Apple's life and work reflects, better than many scholars I know, the embodiment of this practice and principle.

State and Education: Schooling as Sites of Contestation

The only absolutely certain thing is the future, since the past is constantly changing. (Yugoslavian aphorism)[23]

Studying the contributions of Apple in a sequence of books that were inaugurated with *Ideology and Curriculum*, there are other analytical premises we have learned. Perhaps the most important is that particularly during the 20th century, the education system and practices were sustained, prepared, organized, and certified by the state. In fact, public education is a state function not only in terms of the legal order or financial support, but the specific requisite qualifications and certification of the teachers, textbooks, and coursework for the basic curriculum are also controlled by state agencies and defined in the context of specific politics of the state.[24] Changes in the politics of schooling since *Ideology and Curriculum* was written, however, need to be documented and analyzed. Let me offer some insights into these changes and the new challenges they present.

Some radical democratic or progressive educators, including some following the Freirean tradition, at some point in their struggle for liberation have left school settings with the intention to change the systems of public education from the outside. This has occasionally resulted in the New Right progressively taking more control of the available "spaces" within academic institutions and school systems. This positioning has been helped by the logic of administrative and technical control, which challenges through instrumental knowledge any form of reflexive knowledge (á la Habermas) and creates new conditions for the manipulation of consciousness rather than consciousness raising. Apple spoke with prescient voice about this then new and emerging form of technical control in *Ideology and Curriculum*.

Word and Images: Is School Knowledge Relevant?

Representations privilegue, those who have some control over self-representation, and they are largely framed within dominant modes of intelligibility. (Henry Giroux)[25]

A third important change since *Ideology and Curriculum* was written is the more prominent role that image is taking in contemporary societies, overwhelming the traditional role of the written word. Mass media and the digital culture are playing a most prominent role in the socialization of children and youth, usually reinforcing hierarchies and power elites and challenging some of the principles of schooling as purveyors of knowledge and as means of social mobility, equity, and equality. They are several corollaries to this observation. Even if schooling could be considered a mostly social reproduction of values, practices, habits, dexterities, or knowledge, in itself it is losing ground as part and parcel of the socialization devices compared to the mass media and digitalization. The schools are losing relevance; the written word is losing relevance facing the culture of the images; even the curriculum as official knowledge is losing relevance facing the hidden curriculum of the mass media. There is a growing sense of fragmentation and isolation in terms of social relationships and relationships of learning and knowledge. There is a kind of solipsism, which may in the end result in political apathy, nihilism, and social disorganization. There is an increased power of unconventional relationships taking over *le quotidian* of people (e.g., from gang behavior to growing converts to born-again Christianity). There is, finally, a breakdown in family relationships, in the connections between youth culture and adult culture, in the connections between teachers and pupils, in the structured mechanisms of social control, in the rule of the law and the Constitution, and in community intimacy, neighboring and joining.

In short, while schooling may be mostly part and parcel of institutional networks of social reproduction and hegemony, and mass media appears as a more powerful means of social reproduction than schooling, what is being reproduced is not even the traditional, conservative cultures or traditional themes of schooling but disorganized communities, fragmented selves, isolated individuals, nihilism, and the utopia of apocalypse as reflected in the recent school shootings in the United States (Columbine High School in Colorado is a case in point, but unfortunately there are too many other examples of schools shootings in the United States).

Public School as a Common Good: The Role of Teacher Unions

Justice and freedom do not mutually support each other. (Nico Stenr)[26]

Another important change is the new role of teacher unions defending the common good rather than simply their membership's corporatist interests.[27] The role of teacher unions in the world is shaped by their confrontation to the dominant research agenda for educational reform. This hegemonic agenda for reform is basically orchestrated around two premises: a model of privatization of public education addressing what is perceived as the crisis of public education and the competing dynamics of centralization-decentralization in the articulation of educational reforms worldwide.

Unions react to these policy changes in diverse ways. These tensions are translated into the responses of teachers and teacher unions to the centralization/decentralization and public education/privatization tensions, and by another important dichotomy in teacher unions, the conflict between unionism and professionalism. Centralization and decentralization dynamics affect the relationship between teachers and the state in several ways, including the state's provision of educational services, the setting of national goals and curricula, bargaining processes, and professional autonomy. The unionism versus professionalism debate relates to the conflicting role of teachers as laborers and as professionals and includes issues of skilling and deskilling of teachers, working conditions, and participation in educational reform processes. Two key tensions are identified in the interaction between teacher unions and the state: centralization versus decentralization and unionism versus professionalism in the life of teacher unions.

Centralization versus decentralization tensions relates to whether teachers unions should support or resist the decentralization processes pushed by governments. This is not an easy task for two reasons: (a) because decentralization policies are usually complemented with the reinforcement of centralized structures, and (b) because, in principle, decentralization may empower teachers as professionals, but may also hinder them as workers. This leads to the second dilemma faced by unions: to what extent can they advance an agenda that defends both the rights of teachers as workers and as professionals without incurring contradictions?

Education as Liberation

Who are better prepared than the oppressed to understand the terrible significance of an oppressive society? Who suffer the effects of oppression more than the oppressed? Who can better understand the necessity of liberation? They will not gain this liberation by chance but through the praxis of their quest for it. And this fight, because of the purpose given it by the oppressed, will actually constitute an act of love opposing the lovelessness, which lies at the heart of the oppressor's violence, lovelessness even when clothed in false generosity.[28]

Perhaps the most important change since the first edition of *Ideology and Curriculum* is the question of the impact of globalization in educational settings. One may wonder whether the reproductive nature of hegemony is now augmented with the phenomenon of globalization. The dialectics of the global and the local show that the school, rather than being a space for emancipation, continues to be a space for authoritarianism, control, social reproduction, and disciplinary behavior.

The dynamics of the global are highly contradictory to the dynamics of local control of educational establishments, and this process is posing challenges that most educational establishments are unable or unwilling to meet. In fact, one may argue that the most salient pattern in the local-global social dynamics is the hegemonic political economy model of globalization (neoliberalism) encountering the growing "localization" and fragmentation of the politics of culture and education—which continues to show its local, provincial, or national prevailing and fragmented dynamics. That economics is growing globally and politics is growing locally crossing the spaces of the nation-state and the international system entails contradictions galore.

This is not surprising, considering the orientation of recent U.S. administrations. The Clinton and Bush neoliberal administrations have created the conditions for free trade, taking advantage of bilateral and multilateral institutions such as the International Monetary Fund or the World Bank, as a way to expand U.S. business hegemony in the world. Yet one implication is the growing outsourcing of jobs, and what Apple and others have described as the lifestyle of affluent urban workers and globalized corporate sectors seeking cheaper products or lower taxes even at the cost of undermining local communities.

HEGEMONY, POWER, AND CITIZENSHIP IN THE AGE OF GLOBALIZATION

Once the foundations of a building are undermined, anything built upon them collapses of its own accord. (Descartes)

This brings me to the final point of this chapter: the new sources of hegemony in the global world and the new role of neoimperial power of the United States. I submit that these changes should play a major role in the current analysis and practice of the politics of culture and education and by implication in democratic citizenship.[29] The first chapter of Apple's classic book is titled "Analyzing Hegemony." Apple wanted to demonstrate, joining a number of critical educators, from critical readings of John Dewey to most of the work of Paulo Freire, that education is a political act. As such, education plays a role in social reproduction of knowledge and power and in the constitution of hegemony, that is: "manifest and latent or coded reflections of modes of material production, ideological values, class relations, and structures of social power—racial and sexual as well as politico-economic—on the state of consciousness of people in a precise historical or socio-economic situation."[30]

Apple, following Gramsci's theoretical insights through the lenses provided by cultural studies and the contribution of Raymond Williams, studies the linkages of hegemony and education. Apple defined hegemony as "an organized assemblage of meanings and practices, the central, effective and dominant system of meanings, values and actions which are lived."[31] From this perspective, Apple goes on to explore the dynamics of hegemony, power, and control in the curriculum and teachers' training. In addition, Apple focuses on how ideology plays a role in molding consciousness, and how knowledge and power intersect in the realm of cultural politics, particularly in schooling and education. His focus is structural and cultural, trying to find a balance between the most structuralist, and some people would argue, economist critical readings of schooling, with those whose analyses focus on culture, while trying to understand the role of human agency in education, power, and knowledge production. Yet, in reading his book one can conclude that Apple has a very specific focus, that is, the dynamics of schooling in capitalist societies. Indeed, Apple also has a very specific focus on the intersection of issues of race, class, gender, and sexuality in the process of schooling (e.g., dominant models of management, evaluation, research, curriculum work, and so forth), and in the construction of commonsense in the process of ideological and cultural reproduction in the United States. One should also be careful here because the resonance and reception of Apple's work extend well beyond the borders of the country in which it was originally conceived and where he lives.

Twenty-five years ago, this discussion in the United States was indeed path-breaking, and many of us have learned from Apple the key concepts to explore critically the relational connections between education, power, and social reproduction.[32] What is now drastically different, if one were to write *Ideology and Curriculum* again, are the implications of the new social order in the construction of hegemony and the new role that one of the most advanced industrial societies, the United States, is having while behaving as a neoimperialist power.

The complexity of these processes, one may argue, is, simply put, that all bets are off. While criticizing social reproduction, critical educators have been struggling to promote equity and equality in schools, along with achievement of a good quality education. To this extent, we believe that better research findings, more consistent policy, better school management, teacher training, curriculum and instruction theories, and textbooks make a difference. Yet, what difference do better schools make for the betterment of our society if the overall orientation of the U.S. government is to achieve global hegemony through the use of brutal force (disguised through military new euphemisms such as "smarts bombs"), and to act as a world policeman in a neoimperialist fashion? What difference do schools make in the training of children and youth who, eventually, will become the new centurions in the new century? What difference do schools make in the education of people of color if they will become "green card Marines" in the imperial army? What difference do schools make in promoting social mobility if there are no jobs for the graduates because most of the best jobs have been outsourced into a globalized market, benefiting from the surplus value of globalized corporations?[33] What difference do schools make in promoting multicultural traditions if, as many scholars have argued, there is only one dominant, hegemonic culture in capitalism, and that is the commodification of labor and knowledge and the culture of class?[34] What difference do schools make if, as some have argued, they represent the broken promises of public education?[35] What difference do schools make if in betraying the principles of the Enlightenment, under the burden of heavy school and union bureaucracies, with schools located in run-down buildings, managed by self-serving politicians, stuffed by a technocratic curriculum, demoralized by administrators and teachers, and tested-to-death, disenfranchised students, with overworked and underpaid parents, and assailed by the world of business as another site for profit taking, schools have abandoned the key tenets of reasonability and utopia?

These are, indeed, some of the pressing questions of today, questions that certainly Apple's *Ideology and Curriculum*, and his many important books that followed, helped to establish an understanding of the ebb and flow of social and political struggles in schools. Yet these are new questions that demand from us more theoretical and innovative thinking and research, but more important, more decisive, ethically consistent, and efficient political actions to answer them; questions that if we[36] are unable to answer, both theoretically and practically, will leave schools, students, parents, teachers, and local communities exiled from the soul of democracy and freedom.

Is there any theoretical guidance to address this conundrum? As a response, and in closing, let me offer one of the most insightful epistemological quotes from Karl Marx's *Grundrisse* that, although complex and perhaps difficult, may help educators to frame theoretically the issues involved:

> The concrete is concrete because it is a combination of many determinations, i.e., a unity of diverse elements. In our thought, it therefore appears as a process of synthesis, as a result, and not as a starting point, although it is the real starting point and, therefore, also the starting point of observation and conception. … Hegel fell into the error, therefore, of considering the real as the result of self-coordinating, self-absorbed and spontaneously operating thought, while the method of advancing from the abstract to the concrete is but the way of thinking by which the concrete is grasped and is reproduced in our mind as concrete. It is by no means, however, the process which itself generates the concrete.[37]

ACKNOWLEDGMENT

I would like to thank Eden Celeste Flynn for her valuable comments to a previous version of this chapter.

NOTES

1. Chandra T. Mohanty, *Feminism without Borders: Decolonizing Theory, Practicing Solidarity* (Durham, NC: Duke University Press, 2003), p. 6.
2. Michael Apple, Raymond Allan Morrow, and Carlos Alberto Torres, "Education, Power and Personal Biography: An Interview with Michael Apple," *Phenomenology + Pedagogy* 8 (1990). Reprinted in M. Apple, *Official Knowledge: Democratic Education in a Conservative Age* (New York: Routledge, 1993).
3. Carlos Alberto Torres, *Education, Power, and Personal Biography: Dialogues with Critical Educators* (New York: Routledge, 1998).
4. In my book with Ray Morrow, we compared and contrasted the works of Michael Apple and Henry Giroux as exemplary of the developments of critical pedagogy in the United States in the 1990s. Raymond Allan Morrow and Carlos Alberto Torres, *Social Theory and Education: A Critique of Theories of Social and Cultural Reproduction* (New York: SUNY Press, 1995).

5. In 2004, as president of the Research Committee of Sociology of Education, I sponsored a Mid-Term Conference of Sociology of Education of the International Sociological Association (ISA) organized in Buenos Aires, Argentina. The conference was organized by the Paulo Freire Institute–Argentina, the University of Buenos Aires, the Centro Hipermediático Experimental Latinoamericano (cheLA), the University of Buenos Aires, and the Argentinean Teacher Union (CTERA). This conference was very well attended with more than 700 papers submitted and a very large audience over three days of work. The conference organizers insisted that they wanted to have Apple as the keynote speaker opening the meeting titled "Globalization, Education, Resistance and Technologies: The Social Responsibility of the Sociology of Education Regarding the Emergent Social Movements." They wanted Apple to talk about the scholarship of class, race, gender, and the state in the context of globalization. Michael, who was then at the University of London, could not attend but generously agreed to be interviewed by telephone. I translated that dialogue into Spanish. The conference was attended by a large group of South American graduate students, teachers, and scholars who were eager to listen to his opinions and very much celebrated his analyses. Apple previously agreed to send a text that opened the program of the event, published in Spanish and English, developing some of the key theses of his new introduction to the third edition of *Ideology and Curriculum* (New York: RoutledgeFalmer, 2004).

6. Michael Apple, *Ideology and Curriculum, Third Edition.* (New York: Routledge Falmer, 2004) p. 5.

7. Carlos Alberto Torres, *Globalization, Education and Transformative Social Justice Learning: A Preliminary Draft of a Theory of Marginality.* Paper prepared for the Fifth International Conference on Transformative Learning., Teachers College-Columbia University, New York, October 2003, p. 4

8. This topic has been insightfully addressed by Herbert Marcuse in his classic *One-Dimensional Man*, a book that marked the thinking of a generation of critical scholars (see the edition with a new introduction by Douglas Kellner [Boston: Beacon Press, 1991]). In the same vein, Freire contrasted the roles of education and extensionalism (and the practice of technocratic leadership) in his *Education for Critical Consciousness* (New York: Continuum, 1996). Two important contributions to critique the political expedience of technocracy using a theory of the state are Philip Corrigan ed., *Capitalist State Formation and Marxist Theory* (London and Melbourne: Quartet Books, 1980) and the by now classic work of Claus Offe, *Contradictions of the Welfare State*, ed. John Keane (London and Sydney: Hutchinson, 1984).

9. As Raymond Morrow and David Brown define with their characteristic precision, "The use of the notion of rationalization was originally developed by Max Weber, who distinguished between formal or instrumental rationality and substantial rationality. *Instrumental rationality* referred to the efficiency of the means realizing given ends (values), where efficiency was based on calculations and expertise was based on scientific techniques. In contrast, *substantial rationality* referred to ultimate value claims and therefore could not be based on formally rational procedures at all." Raymond Allen Morrow with David D. Brown, *Critical Theory and Methodology* (Thousand Oaks, CA: Sage Publications, 1994), p. 100.

10. Carlos Alberto Torres, "Globalization, education, and citizenship: solidarity versus markets?" *American Educational Research Journal* 39, no. 2 (2002): 363–78; Carlos Alberto Torres, "The State, Privatisation and Educational Policy: A Critique of Neo-Liberalism in Latin America and Some Ethical and Political Implications," *Comparative Education* 38, no. 4 (November 2002): 365–85; Carlos Alberto Torres, R. S. Pannu, and M. Kazim Bacchus, "Capital Accumulation, Political Legitimation and Educational Expansion," in *Education and Social Change*, ed. J. Dronkers (Greenwich, CT and London, England: JAI Press, 1993) (International Perspectives on Education and Society, volume 3).

11. Raymond Morrow and Carlos Alberto Torres, *Social Theory and Education: A Critique of Theories of Social and Cultural Reproduction;* (Albany, NY: State University of New York Press, 1996); Raymond Morrow and Carlos Alberto Torres, "Education and the Reproduction of Class, Gender and Race: Responding to the Postmodernist Challenge," *Educational Theory* 44, no. 1 , (1994): 43–61 Included as a chapter in C. A. Torres and T. Mitchell, eds., *Sociology of Education: Emerging Perspectives*, ed. C. A. Torres and T. Mitchell (Albany: State University of New York Press, 1998).

12. Theories of resistance, theories of multiculturalism, critical pedagogy, neo-Marxism in education, critical theory, several strains of feminism, post-colonialism, and even most of the work in postmodernism, are all tributaries of (in either agreement to and extension of the analyses or in contradistinction to) the theoretical matrix opened up with theories of social reproduction. For an extensive discussion of this problematique, see Morrow and Torres, *Social Theory and Education: A Critique of Theories of Social and Cultural Reproduction*. See for instance, Michael Apple, ed., *Cultural and Economic Reproduction in Education: Essays on Class, Ideology and the State* (London and Boston: Routledge and Kegal Paul, 1982). Here is one of the most brilliant chapters by Apple, one that, particularly given the technocratic nature of U.S. education and policy, has not received the attention that it deserves, "Curricular Form

and the Logic of Technical Control: Building the Possessive Individual" (pp. 247–274).

13. There is no question that this tradition has grown in the United States and elsewhere and is impacting research and graduate education, teachers' training, curriculum work, and eventually may reach the realm of policy making. It will be difficult, however, to provide a systematic bibliography of key works in critical theory applied to education. Every selection of books that represent that tradition is arbitrary. I made my selection of those contributions by interviewing those 12 authors who, in my opinion, helped in this country and internationally to establish the critical tradition after the 1960s. This analysis is documented in Carlos Alberto Torres, *Education, Power and Personal Biography:. Interviews with Critical Educators* (New York: Routledge, 1998).

14. Michael Apple, "The New Sociology of Education: Analyzing Cultural and Economic Reproduction," *Harvard Educational Review* 48, no. 4 (November 1978): 502.

15. Michael Apple, "Ideology and Practice in Schooling," *Boston University, Journal of Education* 168, no. 1 (1986): 9–11.

16. Michael Apple, *Official Knowledge: Democratic Education in a Conservative Age* (New York: Routledge, 1998). Michael Apple, *Educating the "Right" Way* (New York: Routledge, 2000).

17. *New York Review of Books*, November 18, 2004, p. 38.

18. Antonio Gramsci, *The Antonio Gramsci Reader: Selected Writings 1916–1935*, ed. David Forgacs, with a new introduction by Eric Hobsbawm (New York: New York University Press, 2000), p. 357.

19. Amilcar Cabral, "The Role of Culture in the Liberation Struggle," in *Political Education in Africa*, ed. M. Arruda et al. (Toronto: Latin American Research Unit [LARU], No. 3, June 1977).

20. See for instance, Robert Rhoads and Carlos Alberto Torres (eds.), *The University, State, and Market: The Political Economy of Globalization in the Americas* (Stanford: Stanford University Press, 2006).

21. Michael Apple himself, in one of his last books *The State and the Politics of Knowledge* (New York: RoutledgeFalmer, 2003), documents the new developments in the Third World, particularly in Brazil, with the new projects around the World Social Forum and the World Educational Forum. With Rob Rhoads we have analyzed this phenomenon jointly with other authors—see chapters by Boaventura de Sousa Santos, Noam Chomsky, Atilio Boron, and Robert Rhoads, and Carlos A. Torres in the Rhoads and Torres's book mentioned in note 20). A most intriguing process of expropriation of bankrupted enterprises in Argentina by their former workers and the reconstitutions of them in workers cooperatives, including a fascinating new model of workers education, is well presented in the documentary movie, *The Take,* produced by Canadian

Journalists (2005). Moreover, in the context of the failure of neoliberalism so well exemplified in the failure of the Argentina economic model, new energies have been orchestrated around new social movements, such as the *Movimento Barrios de Pie* in Argentina or, on parallel lines, the *Movimento Sem Terra* in Brazil.

22. Carlos Alberto Torres, "NCLB: A Brainchild of Neoliberalism and American Politics," *New Politics* 10, no. 2 (Winter 2005): 94–100.

23. A Yugoslavian aphorism cited by Immanuel Wallerstein in "A Left Politics for the 21st Century? or, Theory and Praxis Once Again," *Democratie* (Binghamton: Fernand Braudel Center, University of New York, 1999), p. 1.

24. Carlos Alberto Torres, *Democracy, Education and Citizenship: Dilemmas of Citizenship in a Global World* (Lanhman, MD: Rowman and Littlefield, 1998), p. 14.

25. Henry Giroux, "What Might Education Mean after Abu Ghraib: Revisiting Adorno's *Politics of Education.*" *Comparative Studies of South Asia, Africa and the Middle East,* 24, no. 1 (2004): 3–19, quote on p. 8.

26. Nico Stehr, "Is Civil Society a Daughter of Knowledge? Worlds of Knowledge and Democracy" (Essebm, Germany: Kulturwissenshafliches Institut, November 2004, manuscript).

27. Carlos Alberto Torres, Seewha Cho, Jerry Kachur, Aurora Loyo, Marcela Mollis, Akio Nagao, and Julie Thompson, "Political Capital, Teachers' Unions and the State: Conflict and Collaboration in Educational Reform in the United States, Canada, Japan, Korea, Mexico, and Argentina" manuscript, Los Angeles (2004).

28. Paulo Freire, *Pedagogy of the Oppressed* (New York: Continuum, 2000), p. 5.

29. Henry Giroux offers a significant contribution, analyzing the situation of U.S. forces in Iraq and the events of Abu Ghraib. (see Giroux, "What Might Education Mean after Abu Ghraib: Revisiting Adorno's *Politics of Education,*" drawing from Adorno's compellng suggestions in Theodor W. Adorno, "Education after Auschwitz," *Critical Models: Interventions and Catchwords* [New York: Columbia University Press, 1998], pp. 191–204.)

30. Michael Apple, *Ideology and Curriculum* (New York: Routledge & Kegan Paul, 1979), p. 1.

31. Ibid., p. 5.

32. One could think of few other books with the range of explanatory capabilities and impact of *Ideology and Curriculum*. I should note, *noblese oblique*, Basil Bernstein, *Class, Codes and Control*, 3 vols. (London: Routledge & Kegan Paul, several years); Samuel Bowles and Herbert Gintis, *Schooling in Capitalist America* (New York: Basic Books, 1976); Pierre Bourdieu and Jean Claude Passeron, *Reproduction in Education,*

Society and Culture, trans. R. Nice (London: Sage, 1977); and Martin Carnoy and Henry M. Levin, *Schooling and Work in the Democratic State* (Stanford, CA: Stanford University Press, 1985).

33. Nicholas C. Burbules and Carlos Alberto Torres, eds., *Globalization and Education: Critical Perspectives* (New York: Routledge, 2000).

34. Cameron McCarthy, *The Uses of Culture: Education and the Limits of Ethnic Affiliations* (New York: Routledge, 1998); Rusell Jacoby, "The Myth of Multiculturalism," *New Left Review* 208 (1994): 121–126; Carlos Alberto Torres, *Democracy, Education and Multiculturalism: Dilemmas of Citizenship in a Global World* (Lanham, MD: Rowman and Littlefield, 1998).

35. Greg Dimitriadis and Dennis Carlson, eds., *Promises to Keep: Cultural Studies, Democratic Education and Public Life* (New York: Routledge, 2003).

36. I use the pronoun "we" here not only as a rhetorical device, but as a signifier of political commitment to social justice of a very heterogeneous group of people who care about public education and are committed to address the injustices of social life in capitalist social formations. One may argue that by doing so, one has no choice but to address all forms of domination, as reflected in the contributions of Freire's *Pedagogy of the Oppressed.*

37. Karl Marx, *Grundrisse* (Harmondsworth & London: Penguin Books & New Left Review, 1973), p. 101.

II

Contemporary Theoretical Challenges

4

RIDING TENSIONS CRITICALLY

Ideology, Power/Knowledge, and Curriculum Making

YOSHIKO NOZAKI

INTRODUCTION

The central problem of curriculum is what we should teach,[1] and a curriculum theory, by clarifying concepts involved and unpacking the nature of the problem (and the problems arising from it), should provide some justification and practical guidance for the choices we make as to what to teach (Kliebard, 1992). If we decide to teach knowledge rather than something else, it is imperative to unravel the issues concerning the nature of knowledge. Indeed, since the 1970s, a number of scholars in the field of education have examined critically the knowledge taught in schools as social construction and the link between that knowledge and social control (e.g., Apple, 1979, 1985; Whitty, 1985; Young, 1971). In this movement, Michael W. Apple has constantly taken the lead, articulating with theoretical force the need for educational research examining the selective traditions of curriculum knowledge and the linkages between knowledge made available to students and economic and political power.

In recent years, with postmodern theories exerting a strong and profound influence on the field, research on curriculum theory and practice has come to an unavoidable confrontation with the episte-mological and methodological (often referred to "theoretical") issues involved in knowledge production, selection, and organization. Can a particular epistemology, or methodology, of knowledge serve suffi-ciently as a curriculum theory, especially when developing a curricu-lum for social change? This chapter begins with an examination of the concept of ideology and proceeds to discuss Michel Foucault's alterna-tive approach to the problem of knowledge. It then examines R. W. Connell's idea of standpoint theory for counter-hegemonic curriculum development and Foucault's idea of genealogy. Foucault's geneaology is conceived as a theory for historical inquiry; however, in my view, it makes for a viable curriculum theory. The chapter concludes by sug-gesting the use of the metaphor "riding tensions" in dealing with the epistemological and methodological issues in curriculum making.

THE CONCEPT OF IDEOLOGY AND ITS THEORETICAL TENSIONS

The concept of ideology has been widely debated and variously inter-preted among researchers in social sciences in general and Marx-ist scholars in particular. It was Marx who reinvented the concept by making the connection between ideology and social contradictions. With Marx, however, the concept was used in at least two contentious ways: sometimes it was used to mean "illusion, false consciousness, unreality, up-side-down reality," while at other times it was "the set of ideas which arise from a given set of material interests or from a defi-nite class or group" (Williams, 1983, pp. 153–157; see also Apple, 1979, pp. 20–24).

This basic split in usage gives the concept a central theoretical ten-sion: Should ideology be used critically and somewhat negatively (such as, for example, "false consciousness"), or should it be used descrip-tively with positive connotations (such as, for example, a "worldview" or "perspective" expressing the value of a particular social group)? This is, in essence, to ask whether knowledge is the opposite of ideology, or if it is ideological to begin with. Additional theoretical tensions are also identified: (1) Is ideology conceived of as the antithesis of science, or is science ideology? (2) Is ideology a subjective, psychological phe-nomenon or an objective, social phenomenon? (3) Is ideology a specific element in the "superstructure" of society, or is it identical with the whole sphere of culture? (4) Is ideology tied to class, and if so, in what sense? (e.g., Barrett, 1991; Larrain, 1979).

To be sure, philosophers (in particular, epistemologists) have long since asked these questions concerning the nature of knowledge and its determinants.[2] It is beyond the scope of this chapter to discuss the various positions that have been taken in the philosophical debates; however, it is worth mentioning past Marxist approaches to the questions. In Marxist traditions, the economic relation occupied (and perhaps continues to occupy) a major position in considering the notion of determination. In so-called economic reductionism, the edifice metaphor of base and superstructure was simplified in such a way that the "superstructure"—for example, all cultural and political institutions, relationships, and activities, including schools—was conceived of as the straightforward "reflection" of economic relations of production.[3] Objections to this position have long been raised by a number of theorists, including Antonio Gramsci and Louis Althusser, who have argued that culture and ideology have their own histories and are not totally determined by economic relations (i.e., the "relative autonomy" of ideology); instead, there are a number of determining factors in operation (i.e., "overdetermination"). To a significant degree, these concepts have reformulated the edifice metaphor.[4]

Nonetheless, the idea of class—or economic relations and material conditions—has remained connected in some way to the concept of ideology. "If a theory of ideology were to be useful," Michele Barrett (1991) suggests, "it would most certainly have to be applicable to understanding the cultural, ideational and subjective experiences of people in terms other than ... those of social class" (p. 158). In this regard, some critics (notably Ernesto Laclau and Chantal Moufee, 1985), in extending some of Gramsci's ideas, have argued that ideology has "no necessary class belonging," that ideology *is not necessarily* related to social class. Their attempt has clearly opened up ways to develop and examine political discourse through multiple lenses, in a nuanced manner; it may, however, at least to some, "represent a ... collapse of the Marxist model" (Barrett, 1991, p. 80). In any case, the theoretical tensions surrounding the determination of human knowledge and consciousness will continue to exist, even if class reductionism were to be overcome.[5]

The concept of ideology invites further theoretical tensions, since it implies a distinction between true and false. If ideology is false consciousness, which or whose knowledge is valid, correct, or true? If ideology is an expression of a worldview, should any such worldview be given the same epistemological status? Here, the epistemological question intersects the question of "science." To be sure, "science" in this usage has a broader meaning than it usually does in English: it "denote[s] a systematic approach to any sphere of knowledge, including the humanities, guided by methods of investigation accepted by a community of scholars" (Iggers, 1997, p. 17).[6]

To raise a question of science is to approach the problem of ideology (or the problem of knowledge) from a different arena with some additional problematics and premises. In this arena, while the view that science is opposed to ideology has been influential (e.g., "scientific methods" guaranteeing a knowledge of a reality made up of "objective facts"), many critics working from a variety of positions have spoken of "science as ideology" (see also Larrain, 1979, pp. 172–211). Although the debates on the nature of science may continue, it seems safe to suggest that any inquiry in a given field of science begins with a choice of question(s), and that this recognition suggests the social and political implications of science—at least in many fields of social sciences. Moreover, any method or methodology used in a particular science involves a set of accepted rules, procedures, and technologies, which are not entirely value-neutral. A good case in point is women and science(s). Many feminist studies have demonstrated that the assumptions embedded in scientific inquiry, methodology, and methods have historically, by and large, served men's interests. Should women, then, oppose science, since it has served to maintain the patriarchy? Or should women transform science, in terms of its concepts, content, and methods? (See also Haraway, 1991; Harding, 1991.)

These questions point out that the epistemological and methodological tensions concerning knowledge and ideology, including the question of science, have direct implications for political struggles. They also point to the tensions that exist in the role(s) of intellectuals, including educational researchers and practitioners, in those struggles. In recent politics, voices of socially subordinate groups speaking about their particular experiences and claiming their own knowledges have become extremely influential. Their knowledges are often seen as privileged, and are supported by some version of so-called standpoint theory. (Indeed, as I discuss below, the standpoint theory can be a powerful curriculum theory.) On the one hand, the concept of ideology in its descriptive usage may allow intellectuals (or educators for that matter) to support such voices and truth claims positively. On the other hand, its critical usage asks them to examine and assess the truth claims carefully and rigorously. Sometimes such a critical examination becomes (or comes to be seen as) an act of intellectual arrogance; however, to lose entirely the critical edge in dealing with the matter of knowledge(s) could result in a highly relativistic position—that all truth claims are equally valid (see also Barrett, 1991).

The concept of ideology seems to be both enabling and disabling at the same time: enabling in that it helps illuminate the theoretical tensions and complexity (in some cases very well) concerning the problem of knowledge; disabling in that it leads to a series of dilemmas that are not easily overcome. In addition, while it is undeniable that the concept (with various meanings) has played an important role in social, political, and intellectual debates and criticism, in part because of its history, it is hard to "shake off" some of the connotations (e.g., the edifice metaphor) that are now seen as inadequate by many Marxists themselves (Barrett, 1991, p. 168). It is perhaps worth examining alternative approaches to the issue of knowledge to see how the theoretical tensions can be addressed differently. Below, I would like to discuss one such alternative proposed by the French philosopher Michel Foucault, who has brought about a clear paradigm shift in the discussion of knowledge.

MICHEL FOUCAULT AND THE
THEORY OF POWER/KNOWLEDGE

Foucault (1980) states that "ideology" is "a notion that cannot be used without circumspection" (p. 118).[7] Note that in saying that he is arguing against the critical—rather than descriptive—usage of the term: "like it or not, [the concept] always stands in virtual opposition to something else which is supposed to count as truth" (p. 118). In his view, it is an error to assume that "knowledge can exist only where the power relations are suspended"; rather there is the nexus of power and knowledge. As he puts it:

> Perhaps we should abandon the belief that ... the renunciation of power is one of the conditions of knowledge. We should admit rather that power produces knowledge ... ; that power and knowledge directly imply one another. (Foucault, 1979, p. 27)

Foucault (1980) defines his problem as a "politics of truth" that addresses "the effects of power and the production of 'truth'" (p. 157). (In doing so, he contrasts his problem to that of ideology, which he wittily calls "economics of untruth.") Foucault offers the concept of discourse, which in itself is "neither true nor false," and this allows him (and us) to launch a new kind of study concerning the question(s) of knowledge—a historical research to see "how effects of truth are produced within discourses" (p. 118). In his view, "truth" should be seen as "a system of ordered procedures for the production, regulation, distribution, circulation and operation of statements," a system that is "linked in a circular relation with systems of power which produce and sustain it, and to effects of power which it induces and which extend it." He terms this circular relation (and the power relations it helps maintain) as a "regime of truth" (p. 133).

It should be noted here that Foucault does not mean that because of the existence of a power-knowledge nexus there is no such thing as truth. To do so would be to follow the logic he refutes—the logic holding that true knowledge must be free of power. Jon Simons (1995), a scholar in political philosophy, points out that Foucault's argument about "the mutual constitution and enmeshment of power and knowledge" should not be taken to suggest that "all human scientific truth ... is untrue," but, instead, that "efforts to justify theories epistemologically cannot be disentangled from their political effects" (p. 92). The fact that "the relation between legitimate power and scientific truth is intense, constant, and highly organized ... does not undermine the epistemological validity of the truths told about human beings" (p. 44).

In other words, Foucault's "antiscience" position needs to be assessed carefully. No doubt that for Foucault (1988) science "has become institutionalized as a power," and as such it "forces [one] to say certain things" (pp. 106–107).[8] Foucault makes this point clearly and provocatively. Still, his position does not seem as radical as it sounds at first. He is concerned with the wider effects of the sciences (and the truths they produce) in terms of the subjection and domination that take place in a given society, not with the sciences per se. For example, Foucault (1980) defines "genealogy," his alternative approach to history, as "precisely antisciences," but it is not to defend "ignorance and non-knowledge" or to "deny knowledge." It is "the insurrection of knowledges" that are opposed to the effects of the centralizing powers, which are linked to the institution and functioning of an organized scientific discourse within a society such as ours (pp. 83–84).

This resonates well with Foucault's discussion on the role of the intellectual in a contemporary society, in which he argues that the (political) role of the intellectuals is "not to criticize the ideological contents ... linked to science," not "to ensure that his [sic] own scientific practice is accompanied by a correct ideology," but "ascertaining the possibility of constituting a new politics of truth" (Foucault, 1980, p. 133). This does not mean that there could be an ideologically free science. Rather, the idea is to disconnect it from the forms of hegemony (and by implication, I would say, to reconnect it to the counterhegemonic projects). As he explains:

> It's not a matter of emancipating truth from every system of power (which would be a chimera, for truth is already power) but of detaching the power of truth from the forms of hegemony, social, economic, and cultural, within which it operates at the present time. (Foucault, 1980, p. 133)

Foucault's idea per se may not be completely novel, especially for critics who have taken the position of knowledge as ideology, and who have struggled, successfully or not, for remaking the sciences from the perspectives of socially subordinate groups. Nevertheless, in my view, Foucault (re)articulates the view so clearly by reframing the problem of hegemony in relation to his notions of politics of truth and regime of truth, and he should certainly be credited for that.[9] In any case, the real issue—where the theoretical tensions would play out—goes perhaps to the specifics of his proposal for that "detaching."

Here it is important to note that Foucault (1980) identifies two kinds of "subjugated knowledge": an "erudite knowledge" and "local memories" (pp. 81–83).[10] The former is a knowledge "buried" in the prevailing tendency of history studies (which he calls "functionalist coherence" and "formal systemization"), which can be revealed by erudite and specialized scholarship and criticism. The latter is a "local, popular, disqualified knowledge," "a whole set of knowledges that have been disqualified [by science] as inadequate to their task or insufficiently elaborated" (p. 82). His examples are the knowledges of the psychiatric patient, of the ill person, of the nurse, and of the doctor, as opposed to the knowledge of medicine. The erudite knowledge and local memories are the basis of genealogy. As Foucault (1980) declares: "Let us give the term *genealogy* to the union of erudite knowledge and local memories which allow us to establish a historical knowledge of struggles and to make use of this knowledge tactically today" (p. 83).

Foucault suggests here the (counter-hegemonic) need to bridge the knowledges, memories, and voices of the socially subordinate and the scientific truths. As a general statement, this may not be entirely new, since a number of critical and feminist activists and scholars (with some standpoint theories) have attempted to do the same (though, as I describe below, some specifics of genealogical approaches are in fact new in their antiessentialist orientation). What is new at this general level is that he clearly (re)affirms—in the context of "antiscience," in opposition to the dominant regime of truth—the significance of intellectual expertise.

Of course, Foucault means to link it to the voices and perspectives of the socially subordinate, but, in a sense, his formulation makes the tension between the two kinds of knowledges (and epistemologies) more explicit. Who in the end would be the producer(s) of knowledge, and on what ground? Concerning this point, John Fiske (1996) observes—and I would agree—that Foucault seems to believe that it is "academics like himself" who can write a genealogical history (i.e., produce counter-[hegemonic] knowledges).[11] In any case, it seems that we still face theoretical tensions, including the question of epistemology, determination, and science, even if we take Foucault's position (not to mention that Foucault advances one kind of epistemology, and that his own study of history contains truth claims, however nuanced).

The theoretical tensions embodied with the concept of ideology reappear in Foucault's theory of power/knowledge. Then how do such tensions reappear in curriculum making, when one uses a particular theory as its guiding principle? In the following pages, I examine first R. W. Connell's argument for using the standpoint of the socially subordinate as a guiding principle for counter-hegemonic curriculum projects, then Foucault's idea of genealogical approaches to history.

STANDPOINT THEORY AND COUNTER-HEGEMONIC CURRICULUM MAKING

R. W. Connell (1993) begins his book *School and Social Justice* with a question: "What are our design principles for a school curriculum that will lead towards social justice?" His answer is to employ a strategy of "inverting hegemony" that "seeks a way of organizing [educational] content and method which builds on the experience of the disadvantaged" (p. 38). This strategy enables teachers to develop counter-hegemonic curricula that embody the interests and perspectives of the socially subordinate groups. Connell justifies it in terms of what is called "standpoint theory," an epistemology that basically argues the link between one's lived experience and grounding of knowledge.

In this theory, as Connell (1993) states, "the position of those who carry the burdens of social inequality" serves as "a better starting-point" for the construction of knowledge about the society than "the position of those who enjoy its advantages" (p. 39). "At its simplest," he argues, the standpoint(s) of the socially subordinate yields "experiences and information not normally available to the dominant groups, and therefore overlooked or marginalized in their constructions of knowledge" (p. 39). In other words, the traditional mainstream curriculum excludes the knowledge(s) of the socially subordinate groups, whereas a counter-hegemonic curriculum inverting hegemony brings out that knowledge(s). In Connell's view, the latter is at least better than the former in "being more comprehensive, truer to life 'as it really happened.'" For example, a school history curriculum that includes histories of socially subordinate groups (e.g., ordinary people and women) is more comprehensive than the traditional school history curriculum centering on the deeds of famous men.

Moreover, to take the standpoint(s) of the socially subordinate is to acquire "intellectual power" in constructing knowledge. Citing Georg Lukacs, Connell (1993) discusses the point of view of the proletariat as a classic example. According to Connell, Lukacs argues that the structural location of the working class allows workers to gain, in concrete terms, the most significant insights into the mechanisms of capitalist exploitation, without which the dynamics of class relations cannot be fully comprehended. However sophisticated, philosophers' views are blocked by their privileged locations in the capitalist world. Proletariat views and insights arising from their experience and action (standpoint) are necessary to overcome such blockages (p. 40).

Although Lukacs makes his case for the standpoint of the proletariat in understanding class relations, Connell (1993) argues that the general point—the intellectual power of standpoint held by the socially subordinate—also applies to other kinds of social relations such as gender, race, and sexuality. As he explains:

> [W]e think through economic issues from the standpoint of the poor, not of the rich. We think through gender arrangements from the standpoint of women. We think through race relations and land questions from the standpoint of indigenous people. We think through questions of sexuality from the standpoint of gay people. (p. 43)

That is, developing a counter-hegemonic curriculum might mean considering a number of standpoints, depending on the kinds of social relations one wishes to address in a given curriculum. As Connell (1993) puts it, "curricular justice" requires counter-hegemonic projects across the whole spectrum of social inequality. "No institutionalized pattern of social inequality is in principle exempt from it," says Connell. And such a situation would, in turn, result in "great diversity in what is undertaken" in practice (p. 44).

Connell's argument is accessible and persuasive. It is pre-eminent over others in its explicit interests (and success, in my view) in articulating a clear guiding principle for counter-hegemonic curriculum making. However, it is also important to note that the theoretical tensions (and dilemmas) concerning knowledge are present even in his successful argumentation. For example, the notion of standpoint(s) carries a form of essentialism regarding the relation between one's structural position and his or her knowledge(s). A case in point here is the notion of "the standpoint of women." The notion implies the singularity, or coherence, of such a standpoint and the knowledge it yields. However, "women" are not an internally monolithic group. Thus, the insights arising from their experience and action not only vary but also in some cases contradict each other. Here we face a question of method for selecting and organizing knowledge(s): How do we choose one set of insights over others? Do all "insights" have the same epistemological status? And how do we organize contradictory knowledges?[12]

Connell (1993) touches on the question of method, but not extensively. While suggesting that "an understanding of the central mechanisms producing a social structure is available through the experience of the groups subordinated by those mechanisms," he is careful not to equate "experience" with "knowledge." The latter, in his view, involves "constructive intellectual work," for which the disadvantaged groups may not possess "tools." As he puts it:

> To say this understanding is "accessible" through a group's experience is not to say it is necessarily produced in fact. Producing it, and then generalizing it, requires constructive intellectual work. And this is not easy for disadvantaged groups to do, precisely because of their disadvantage: most of the tools of intellectual work are in other people's hands. (p. 41)

Connell continues, "The complex issues that arise at this point are very lively ones for teachers in disadvantaged schools." Connell does not, however, go further to identify the complex issues he foresees or the specifics of the roles teachers might play. His answer is simply that "[t]he task is complex and difficult, but possible" (p. 41).

Connell (1993) seems to be hinting that teachers could (help) produce and organize the knowledges of the socially subordinate.[13] If he believes in the teacher's ability to overcome the "complex and difficult issues," this belief does not necessarily derive from his sheer, unfounded optimism. He has conducted research with schoolteachers in several educational projects, and that experience may have given him a degree of trust in teachers' abilities.[14] Having said that, however, I do find it somewhat frustrating to see him stop short of discussing the nature of "the complex and difficult issues" and the ways teachers can and should deal with them, as the role(s) played by the intellectuals (teachers, in this case) is one of the major theoretical tensions in producing, selecting, and organizing knowledge.

Another tension exists in the way Connell (1993) addresses the relationship between political struggles and knowledge. On the one hand, he suggests the social and political nature of curriculum, as "social division and social power shape the production and distribution of knowledge," and as "the way knowledge is organized has social consequences" (p. 34). On the other hand, Connell argues that the "political outcome" is not the aim of counter-hegemonic curriculum projects. As he puts it:

> There have been education systems where the political outcome is the key criterion for curriculum choice. This was the case in the Soviet Union, and the far right in the U.S. is doing its best to impose the same logic in that country. It is important to avoid this, as it would abandon the element of independent truth in, for instance, scientific accounts of the world. (p. 45)

Some may wonder if the last sentence points to another tension—"science and ideology," and I think this is the case. Connell appears to be aware of the theoretical tensions he confronts, and interestingly he refers to Foucault:

> Knowledge is a social product. ... What is known, by whom, about whom, with what effects—these are social, indeed political, questions. To say this is not to say, as some skeptical epistemologists do, that *truth* is eliminated as an issue, or becomes an effect of power. I don't go all the way with Foucault; I think that truth is in many circumstances a subversive force that disrupts power/knowledge regimes. (If it were not, we would not see so much energy expended by governments and corporations in controlling knowledge.) (p. 109)

Foucault might somewhat disagree with Connell's interpretation of his position, since, as I have discussed above, "truth" is the most important issue for him, and it is also his contention that in certain occasions "playing the game(s) of truth" is the only way to "avoid ... the effects of a domination" (Foucault, 1991, p. 15). At any event, it seems that the theoretical tensions and struggles are present, overtly or not, in Connell's curriculum theory, and one can wonder whether it would have been more helpful had Connell gone further to elaborate his position. In particular, some of his readers (teachers and curriculum planners) who face these tensions in their everyday practices might have wished to hear it.

Connell (1993) offers a viable theory for counter-hegemonic curriculum making. His argument is strong, given its clarity in explaining the notion of the standpoint(s) of socially subordinate, its relationship to counter-hegemonic knowledges, and its significance to curriculum development. In my view, two major issues at least arise and remain to be considered with care, however. One issue concerns the essentialism the notion of standpoint (of a particular group) almost inevitably carries. Does Connell's curriculum theory overcome it without diminishing its clarity? The other concerns the epistemological and methodological tensions and their persistence. Even though Connell addresses them at times, the tensions never seem to go away. Here it would be worthwhile to examine Foucault's proposal for the genealogical study of history as it is read as a curriculum theory. Although Foucault is also concerned with ways of producing, selecting, and organizing the counter-hegemonic knowledge(s), he takes a different path than Connell, placing "antiessentialism" at the core of his argument.

GENEALOGY AS "EFFECTIVE" CURRICULUM

Although Foucault refers to "genealogy" in more than several essays and interviews, it is in his essay "Nietzsche, Genealogy, History" (Foucault, 1977, pp. 139-164) that he explains his idea of "genealogy" extensively and in more specific terms. Foucault suggests genealogy as a new approach to historical studies. For him, it is not to deny history (and a study of history) altogether; rather, it is to overcome what he calls "the search for origins"—the metaphysical and teleological moves and orientations he observes in historical studies (p. 140). He states that the pursuit of origins is "an attempt to capture the exact essence of things, their purest possibilities, and their carefully protected identities." It is a pursuit that assumes "the existence of immobile forms that precede the external world of accident and succession" (p. 142). Such a position, for him, is merely the historians' extension of their "faith in metaphysics." Foucault's alternative is to find "disparity" (differences) at the historical beginnings of events (p. 142). To find "disparity" is to see such beginnings as "derisive and ironic, capable of undoing every infatuation," and to attend to "vicissitudes of history," the multiplicity, complexity, unpredictability, and twists and turns of history (p. 144).

Two examples of genealogy help us to clarify Foucault's point. The first is the analysis of "descent" (*Herkunft*). According to Foucault, the analysis of descent often involves a consideration of race or social type, but it directs attention to the differences—not to the essential identity—that exist at its early stages of development:

> [T]he traits it attempts to identify are not the exclusive genetic characteristics of an individual, a sentiment, or an idea, which permit us to qualify them as "Greek" or "English"; rather, it seeks the subtle, singular, and subindividual marks that might possibly intersect in them to form a network that is difficult to unravel. (1977, p. 145)

Hence, rather than finding or constructing the image of the original unified and coherent identity, the search for descent "dissociat[es] the self," "disturbs what was previously considered immobile," "fragments what was thought unified," and "shows the heterogeneity of what was imagined consistent with itself" (p. 145). In short, it is to look at the heterogeneity (differences), rather than the homogeneity (identity), within a particular unit or subject matter.

Foucault's second example of genealogy is an examination of "emergence" (*Entstehung*). The analysis of emergence as he conceives it is not performed in terms of historical development (of the origin), but in terms of the emergence of disparity (e.g., different interpretations) in certain historical processes. According to Foucault, the emergence of disparity, such as different interpretation, arises because of confrontations between societal forces, and thus its analysis "must delineate ... the struggle these forces wage against each other or against adverse circumstances, and the attempt to avoid degeneration and regain strength by dividing these forces against themselves (1977, pp. 148–149).

Foucault, calling history as it is traditionally practiced "traditional history," calls history transformed into the genealogical study of history "effective history." (Here, the parallel would be "traditional curriculum" and "effective curriculum.") The former is the attempt to understand history in terms of "continuity"—the continuity of the original unified and coherent essence of things. He criticizes traditional history as having "theological" or "rationalistic" aims; that is, "dissolving the singular event into an ideal continuity ... as [a] teleological movement or a natural process" (1977, p. 154). Contrary to this, effective history is characterized as an attempt to "[place] within a process of development everything considered immortal in man" (p. 153). It is to bring "discontinuity" into history by historicizing those things regarded as natural and timeless, and so it deconstructs the image of original unity. In short, effective history "divides our emotions, dramatizes our instincts, multiplies our body and sets it against itself" (p. 154).

Effective history differs from traditional history in other important ways as well. It directs its attention to the multiplicity, complexity, and randomness of history (in Foucault's words, the world is "a profusion of entangled events"). It also attempts to understand the larger history by examining what is close (for example, the body, the nervous system, nutrition, digestion, and energies), instead of by "a contemplation of distance and heights [such as] the noblest periods, the highest forms, the most abstract ideas, the purest individualities" (1977, pp. 155–156). That is, effective history can focus on more ordinary, everyday practices, which traditional history has tended to disregard, but which are crucial for understanding multiple forms of power relations and the ways they work.

By now it should be clear to readers that Foucault argues for antiessentialist studies of history. It is a theory for producing, selecting, and organizing genealogical/historical knowledges (and so it can serve as a curriculum theory). A genealogical approach is used to reveal multiplicity, complexity, and incoherence, and to show struggles that have taken place over these differences. Recall that Connell's standpoint theory, which aims at constructing the knowledge(s) of the socially subordinate, runs into the problem of essentialism. Like Connell, Foucault is concerned with counter-hegemonic knowledge(s), but he offers a different approach, one that seems quite viable, at least in principle.

Some details of his genealogical approach, particularly of their methods and methodology, need to be discussed here. Foucault (1977) holds a position of knowledge as perspective (and this is consistent with his theory of power/knowledge). Genealogical history, or effective history, is "explicit in its perspective and acknowledges its system of injustice," rather than hiding its intentions and perspectives and pretending to be neutral. It reveals that all forms of scientific consciousness "are aspects of the will to knowledge," and that the "will to knowledge does not achieve a universal truth." What happens in the development of knowledge is, in fact, a "sacrifice of the subject of knowledge," that is, the pursuit of knowledge cannot be tied to the constitution and affirmation of a subject free from power (or injustice), but to "the destruction" of such a subject. Foucault criticizes the contradiction inherent in the traditional approach to objectivity among historians: in order to invoke "objectivity," they must mask their own perspectives, preferences, and will to knowledge at the beginning of their inquiry (pp. 156–157, 160, 162–163).

Foucault (1977), however, is not as critical of the methods of traditional history as he is of historians' pretenses of objectivity. In fact, in his view, the existing approaches of history—or at least that part of it which he (following Nietzsche) calls the "historical sense"—can play an important role (or become a "privileged instrument," in his words) in genealogy if their metaphysical, or essentialist, tendencies are corrected (pp. 152–153). Moreover, in his view, traditional history, including its methods and approaches, can be made over into genealogy. In a sense, the latter requires the mastery of the former. As he states, "it is necessary to master history so as to turn it to genealogical uses" (p. 160).

Foucault (1977) further suggests the importance of a struggle over, and by way of, a system of rules (e.g., the rules of law, or a science). "Rules," in his view, are "empty in themselves, violent and unfinalized; they are impersonal and can be bent to any purpose." To get a hold on them, therefore, becomes essential:

> The successes of history belong to those who are capable of seizing these rules, to replace those who had used them, to disguise themselves so as to pervert them, invert their meaning, and redirect them against those who had initially imposed them. (p. 151)[15]

For Foucault, the emergence of different interpretations indicates the confrontation of forces (and the reversal of their relationships in the play of dominations), since an interpretation is only possible by appropriating a system of rules (of a science).

Recall that, for Foucault, genealogy is the union of erudite knowledge and local memories, that he is not antiscience (or "antihistory" in this case), and that, for him, it is important to "detach" the power of science from the existing hegemony. In this sense, Foucault makes consistent arguments concerning the role of science in counter-hegemonic struggles. This does not mean that there are no theoretical tensions, however. One may remember, for example, one of the theoretical tensions discussed in previous sections: Who can produce (counter-hegemonic) knowledge(s) and on what grounds? Although Foucault's "Nietzsche, Genealogy, History" (1977, pp. 139-164) essay provides more specific ideas for genealogy, it does not exactly address this tension. Rather, it seems that the essay implies that historians who have converted into genealogists are more likely to produce genealogical knowledges.[16] Of course, there is a difference between suggesting that counter-hegemonic knowledge(s) in a contemporary society cannot be produced without the specific expertise of intellectuals and suggesting that only such intellectuals can produce knowledge(s). But the tension is there.

The question of science seems to remain contentious also, especially in terms of the "neutrality" of accepted methods and procedures. Foucault suggests that the methods can be used for a different (political) purpose and that rules are "empty" in themselves—and I would agree in part. However, that does not necessarily mean that they, themselves, are free of power (and injustice). A number of feminists have shown that existing methods in a given science have been the major problem, and that discussions on feminist methods and methodologies have been a constant among them. A struggle over "rules," which Foucault sees as important, may better precipitate a struggle for a change in rules.

Finally, as I see it, there is a tension surrounding antiessentialism. To be sure, for Foucault, the knowledges produced through genealogies are not "absolute," but "tactical" and "effective," meaning that they should be used tactically to produce certain effects of power that are contour-hegemonic. This position seems to suggest that there are times when genealogical knowledges are not effective (counter-hegemonic), and that during these times, there is even a possibility that they can be used for the maintenance of a particular hegemony. Foucault is right to critique the traditional history and its political effects. Perhaps there is also a need to examine the use of genealogy, including its antiessentialism, with regard to the situations in which those genealogical knowledges were (and are) produced and circulated, for what purposes, and with what kinds of political effects.

CONCLUSION

Epistemological and methodological issues concerning knowledge have dominated the recent debates over postmodern theories in education in general, and research on curriculum theory and practice in particular. Apple (2000), while acknowledging that he has "inflicted [his] share of theoretical labors on audiences throughout the world" for years, expresses his reservations about the recent trend toward (postmodern) metatheories among the critics (p. 6). In his view, the debates have become an intellectual exercise (and power game) among the (elite) academics, and so divorced from actual practices and politics (pp. 6–7). I would agree with him; however, I am a little wary of a possible implication lurking here—albeit indifferently—that theory is not practice, not an actual struggle. The relationships between theory and practice could only be partial and fragmentary, and as such, theory is a struggle in its own right, one that is fought locally and regionally in a specific field alongside those who struggle for, or against, power (see also the conversation between Foucault and Deleuze in Foucualt, 1977, pp. 205–208). I would suggest, therefore, that research on curriculum continue to engage in theory, and that sometimes it can exclusively focus on, say, postmodern theories.

As nature and function of theory varies from one field to another, approaching curriculum theory requires an understanding of what it is and how it functions. Although disagreement and confusion have been commonplace on this subject, I find Herbert M. Kliebard's description most helpful. According to him:

> [A curriculum theory] does not provide us with an immediate printout of a new and foolproof curriculum. It is not a powerful drug that will cure the ills that plague modern programs of study. It does not relieve us of the necessity to make ad hoc decisions based on practical experience. It does provide us with a central principle. That principle addresses itself to the question of what we *ought* to do when we teach children and youth. (Kliebard, 1992, p. 180, emphasis in original)

The recent postmodern debates in curriculum seem to bring with them some kind of inclination for a theory that produces an epistemology-proof curriculum, one that can repel the problem(s) of knowledge once and for all, and, if so, this is problematic. As discussed above, a particular theory of knowledge (such as the standpoint theory in Connell's case and Foucault's genealogy) can work as a guiding principle to choose and organize knowledges to be taught. However, the epistemological and methodological problem(s) of knowledge will be likely to reappear regardless of the theory employed, suggesting that the use of a particular epistemology as a curriculum theory cannot eliminate the theoretical tensions that exist in curriculum making. In other words, the problem(s) of knowledge is not something that can and should be solved, or "proofed," but something that is always—at least potentially—present in any curriculum development and practices, requiring a constant theoretical examination and deliberation.

A new metaphor is needed to address the issues of knowledge in curriculum making. The metaphor I suggest is to carry and play—or "ride" (Simons, 1995, p. 3)—the theoretical tensions throughout a curriculum project, be it theoretical inquiry, the study of a subject matter, or the planning and teaching of a lesson. The metaphor of "riding tensions" has some merits. For one thing, the metaphor refers to an action, and as such it presupposes that a human agency is involved in curriculum planning and practices, teaching and learning. For another, the metaphor conveys a need for everlasting (almost habitual) motions, reflections, and reassessments in order to maintain the tensions needed to keep riding. A lack of adequate tensions may result in one's falling off; tightening them too much may lead to the collapse of one's project. Moreover, those of us interested in an education for social justice, equality, and liberation should ride the tensions critically. The metaphor urges us to experience teaching and learning as a process of "riding tensions" (not "eliminating problems"), there are needs to develop a different set of skills and knowledge to keep us riding critically. The epistemological and methodological issues of knowledge should be raised—say, in terms of race, gender, and class—from critical perspectives at every moment in the process of making a curriculum and putting it into practice.

NOTES

1. This central question is followed by a series of related questions, including "Why should we teach this rather than that?" and "What rules should govern the teaching of what has been selected?" (Kliebard, 1992, p. 174).

2. One example is the idealism versus realism debate. Epistemologists ask questions that are related to how we come to know what we know, and what the relationships among the existence of the world, our experience, our mind, and knowledge are.

3. Williams (1980) describes reductionism as a doctrine holding that "the economic base determines the social relations which determines consciousness which determines actual ideas and works" (p. 19).

4. The concept of "relative autonomy" was originally used by Karl Korsch and became well known through Gramsci's writings. Althusser reworked the concept and developed other concepts as well, including "overdetermined contradictions" and "articulation." See also Apple (1985).

5. One such tension, for example, concerns the relationship between social structure(s) and human agency. The social structure(s) here may include not only economic but also political, cultural, and even cognitive structures.

6. "Science" here includes "history," as the term "historical science" is commonly used in continental Europe as well as East Asia.

7. There are two major reasons for Foucault to object to the concept: its epistemological implications for the distinction between ideology and (true) knowledge, and its link to (Marxist) economic determinism and reductionism (Foucault, 1980, p. 157). In addition, Foucault has a third reason for his objection: the ideology necessarily refers to something of the order of a subject (i.e., the construction of the consciousness of the subject) (p. 118).

8. To be sure, Foucault's "antiscience" is targeted against "human sciences" not "exact sciences" (though he suggests that the latter did not develop without human needs).

9. Barry Smart (1986) argues that Foucault's reformulation "constitutes a major contribution to the development of both a critical understanding of and a challenge to prevailing social, economic, and cultural forms of hegemony" (p. 171).

10. Foucault makes his case in the study of history, but his argument can be applied to other scholarly fields in the humanities and social sciences, including curriculum studies.

11. Fiske (1996), however, speculates that Foucault would have been quick to recognize the limitation of his arguments if he had had the opportunity to encounter the work of the socially subordinate—such as those circulated through the Black Liberation Radio—grounded in a particular social position.

12. In my view, the same point applies to Connell's idea of counter-hegemonic projects across the whole spectrum of social inequality. Although Connell allows the diversity of such projects, it is quite likely that contradictions arise between knowledges organized in different curricula.

13. In fact, later Connell (1993, pp. 113–114) argues that teachers in general can be seen as knowledge producers in the area of curriculum development and implementation and the characters and backgrounds of their students. This view, however, falls slightly short of specifying their role(s) in producing and organizing the knowledges of subordinate groups.

14. Connell (1993), for example, was involved in research on an Australian national study of the Disadvantaged Schools Project, through which he encountered a number of school-level curriculum and planning projects carried out by teachers (pp. 101–108, 129–132).

15. The emergence of different interpretations is an "event" (Foucault, 1977, pp. 152, 154).

16. Foucault's discussion of genealogy, specifically how it produces knowledge(s), and the way he discusses it, leaves a fairly strong impression that genealogy is an activity of specialists. In another essay, Foucault maintains that the question of who exercises power cannot be answered without examining how it is exercised. If we were to apply part of his insight to this case, it could be said that, after all, genealogists were the producers of knowledges.

REFERENCES

Apple, M. W. (1979). *Ideology and curriculum*. London: Routledge and Kegan Paul.

Apple, M. W. (1985). *Education and power*. Boston: Ark Paperbacks.

Apple, M. W. (2000). *Official knowledge: Democratic education in a conservative age* (2nd ed.). New York: Routledge.

Barrett, M. (1991). *Politics of truth: From Marx to Foucault.* Stanford, CA: Stanford University Press.

Connell, R. W. (1993). *School and social justice.* Toronto: Our Schools/Our Selves.

Fiske, J. (1996). Black bodies of knowledge: Notes on an effective history. *Cultural Critique, 33,* pp. 185-212.

Foucault, M. (1977). *Language, counter-memory, practice: Selected essays and interviews.* (Donald Bouchard and Sherry Simon, Trans.; Donald Bouchard, Ed.). Ithaca, NY: Cornell University Press.

Foucault, M. (1979). *Discipline and punish: The birth of the prison.* (Alan Sheridan, Trans.). New York: Vintage Books.

Foucault, M. (1980). *Power/knowledge: Selected interviews and other writings, 1972-1977.* (Colin Gordon, Ed.). New York: Pantheon Books.

Foucault, M. (1988). *Politics, philosophy, culture: Interviews and other writings, 1977-1984.* (L. D. Kritzman, Ed.). New York: Routledge.

Foucault, M. (1991). The ethic of care for the self as a practice of freedom. In J. Bernauer & D. Rasmussen (Eds.), *The final Foucault* (pp. 1-20). Cambridge: The MIT Press.

Haraway, D. J. (1991). Situated knowledges: The science question in feminism and the privilege of partial perspective. In D. J. Haraway (Ed.), *Simians, cyborgs, and women: The reinvention of nature.* New York: Routledge.

Harding, S. (1991). *Whose science? Whose knowledge?: Thinking from women's lives.* Ithaca, NY: Cornell University Press.

Iggers, G. G. (1997). *Historiography in the twentieth century: From scientific objectivity to the postmodern challenge.* Hanover and London: Wesleyan University Press.

Kliebard, H. M. (1992). *Forging the American curriculum: Essays in curriculum history and theory.* New York: Routledge.

Laclau, E., & Mouffe, C. (1985). *Hegemony and socialist strategy: Towards a radical democratic politics.* London: Verso.

Larrain, J. (1979). *The concept of ideology.* London: Hutchinson.

Simons, J. (1995). *Foucault and the political.* London and New York: Routledge.

Smart, B. (1986). The politics of truth and the problem of hegemony. In D. Couzens Hoy (Ed.), *Foucault: A critical reader* (pp. 157-173). Oxford: Blackwell.

Whitty, G. (1985). *Sociology and school knowledge: Curriculum theory, research and politics.* London: Methuen.

Williams, R. (1980). Literature and sociology: In memory of Lucien Goldmann. In *Problems in materialism and culture: Selected essays* (pp. 11-30). London: Verso.

Williams, R. (1983). *Keywords: A vocabulary of culture and society,* revised edition. New York: Oxford University Press.

Young, M. F. D. (Ed.). (1971). *Knowledge and control: New directions for the sociology of education*. London: Collier-Macmillan.

5

ARE WE MAKING PROGRESS?

Ideology and Curriculum in the Age of No Child Left Behind

DENNIS CARLSON

It was Fyodor Dostoyevsky, over a century ago, who warned in *Notes from Underground* that those who would lead people in the pursuit of progress often hold out the vision of some "crystal palace" that awaits us all if we just buckle under, work hard, and think positive—a crystal palace built by science and managed by social engineers. One problem, according to Dostoyevsky, is that the crystal palace is always something projected into the future. In the meantime, we are told we have to put up with a "chicken coop." Or we are told that the chicken coop we inhabit is really already a crystal palace. At any rate, people continue to live and work in chicken coops; and for all the talk of progress, the roofs keep letting in more rain each year. Another problem with the myth of progress toward a crystal palace is that any system that claims to have all the answers, or solve all our problems—if we just put our faith in science, or the free marketplace, or the system managers—is not ultimately worth supporting. For it is associated with an undemocratic belief that the current system cannot be questioned, and that conflict and dissent are bad. There is to be no conflict in the crystal palace, for all conflict is to be therapeutically managed or controlled through scientific behavioralism. Of such a crystal pal-

91

ace, Dostoyevsky wrote, "it will be impossible to put out one's tongue at it even on the sly."[1] And what's the good of living in a system that one cannot criticize, that one cannot raise a protest against? Finally, Dostoyevsky prophetically warned that building the crystal palace will lead to a dehumanizing way of thinking about humans, their desires, and their needs, an outlook that reduces human motives to "an average of statistical figures and scientifico-economic formulas."[2] Social engineers and scientific managers in both the state and industry were becoming the new leaders of progress even in Dostoyevsky's time, and it was their vision of a crystal palace that he feared would dominate the modern era ahead.

I think of Dostoyevsky often these days when I hear so much talk of progress in public education—particularly progress in urban schools serving those marginalized by class, race, and ethnicity. We are told again and again by education officials in the state and by their corporate "partners" in school reform that progress is being made in raising standards, in narrowing achievement gaps, in making teachers, principals, and school districts more accountable to the public, in aligning the curriculum with the test, and in other ways working toward the national goals set forth so boldly in the No Child Left Behind (NCLB) legislation. Admittedly, policy makers and politicians are quick to point out there are still some problems we have to "iron out" in achieving this goal, in rebuilding the nation's schools as crystal palaces in which no one is left behind and success is available to all.[3] But with more data analysis and more hard work on everyone's part, we are making progress. Indeed, President George W. Bush's generic response to all questions about his administration's policies—whether educational or military—has been that we are "making progress," and just need to "stay the course." Somewhere down the road, we are told, if teachers and students work hard enough and people demand that schools be held accountable, the nation's public schools will be crystal palaces. In the meantime, urban educators and students are also told they will have to continue to inhabit chicken coops, being content for now to visit some model crystal palace schools that have been reorganized to ensure high standards, accountability, and "success for all." At times such as this I am inclined to think that if this is considered progress, and this *is* the crystal palace, then perhaps we can do without so much progress.

It is not that I am willing to abandon the language or the project of democratic progress entirely—far from it. As a progressive, that would be more than a little contradictory. But progressives of the democratic sort will have to be careful to clearly distinguish their version of progress from the version that currently holds sway. They will need to engage in a battle over the meaning of progress, as part of a larger cultural battle over the meaning of democracy in the United States. Words such as progress have no essence, no fixed, given, stable, or unified meaning. From a poststructural perspective, the meaning of language is only to be found in the uses to which it is put historically and the interests it serves.

This is where the work of Michael Apple has played such an important role among democratic progressives in the United States, beginning with *Ideology and Curriculum*. Apple has been, from that groundbreaking text up through his most recent work, interested in a critical analysis of dominant reform discourses of "progress" in U.S. education and public life and has sought to affirm an alternative collective memory of democratic progress. If most of his effort has been devoted to a critique of hegemonic constructs of progress, this is perhaps understandable. For until dominant discourses and practices in education have been effectively unmasked and demystified, revealed for what they are and the interests they serve, it may be impossible to get very far in forging a new progressivism in the United States.[3]

In discussing the importance of *Ideology and Curriculum* to such a project, I must mention the changes in the field of critical educational studies since that book was first published. Over the past decade or two, poststructuralist theory has profoundly influenced and redirected critical educational studies; and we must begin by asking: What is the continuing relevance of the structural neo-Marxist theory Apple drew upon to develop his argument in *Ideology and Curriculum* in light of the poststructural shift in theorizing? One answer is that a structural theory of schooling in advanced capitalist society is still very useful, in fact essential, in developing a comprehensive theory of how schools work to produce and reproduce class, as well as race, gender, sexual, and other inequalities. There are real material structures, including economic, political, and educational structures that need to be accounted for in understanding how schools work and the forces that block transformative change. Sometimes, as Apple has pointed out, poststructuralists sound as if the only thing that matters is discourse and subjectivity, or that discourse and subjectivity are freer and more open than they really are. Furthermore, for all the limitations of structuralist theories of schooling, because of their deterministic tendencies and the fact that they overfix, overunify, and overgeneralize about the schooling process, these theories do provide a useful "big picture" of how the system works to reproduce itself. The important thing to remember is that we have created this picture; and that the picture is not reality, not the thing it claims to represent. If this picture proves useful in understanding how schools work and how they might be transformed, then it is worth studying. But when we turn to intervention in public schools and engage in the battle over the meaning of a democratic public education in our times, then I believe a poststructuralist theory better serves us and opens up more democratic possibilities.

What makes Apple's use of structural theory progressive is that he has always placed it in the service of a basically poststructural theory of U.S. cultural politics, anchored in the work of Antonio Gramsci. The fact that Gramsci has survived the much-heralded "death of Marxism" and has had such a major influence on poststructural scholarship (although certainly less so than Michel Foucault) is related to his concern with understanding cultural formations and cultural leadership in terms of historical battles between dominant and marginalized, hegemonic and counter-hegemonic, social movements.[4] Within the context of this battle, words and narratives have no fixed, unified, or stable meaning, only a meaning that is articulated with a "commonsense," a taken for granted discourse that produces certain truths about the nation and its history, truths that are used to construct a national narrative of progress. Gramsci also recognized the importance of forging a progressive commonsense through a convergence of interests linking sexual, gender, ethnic, regional, and religious politics to class politics. If class was for Gramsci, in the last instance, the glue that holds democratic counter-hegemonies together, he also insisted that democratic politics could not be reduced to class and that different struggles have their own relative autonomy and histories of development.

All of this, I would argue, makes Gramsci much more poststructural than structural in his analysis. At the same time, I realize that many, if not most, progressives would probably not think of Gramsci or Apple as poststructuralists. Partially this is because poststructuralism is often understood as a movement beyond Marxism. If this often has been the case, it is not necessarily so. In my view, Marxism is best articulated in poststructuralist terms, although in such terms it can no longer proclaim itself as the one and only metanarrative in critical educational studies, and it must leave determinism and the trope of unity behind. Another reason why Apple in particular is not generally considered a poststructuralist is that he has been among those critical of some of what passes for poststructuralist analysis in education these days, and of "post" discourses in the academy more generally. This in turn is partially related to what Apple has called the "politics of representation."[5] Often what passes for poststructural analysis in the liberal arts academy these days relies on a rhetorical style that is esoteric, abstract, and elitist—a language that does not circulate well outside the academy. For Apple, and for me, the question has never been whether the poststructuralist turn in educational theory is good or bad for progressivism per se. For one thing, it would not be very poststructural to pose the question in such a binary fashion. It is more poststructural to ask: How has poststructural analysis been used, what interests has it served, and what have its effects been.[6] Apple has an interest in poststructuralism's potential to open up opportunities to understand education as contested, to see truth as something that is produced by power and deployed strategically within concrete situations, and to see space for the interruption of the "normal" meaning-making process in schools and other educational sites.

In what follows, I want to return to some of the structural theory Apple relied so heavily upon in *Ideology and Curriculum* to flesh it out in a more poststructural form, informed by Foucault as well as Gramsci. Apple himself has taken up this project in his more recent work, so what I have to offer is only meant to help develop some elements of this project. By way of doing that, I also want to explore the continuing relevance of the neo-Marxist structural reproduction theory of schooling in the age of No Child Left Behind. In some ways, it seems like much has changed since the late 1970s when *Ideology and Curriculum* was written. There have been at least two, some would say three, rounds of school reform in the aftermath of the Reagan administration's proposal for an overhaul of the nation's schools, *A Nation at Risk* (1983). Educational officials point to progress on all fronts in the war against underachievement and "functional illiteracy" now that we have more sophisticated standardized tests to assess student learning and a better management information system to identity and target instruction to those who need remediation at an early age. But underneath the veneer of change, little has fundamentally been altered in the commonsense reform discourse that guides progress, and "real" democratic progress has eluded us. For this reason alone, what Apple had to say about ideology and curriculum in the 1970s remains more than pertinent today.

THE QUESTION CONCERNING IDEOLOGY

The first and most immediate question that must be raised in a poststructural rereading of *Ideology and Curriculum* is whether one of the central signifiers of critical theory in the modern era—namely, "ideology"—is worth holding on to anymore. But if we are to let go of it, what is to replace it? Discourse? Already, in the late 1970s, Apple was aware that the language of ideology is "problematic" as he put it. For one thing, there are a number of different traditions that have used a language of ideology, including a functionalist (and vulgar Marxist) tradition that views ideology as nothing more than "false consciousness," and a tradition in sociology associated with Geertz and others that treats ideology as a system of symbols, ideas, and beliefs that make the fabric of everyday social life meaningful and coherent. Then, as Apple argued, there are "interest" theories of ideology rooted in Marxism, and a "strain theory" of ideology associated with Durkheim and Parsons that views ideology as a workable "definition of the situation." What Apple finds useful is the "common ground" among all of these different orientations. In one way or another, he wrote, ideology "always deals with legitimation, power, conflict, and a special style of argument"—one that disguises the real interests it serves and seeks to persuade on the basis of vague and dubious assumptions.[7]

What complicates Apple's usage of the language of ideology, and makes it more poststructural, is precisely his grounding in a Gramscian Marxism. For Gramsci, ideology is the "commonsense" understanding of the world that actually encodes the interests and perspectives of dominant groups. To the extent that hegemony is fairly stable, it is at least partially because this commonsense perspective or worldview permeates and saturates the lived experiences of actors. In public schools, as Apple argued, this commonsense provides a framework to assist teachers and principals in organizing their everyday lives and relations, and it enables them to believe they are "neutral participants in the neutral instrumentation of schooling." At the same time, the economic and political interests served by the hegemonic commonsense are hidden or masked.[8] Apple is led to conclude that "ideology cannot be treated as a simple phenomenon. Nor can it be employed merely as a bludgeon with which one hits an opponent over the head."[9] A basic question, however, remains unanswered in this text—the question of how one can effectively distinguish ideological from nonideological texts, since all texts are interested, all incorporate taken-for-granted beliefs, and all attempt to persuade in their own ways through the use of rhetorical style.

Significantly, Apple has moved slowly but steadily away from the language of ideology toward a language of "dominant discourses" or hegemonic "commonsense," and to the more particularistic language of "authoritarian populism" and "neoliberalism." In his 2001 book, *Educating the "Right" Way*, the language of ideology is missing entirely. When he did use it in the second edition of *Official Knowledge* in 2000, he emphasized that "the first thing to ask about ideology is not what is false about it, but what is true."[10] There is, as Apple often has remarked, some good sense along with bad sense in hegemonic discourses, for they must win the consent of the governed and tap into cultural values that are widely held. For example, one might say that in the hegemonic discourse of NCLB, there is good sense in the provision that schools have to adopt policies to overcome socioeconomic, ethnic, and racial disparities in student achievement.[11] Unfortunately, when this good sense is articulated within a broader hegemonic reform discourse that links it to more accountability and standardized testing, and when it ignores the impact of inequalities generated in the economic sphere, then its progressive potential is severely limited. As Apple observes, the current conservative discourse in education and public life "speaks to a populist impulse, but that impulse has been colonized by the Right in powerful ways."[12]

Is there still some good sense in the language of ideology, or should progressives abandon it and move on to a more poststructural language of hegemonic and counter-hegemonic discourses? I, like Apple, find that at this point it is usually easier to avoid the language of "ideology," since it comes with so much historical baggage. At the same time, I suspect that avoiding the language of ideology is no better than using it uncritically. As Foucault recognized, we actively go out of our way to avoid in discourse something that is still very much part of the discourse as an absent presence (1978).[13] In fact, Gramsci did make some use of the language of ideology, although always with reservation and qualification. In its "negative," antidemocratic forms, Gramsci identified ideology with "a dogmatic system of eternal and absolute truths."[14] Religious dogma is ideological in this sense, but so too, according to Gramsci, is a "vulgar materialist" Marxism that treats ideology as merely "false consciousness" and a reflection of the material base. Again, what is important about Gramsci's use of ideology in this negative form is that he applies it precisely to those discourses in modern science, religion, and politics that claim to be nonideological, that is: depoliticized, objective, authoritative. We may thus speak of scientific Marxism as ideological, along with "authoritarian populism" on the political right. Gramsci did acknowledge that to the extent that ideology represents the commonsense beliefs of a social group or class, then progressives also must have an ideology. But if ideology is to take on this "positive" form, he argued, then it must be an ideology that begins with the assertion that "every 'truth' believed to be eternal and absolute has had practical origins and has represented a 'provisional' value."[15] Beyond this, a progressive ideology would need to be a "philosophy of praxis" involved in the mobilization of power blocs and movements within the "terrain upon which people move, acquire consciousness of their position, struggle, etc."[16]

Because the notion of ideology is so closely linked with the modernist binaries of clarity and distortion, as well as enlightened consciousness and false consciousness, it may not be a term that is worth recuperating. Certainly, Gramsci ended up using the language of ideology sparingly, as Apple does in his later work. If we use the language of ideology, we have to be careful not to drag along with this word all of the historical baggage of scientific Marxism and "false consciousness." As Foucault argued, we risk "investing Marxist discourses ... with the effects of a power which the West since Medieval times has attributed to science."[17] But I think it may be premature to do away with a language of ideology entirely. For one thing, the commonsense understanding of the term ideology still conveys more than just an interested worldview, epistemology, or discourse. If all worldviews distort reality in their own ways, some do so in far more manipulative and deliberate ways than others. Some also mask their interests and biases behind claims to objectivity and expert authority, while others are more upfront about their interests and the values they represent. Finally, some discourses honestly strive to bring a degree of clarity to complex issues, while others are about keeping people living in the dark.

I would say that the language of NCLB is ideological in many of these ways. It represents a kind of "double-speak" that means the opposite of what it says. Thus, No Child Left Behind and Success for All are reform movements that are consistent with a policy of limiting "success" to a few, as U.S. society is made increasingly inequitable. Of course, to charge that this is double-speak would be to imply some degree of deliberate intent to mask the real effects of reform. What we can say is that the Bush administration has made masterful use of double-speak in "packaging" and "selling" the invasion and occupation of Iraq as "Operation: Iraqi Freedom," and that the campaign to "Save Social Security" masks a plan to dismantle it. Much of the rhetorical system of reform under the neoconservative hegemony is about persuading the public to "buy" a bill of goods that turns out to be something other than what people thought they had bought.

In contemporary U.S. educational reform discourse, the so-called Houston miracle has played a prominent ideological role. As governor of Texas, George W. Bush worked closely with corporate leadership in the state to overhaul the state's system of public instruction to bring schools into alignment with the latest approaches to cost-effective management in industry and the changing "needs" of the labor force. Houston was much touted as the exemplary model of this school reform based on a partnership between political and economic leadership in the state. It reported steadily rising passing rates on the new Texas Assessment of Academic Skills (TAAS) test, and seemed to be making remarkable strides in eliminating the achievement gap between white and minority children. When Bush became president, he brought with him to Washington as his new education secretary, Houston's superintendent Rod Paige. The No Child Left Behind law signed by President Bush in January 2002 gave public schools 12 years to match the progress made in Houston's schools in raising achievement levels and narrowing achievement gaps. Now we are beginning to learn more about how the Houston miracle was produced, or more accurately, fabricated, as an ideological text.

A recent investigation of Houston schools by the *New York Times* revealed a "rampant undercounting of school dropouts," along with an overreporting of how many high school graduates were college bound. Although 88% of Houston's student body is black or Latino/Latina, only a few hundred minority students leave high school "college ready," that is, having the college preparatory courses colleges are looking for in applicants. The investigation also revealed that gains on the state's high school proficiency exam were not transferable to other standardized exams of academic achievement.[18] Finally, the *Times* investigation pointed to the fact that whereas the state has billed its high school proficiency exam as setting high standards for students, it was widely acknowledged in the state that it was a "minimum skills" test that was a ticket for a minimum skills job.

What this suggests is that the "Houston miracle" was only the illusion of progress. What real progress there was in raising test scores was produced through a reform that emphasized: frequent rounds of student assessment, remediation, and retesting; a curriculum "aligned" with a particular standardized test; and assessment of teachers and principals on the basis of how effective they are in raising test scores. As most any urban school teacher can attest, if it is higher test scores they want then it is higher test scores they will get, even if it is through "drill 'em and test 'em" approaches that are part of why there is a crisis of underachievement in urban schools to begin with. If the kind of distortion of reality represented in the myth of the "Houston miracle" is what we can expect in U.S. education in the age of No Child Left Behind, then ideology may be an appropriate term to describe it. Even in this case, however, ideology cannot be reduced to a variety of propaganda discourse. It is, in a Foucauldian sense, a discourse that makes utterances about the Houston miracle possible, that produces truths about what constitutes progress and how it will be assessed, and that constitutes power relations in which urban teachers and their students are kept subordinated. It is the taken-for-granted belief system of the new corporate state engaged in opening a field of possible options, and, one might add, closing down other options.

IDEOLOGY AND TECHNICAL CONTROL

One of the most important contributions of *Ideology and Curriculum* was to refocus critical educational studies from a rather narrow concern with the "content" of the curriculum to an analysis of curricular form. Not that what gets included in the curriculum—what Apple called "official knowledge"—is unimportant. In *Ideology and Curriculum*, Apple refers in particular to the important work of Raymond Williams and his idea that ideology works by presenting people with a "selective tradition" of knowledge that includes the narratives and perspectives of dominant groups while at the same time selectively excluding the contributions and perspectives of marginalized groups. While this opens up an important line of inquiry in curriculum studies, Apple has been more interested in how ideological configurations enter into the form the curriculum takes—primarily its technical form, for the curriculum is a particular kind of technology used by teachers and students to produce learning outcomes or "products."

As one might expect, based on what I have already said about ideology, Apple argued that it is precisely those curricular forms and materials that have emerged out of scientific positivism and behavioralism that historically have been the most ideological, even as they claim to be neutral. In fact, there is nothing neutral about "technical, efficiency, and 'scientific' perspectives in curriculum and education in general."[19] Such categories and perspectives are ideological in that they usually have taken the form of the "development of procedures to guarantee certainly and to rationalize and make explicit as many aspects of people's activity as possible." Because they are primarily interested in efficiency, they tend to "exclude other modes of valuing." They promote the idea that "scientific" techniques "are interest-free and can be applied to 'engineer' nearly any problem one faces."[20] Finally (and here Apple prefigured an important poststructural theme), these perspectives, techniques, and categories legitimate a consensus view of the curriculum. They ask for "total agreement on the 'paradigm' to be used in curriculum thought," a kind of scientific metanarrative.[21] Later, Apple would further develop this concern for the technical form of the curriculum with regard to the deskilling of teachers' work through new behavioral, prepackaged curricular programs in *Teachers and Texts* (1986).[22] Technical control not only changes the work of teaching, it enters into the perspectives teachers and other educators use to guide and give meaning to their work.

This analysis of curricular form is obviously consistent with, although not directly influenced by, the work of Foucault on microtechnologies and apparatuses of power. Foucault argued that power "is exercised rather than possessed."[23] It does not exist as some crystallization of interests in a central point (such as the state or economic sphere), but rather circulates through discourses and is ultimately exercised at the extremities, through microtechnologies that attach themselves to real human bodies, in particular institutional sites. In the modern era, Foucault argued, disciplinary discourses and corresponding microtechnologies of power have organized and guided activities in most institutional sites, and they have been closely linked to the rise of the scientific disciplines as well as managerial and production discourses and technologies in the economy and other spheres of social life. In *Discipline and Punish*, he identified disciplinary power as "the specific technique of power that regards individuals as both objects and as instruments of its exercise."[24] Its instruments include hierarchical observation, normalizing judgment, and the ritual of the examination. In the discourse and practice of systems management, we might say that hierarchical observation takes the form of complex management information systems and surveillance technologies designed to keep teachers and students under (in Foucault's words) "an intense, continuous supervision."[25] As for "normalizing judgment," this includes myriad techniques for evaluating, comparing, differentiating, and judging teachers and students according to supposed objective standards, and also those techniques used for correcting their presumed "defects" or "deficits" and awarding both privileges and punishments. Finally, there is the examination, which combines the microtechnologies of hierarchical observation and a normalizing judgment. Foucault is led to conclude that "the school became a sort of apparatus of uninterrupted examination."[26] If the school historically has been organized and even spatially arranged as an examining institution, new behavioralist and systems management technologies take this ritual of examination to new heights. It is not coincidental that the era of NCLB is also the era of high-stakes testing.

How might we weave a neo-Marxist and Foucauldian analysis of technical control and the curriculum? One possibility is suggested by the poststructural Marxist Felix Guattari. He observes that "capitalism does not seek to exercise despotic power over all the wheels of society. ... It is even crucial to its survival that it manages to arrange marginal freedoms, relative spaces for creativity."[27] What gives transnational capitalism its special power, according to Guattari, is its ability to reorder various heterogeneous activities and domains of cultural production, to maintain control not through centralization of power, but through the decentralization of power to the point of production. Control is much more invested, consequently, in microtechnologies, which Guattari refers to as "machines." He does so by way of emphasizing a poststructural concern with processes and the technologies that guide processes, rather than with structure. Schools may then be approached as sites where teachers and students use what Guattari calls "semiotization machines" to decode texts and produce certain objectified and quantifiable outcomes or truths. On the other side of the dominant machines of public education today are the reform discourses and interests of transnational capitalism. These discourses are engaged, according to Guattari, in "de-territorializing" economic machines and information technologies and "re-territorializing" them by applying them to the reorganization of all public institutions.[28] This has a good deal of relevance in interpreting the situation we face in public education and in teacher education, and it is a chilling reminder that public educators at all levels—from elementary school to the university—are being called upon to align their research and scholarship with the "machines" of NCLB.

Recently, at a conference that attracted a number of progressive teachers, I had the opportunity to informally interview a veteran elementary school teacher who teaches in a northern rustbelt city. When I asked her about how the "machines" of NCLB were affecting her own work and the work of other teachers in her building, she told me the following story. Her school, she said, served the poorest of the poor, a mixture of white, African American, and Latino students (87% of whom were classified as living in poverty). Several years ago the state declared her school to be in "academic emergency," which meant that if test scores did not significantly rise and the achievement gap between black, Latino, and white students did not narrow, the school could be closed and teachers could lose their jobs.

In an effort to better "align" the curriculum with the state-mandated proficiency test in the fourth grade, which children had to pass in order to be promoted to the fifth grade and continue on toward the ninth-grade proficiency test, the district had decided several years prior to adopt the popular and influential school reorganization model Success for All (SFA). This model, developed by the behavioral psychologist Robert Slavin, has been particularly popular in schools serving urban and rural poor children. It begins with a highly scripted curriculum, with a focus on reading skills. Textbooks contain the exact words teachers are to say in introducing lessons, questioning students, and assessing learning outcomes. Every teacher in a given grade level is supposed to be on the "same page" at the same time and to move forward at a predetermined pace. Those students identified as skill deficient in particular areas are given special tutoring and remediation—with teachers doing much of the one-on-one tutoring after school hours for $15 an hour. According to this teacher, by the third year of SFA, teachers were getting fed up with the "cookie cutter" approach to teaching and told the principal, in effect, "we're not little robots." They began to deviate from the script and schedule and reassert control over their teaching. It was at this point that the "SFA police," as the teacher referred to them, made a checkup visit to the school. Teachers did their best to "put on a dog and pony show" for the SFA consultants, but in the end, the SFA team announced that the program was not working in the school and blamed the teachers for not sticking to the predetermined script. Consequently, after three years of using the SFA model, SFA withdrew support from the school and district administrators began "shopping around" for another reorganization model that promised to raise test scores.

They found it in the Baldrige reorganization model. Sponsored by the Malcolm Baldrige Foundation, which was established to promote increased productivity and cost-effectiveness in U.S. industry, the Baldrige school reorganization model and the "Baldrige Criteria for Performance Excellence" are now being supported with grant money through the U.S. Department of Education, in collaboration with the Bill Gates Foundation.[29] In Baldrige schools, the official philosophy is that it is up to local school staff to decide how they will go about increasing "productivity," with the proviso, of course, that staff produce a steady stream of quantifiable output data on each student's skill levels, in each subject domain, on a short cycle of assessment. Teachers attend special workshops to learn how to write multiple-choice tests to assess students, along with workshops on how to use new computer programs and management information technologies that monitor and record student "progress." Students are given weekly computer printouts that detail exactly where they stand in each skill area, and class averages are plastered around the classroom walls as constant reminders to teachers and students of how they stand relative to goals for achievement. As part of an action plan to raise achievement among those students most "at risk," the students were pulled out of regular classes and assigned to a special "drill 'em and test 'em" class, where, as might be expected, achievement and discipline problems only seemed to worsen and the teacher assigned to the room felt demoralized and on the verge of quitting. The teacher telling me this concluded by saying that many veteran teachers in the building were beginning to vocalize their discontent, as they had with SFA. Recently, some of the teachers asked a Baldrige consultant: "Why are we doing this? Where is it going?" The consultant, needless to say, was not happy, and the school faced the prospect of being dropped by the Baldrige Foundation, as it had been dropped by SFA. Again, test scores were not rising as expected, racial disparities continued to exist in achievement, and once again, teachers were blamed. Ironically, the Baldrige Foundation website asks educators who might be interested in joining their network of schools: "Do you believe you have been making progress but want to accelerate or better focus your efforts? Try using our simple questionnaire, Are We Making Progress?"

Once more, we can see just how much the technology or "machines" behind such reform movements represent one more elaboration on a systems management theme of progress. Of course, progressives need to ask the question: Are we making progress? For only then can we begin to question how progress has been defined, whose interests it has served, and how the neutral language of progress through systems management has subverted the democratic, liberatory project of public education. We can also begin to question just how much real progress has been made, even in raising achievement levels on standardized tests, by systems management discourses of progress.

CULTURAL CAPITAL AND THE CULTURE OF POVERTY

Along with the technical form of the curriculum, Apple has been inserted in its rhetorical and linguistic form. In *Ideology and Curriculum* he made use of a basically structural theory to sketch out such an analysis, drawing on Pierre Bourdieu's theory of cultural capital as well as Basil Bernstein's theory of class-based linguistic codes. In essence, their argument is that because middle-class students more often have learned valued linguistic codes and registers in the home, they are advantaged in the schooling process. Conversely, those who do not bring a "correct" or "normal" linguistic code with them to school are disadvantaged and more likely to be labeled as having learning deficits. This occurs even as educators appear to merely evaluate students on the basis of universalistic standards of merit. Obviously, this helps explain some of the persistent problem of underachievement among poor African American, Latino/Latina, and Appalachian youth in America. They speak a variety of English that is defined as "incorrect" in the school world and have to choose between affirming their language or distancing themselves from it and the culture that comes with it.

In the interview included at the end of the third edition of *Ideology and Curriculum*, Apple comments upon Bourdieu and Bernstein as structural theorists, and on the continuing importance of structural theory. "I do not want to defend reductive structural analysis," he writes, "but in a period of time when all too many people seem to have lost the collective memory of the gains made by the traditions of structural analysis," it is important to keep these traditions alive (p. 180). On the other hand, Apple remarks of Bernstein's work that it is "rather too structuralist at times." He means by this that "you don't see real people act, nor do you see real social movements in formation and action, nor do you see the processes and results of social transformation" (p. 181). Furthermore, Apple criticizes structural theorists for something he also has criticized poststructuralist theorists for—writing and speaking in a highly abstract and esoteric language which is inconsistent with a democratic politics of representation. Given all of this, structural theories of "cultural capital" clearly are still very important in understanding how ideology works in the age of NCLB. They also help us understand "culture of poverty" rationales for underachievement as ideological. The educator's role, like that of Professor Higgins in George Bernard Shaw's *Pygmalion*, is to uplift the poor by teaching them to speak "good," or "correct," English and manage a middle-class presentation of self.

The belief that it is the role of public schools to "correct" the "bad" English of poor, working class, and racial minority students has long been part of the commonsense that middle class teachers bring with them to the classroom—including many middle class black and Latino/Latina teachers—and it gets ideologically linked to a culture of poverty rationale that understands poor and working class young people as the unfortunate victims of their own cultural deficits. Rather than challenge this deficit theory of language and culture, state education officials and curriculum reformers have been among its most vocal supporters in the age of NCLB, and teachers are exposed to through professional development, in-service workshops, and even university education courses. Perhaps the most recent restatement of a culture of poverty rationale in U.S. education is provided by Ruby Payne—speaker, author, and CEO of "Aha! Process," a training/publishing company. Aha! Process originally worked primarily with industry but has begun to do consulting work with public schools over the past decade.

Her recent book, *A Framework for Understanding Poverty*, is required reading for teachers in many urban school districts across the United States. Indeed a whole industry has emerged to provide staff development training workshops and materials based on ideas developed in the book. When teachers tell me about these workshops and the book, it is often because they felt, as one teacher remarked, "it opened my eyes." Now this is a very interesting choice of words, for it implies that the teacher had become enlightened, and that previously she had been blind to the truth about why poor kids did so poorly in school. Yet, one might argue that what this white, middle class teacher was exposed to in staff development was enlightening only because it confirmed what she already knew, or thought she knew, about poor kids, but had not been able to articulate in a professional discourse.

According to Payne, children who come from "generational poverty" backgrounds are likely to be deficient in a number of resources: financial, emotional, mental, spiritual, physical, support systems, relationships/role models, and knowledge of hidden rules. These "hidden rules" are those "unspoken cues" and "habits of a group" that middle-class people have learned that help them successfully negotiate their interactions in work and school—in other words, social and cultural capital.[30]

Payne argues that educators must take all of the deficits of children of poverty into account, but she focuses on language. Her basic argument in this regard is that the poor do not, or cannot, speak as many "registers" of language as normal, middle-class students. They lack (in particular) the formal register—"the standard sentence syntax and word choice of work and school."[31] Payne provides two examples of stories that she says typify middle-class and poverty language registers. She writes that the latter is "far more entertaining, more participatory and exhibits a richness of character, humor, and feeling," which is absent from the former. At the same time, she writes that the middle-class story structure has "sequence, order, cause and effect, and a conclusion: all skills necessary for problem-solving, inference, etc."[32] Although she is sympathetic to the "richness" of the language of poor children, this is a sympathy that only extends so far. Schools should, according to Payne, privilege the formal register. The problem, of course, is that in doing so, schools are engaged in normalizing practices, in this case the establishment of a white, middle-class linguistic standard or norm and the corresponding devaluation, marginalization, and stigmatization of the language of poor and working-class students, and more particularly the language of poor African American and Latino/Latina youth.

But what are we to do then? Should progressive-minded teachers encourage their students to write and speak in their own preferred linguistic styles and registers? Would that have the effect of further marginalizing and disempowering youth who are already marginalized by class and race? These questions immediately come to the fore whenever I ask teachers to consider that the culture of poverty rationale is ideological because it masks the "real" forces involved in producing poverty and underachievement in the United States. I do not mean to dismiss these questions lightly, for they are questions that have to be asked. In formulating a response, if not an "answer," progressives need to remember Apple's admonition—as I have already said—that there is some good sense along with bad sense in hegemonic discourses. It certainly is true that those young people from generational poverty backgrounds who can adopt middle-class, white linguistic codes and rhetorical styles are more likely to get ahead in U.S. society as it is currently organized and governed. It is also true that these young people will have to work extra hard to do so, and that in the process they will have to distance themselves from their home cultures and what Bourdieu called habitus. Furthermore, linguistic codes and rhetorical styles alone cannot explain the persistence of inequality and poverty in the United States. Much of that inequality and poverty is structurally produced by the economy; so it is not altogether fair to blame the victims for their condition. Furthermore, Payne and those who advance a culture of poverty rationale seek to reduce all inequalities in the United States to socioeconomic inequalities, which can then supposedly be overcome if everyone learns to talk, act, and think in a good, normal middle-class fashion. They forget that race still matters in the United States. Consequently, racial inequalities in achievement are understood in this theory merely as a reflection of the fact that African American and Latino students are less likely than whites to speak "standard" or "correct" English. That obviously oversimplifies a complex issue, and it fails as well to interrogate its own Eurocentric perspective on what is "correct" English.

CONCLUSION: TOWARD DEMOCRATIC PROGRESS

H. G. Wells's 1935 science fiction novel, *Things to Come*, is a story about the efforts by a group of managers, engineers, and scientists in the year 2059 to usher in an age of progress through the application of scientific knowledge to every public problem—from sending a rocket to the moon to organizing and running public institutions. Although Wells was one of the great champions of the modernist vision of progress through science and engineering, he also recognized, as Dostoyevsky had, the problems inherent in applying scientific management to the affairs of humans. Most people in Wells's future have to work much harder than previous generations did, and they have to give up their freedoms and submit to the authority of the five-year managerial plan, like cogs in a wheel. Near the end of the novel, a group of workers stage an uprising against the rule of the engineers—a rebellion that is quickly put down. But not before a leader of the workers can cry out: "What is all this progress? What is the good of progress? ... We must measure and compute, we must collect and sort and count, we must sacrifice ourselves. ... What is it, this progress?"[33] I think those are very good questions to ask and particularly about educational reform discourses that promise progress in the "war" against chronic under-achievement in urban schools serving youth marginalized by class and race. Too often, "progress" is brought about by more standardized testing, by reducing the curriculum to a series of reified and fetishized "outcomes," and by making teachers conform to the managerial plan for school "productivity." Furthermore, it is largely false progress, progress in raising test scores through an aggressive policy of teaching to the test, progress that does not translate into meaningful learning, progress that hides the fact that an increasing number of urban youth are being disempowered and disenfranchised, or at best prepared with the "basic skills" they need to enter the lower rungs of a growing service sector economy.

In the mainstream discourse on progress in the "war" against under-achievement, it is often said that reforms have come in waves. Thus, a first wave of reform is associated with top-down models of accountability designed to raise standards; a second wave is associated with site-based management and free-market approaches to reform; and now a third wave is linked to school reorganization models that promise "success for all." Unintentional though it may be, the metaphor of reform as a wave washing over public schools conjures up images of a hurricane, or even tsunami, sweeping over a landscape and clearing everything in its path. In this case, urban schools, and the teachers, students, and administrators who live and work in urban schools, have been hardest hit. The sad truth is that as long as reform continues to be framed within the currently hegemonic discourses, it will not serve to advance democratic projects or empower urban teachers and their students. Public schools have been heavily influenced throughout the past hundred years by scientific managerial discourses of reform; and they have been heavily involved (often against the best intentions of teachers and other public educators) in the reproduction of class, race, gender, sexuality, and other inequalities. It is the idea and the promise of democratic public education, rather than the dominant practice of public education, that Apple ends up affirming in *Ideology and Curriculum* and in his subsequent work. One of the implications of his work, it seems to me, is that to effectively respond to the crisis of underachievement in U.S. education, progressives will have to unmake much of the "progress" that has been made over the past several decades through wave after wave of neoconservative and neoliberal reform. At the same time they will need to hold on to what progress was made (in the way of affirmative action and a more multicultural curriculum, for example) in the 1960s, and hold on to the collective memory of progressive struggle in the United States along a number of fronts.

In forging a democratic counter-hegemonic discourse of reform in U.S. education, the most immediate and pragmatic response among progressives may well be a politics of individual and collective resistance to the "machines" of urban schooling, including high-stakes testing. This is already beginning to happen in many states and has been associated with, among other things, organized refusals to take state-mandated proficiency tests. Teachers have an important role to play in such movements, as interested "insiders" aligned in solidarity with those students disempowered and effectively disenfranchised by high-stakes testing. As Apple recognized, and as I have long argued, teachers represent a potentially powerful counter-hegemonic power bloc in democratic educational renewal, and there is much good, progressive work to be done in teachers' unions and professional organizations.[34]

At some point, however, progressives also must move beyond critique and resistance toward the forging of a counter-hegemonic movement for progress in the United States, linked to a new commonsense discourse on the renewal of public education and public life.[35] The promise of democratic education and public life in America has been subverted over the past century and continues to be. But it nevertheless provides some scaffolding for constructing a new democratic discourse of educational renewal. That promise, projected upon a new cultural landscape, is about bringing people together across their differences in ways that do not erase difference but that engage them in a collective dialogue. It is about providing opportunities for individuals and groups to engage in the creative production of meaning and to contribute in diverse ways to public life. And it is also about empowering those who have been marginalized by class, race, gender, sexuality, and other markers of difference and identity so that they can develop their fuller potentials as human beings. For Apple, as for Paulo Freire and many of us who still believe in the radical democratic possibilities of the Enlightenment project, the most important thing that a counter-hegemonic discourse must do is reawaken hope and challenge the dominant cynicism and pragmatism of the age. At the same time, it must be noted that no persuasive progressive power bloc or discourse has emerged in education. This is a testimony to just how hegemonic the current reform discourse on progress is. It has become so taken for granted, so much part of people's commonsense understanding of things, so pervasive, and so powerful, that it is difficult to "unthink."

To get beyond the current "stuck point" in progressive cultural politics, I believe poststructural perspectives can be particularly useful.[36] Like other intellectual movements linked to broader movements in the public, poststructuralism is a marker for a broad array of discourses and practices. Nevertheless, poststructuralism does generally imply some form of discourse analysis and some attempt to deconstruct the dominant binaries of "normal science," including the insider/outsider, macro/micro, theory/practice, and mind/body binaries. Poststructural theory also implies that truth, since it is discursively produced and involved in constituting power relations, is never stable, secure, or unified, and never without its opposition.[36] There always are oppositional discourses, practices, and spaces to be found within public schools and other sites in the public, although they might be quite marginalized and poorly linked. Furthermore, there are real limits to how far hegemonic discourses and microtechnologies can control practice. In schools today there continues to be some limited room to carve out "free spaces" organized according to progressive principles of pedagogy, although it may be a shrinking space.[37]

It is the role of the educator and the intellectual to help expand the potential of these oppositional spaces to linkup and become transformative, to produce what Guattari called a "molecular revolution" that emerges out of many small, localized actions of resistance and reimagination. This is the work of both Gramsci's "organic intellectual" and Foucault's "specific intellectual," the strategic work whose object is to expose certain taken-for-granted discourses that dominate and limit people, and to build alliances and affiliations among various struggles against domination. Progressive intellectuals in this sense do not speak in the name of the oppressed, but, as Foucault says, "alongside them, in solidarity with them, in part because others' oppression is often inseparable from their own."[38] Progressive intellectuals of this sort work the boundaries between insider and outsider status, linking what is going on inside and outside public schools, and speaking in solidarity with those whose interests and voices have been silenced in public school reform discourse. The intellectual thus plays a critical role in the devel-

how much progress been has really made? *resisting reformed curriculum.*

opment of what Gramsci called a "philosophy of praxis," a form of scholarship and writing aimed at the critical intellectual development of a group or movement with which the intellectual is aligned in solidarity. The disempowered cannot become empowered until they can organize themselves around a discourse of struggle and affirmation, and according to Gramsci, "there is no organization without intellectuals."[39] This is the tradition within which Apple has continued to work as a public intellectual since publication of *Ideology and Curriculum*, and it is the place and ground from which he speaks and writes. It means that he always manages to find some hope in this time of cynicism and fatalism on the political left in the United States, a hope maintained by returning to the battle over the course and direction of U.S. public life with a renewed conviction that the future is open, and that the democratic impulse in U.S. education and culture has not been extinguished.

NOTES

1. Fyodor Dostoyevski, *Notes from Underground*, trans. Richard Pevear and Larissa Volokhonsky (New York: Random House, 1993), p. 35.
2. Ibid., p. 21.
3. See Dennis Carlson, *Leaving Safe Harbors: Toward a New Progressivism in American Education and Public Life* (New York: RoutledgeFalmer, 2002).
4. See Jane Kenway, "Remembering and Regenerating Gramsci," in *Feminist Engagements: Reading, Resisting, and Revisioning Male Theorists in Education and Cultural Studies*, ed. K. Weiler (New York: Routledge, 2001), pp. 47–66.
5. Michael Apple, *Ideology and Curriculum, Third Edition.* (New York: RoutledgeFalmer, 2004), p. 181.
6. See Dennis Carlson and Michael Apple, "Introduction: Critical Educational Theory in Unsettling Times," in *Power/Knowledge/Pedagogy: The Meaning of Democratic Education in Unsettling Times*, ed. Carlson and Apple (Boulder, CO: Westview, 1998), 1–40.
7. Apple, *Ideology and Curriculum, Third Edition*, pp. 18–19.
8. Ibid., p. 20.
9. Ibid., p. 19.
10. Michael Apple, *Educating the "Right" Way: Markets, Standards, God, and Inequality* (New York: RoutledgeFalmer, 2001). Michael Apple, *Official Knowledge: Democratic Education in a Conservative Age,* 2nd ed. (New York: Routledge, 2000), p. 20.
11. See Sam Dillon, "Under School Law, Push to Close Minority Gap," *New York Times*, May 27, 2005, 1, 19.

12. Apple, *Ideology and Curriculum*, p. 201.

13. This is a theme that is developed in Michel Foucault, *A History of Sexuality*, Vol. 1, trans. Robert Harley (New York: Pantheon, 1978).

14. Antonio Gramsci, *Selections from the Prison Notebooks* (New York: International Publishers, 1971), p. 407.

15. Ibid., p. 406.

16. Ibid., p. 377.

17. Michel Foucault, *Power/Knowledge: Selected Interviews and Other Writings, 1972–1977* (New York: Pantheon, 1980), p. 85.

18. Diana Schemo and Ford Fessenden, "Gains in Houston Schools: How Real Are They?," *New York Times*, December 3, 2003, A1, A27.

19. Apple, *Ideology and Curriculum, Third Edition*, p. 99.

20. Ibid., pp. 102–103.

21. Ibid., p. 111.

22. Michael Apple, *Teachers and Text, A Political Economy of Class and Gender Relations in Education* (New York: Routledge and Kegan Paul, 1986).

23. Michel Foucault, *Discipline and Punish: The Birth of the Prison*, trans. Alan Sheridan (New York: Vintage, 1979), p. 26.

24. Ibid., p. 40.

25. Ibid., p. 174.

26. Ibid., p. 186.

27. Felix Guattari "Capitalist Systems, Structures and Processes," in *The Guattari Reader*, ed. Gary Genosko (Oxford, UK: Blackwell, 1996), p. 235.

28. This language of de-territorializing and re-territorializing machines is developed in Felix Guattari, *Molecular Revolution: Psychiatry and Politics* (London: Penguin, 1984).

29. See Baldrige National Quality Program, *Education Criteria for Performance Excellence* (Washington, DC: Baldrige Foundation, 2003), and Richard E. Maurer and Sandra C. Pedersen, *Malcolm and Me: How to Use the Baldrige Process to Improve Your School* (Lanham, MD: Scarecrow Education, 2004).

30. Ruby Payne, *A Framework for Understanding Poverty* (Highlands, TX: Aha! Process, Inc., 2001), p. 16.

31. Ibid., p. 42.

32. Ibid., p. 49.

33. H. G. Wells, *Things to Come* (New York: Macmillan, 1935), p. 118.

34. See Dennis Carlson, *Teachers and Crisis: Urban School Reform and Teachers' Work Culture* (New York: Routledge, 1992).

35. See Greg Dimitriadis and Dennis Carlson, eds., *Promises to Keep: Cultural Studies, Democratic Education, and Public Life* (New York: RoutledgeFalmer, 2003).

36. I use this term in a way similar to the way Elizabeth Ellsworth does in *Teaching Positions: Difference, Pedagogy, and the Power of Address* (New York: Teachers College Press, 1997).

37. See Lois Weis and Michelle Fine, "Extraordinary Conversations in Public Schools," in *Promises to Keep*, ed. Dimitriadis and Carlson, pp. 95–124; and Dennis Carlson, "Hope Without Illusion: Telling the Story of Democratic Educational Renewal," *International Journal of Qualitative Studies in Education* 18, no. 1 (2005): 21–45.

38. Foucault, *Power/Knowledge*, p. 126.

39. Gramsci, *Prison Notebooks*, p. 334.

REFERENCES

Apple, M. (1986). *Teachers and texts: A political economy of class and gender relations in education*. New York: Routledge and Kegan Paul.

Apple, M. (2000). *Official knowledge: Democratic education in a conservative age* (2nd ed.). New York: Routledge.

Apple, M. (2001). *Educating the "right" way: Markets, standards, God, and inequality*. New York: RoutledgeFalmer.

Apple, M. (2004). *Ideology and curriculum* (3rd ed.). New York: RoutledgeFalmer.

Baldrige National Quality Program. (2003). *Education criteria for performance excellence*. Washington, DC: Baldrige Foundation.

Carlson, D. (1992). *Teachers and crisis: Urban school reform and teachers' work culture*. New York: Routledge.

Carlson, D. (2002). *Leaving safe harbors: Toward a new progressivism in American education and public life*. New York: RoutledgeFalmer.

Carlson, D. (2005). Hope without illusion: Telling the story of democratic educational renewal. *International Journal of Qualitative Studies in Education, 18*(1), 21–45.

Carlson, D., & Apple, M. (1998). Introduction: Critical educational theory in unsettling times. In D. Carlson & M. Apple (Eds.), *Power/knowledge/pedagogy: The meaning of democratic education in unsettling times* (pp. 1–40). Boulder, CO: Westview.

Dillon, S. (2005, May 27). Under school law, push to close minority gap. *New York Times*, 1, 19.

Dimitriadis, G., & Carlson, D. (Eds.). (2003). *Promises to keep: Cultural studies, democratic education, and public life*. New York: RoutledgeFalmer.

Dostoyevsky, F. (1994). *Notes from underground*. (R. Pevear & L. Volokhonsky, Trans.). New York: Random House.

Ellsworth, E. (1997). *Teaching positions: Difference, pedagogy, and the power of address*. New York: Teachers College Press.

Foucault, M. (1977). *Discipline and punish: The birth of the prison* (Alan Sheridan, Trans.). New York: Vintage.

Foucault, M. (1978). *The history of sexuality,* Vol. 1. (Robert Hurley, Trans.). New York: Pantheon.

Foucault, M. (1980). *Power/knowledge: Selected interviews and other writings, 1972–1977.* New York: Pantheon.

Gramsci, A. (1971). *Selections from the prison notebooks.* New York: International Publishers.

Guattari, F. (1984). *Molecular revolution: Psychiatry and politics.* London: Penguin.

Guattari, F. (1996). Capitalist systems, structures and processes. In G. Genosko (Ed.), *The Guattari reader* (pp. 233-247). Oxford, UK: Blackwell.

Kenway, J. (2001). Remembering and regenerating Gramsci. In K. Weiler (Ed.), *Feminist engagements: Reading, resisting, and revisioning male theorists in education and cultural studies* (pp. 47–66). New York: Routledge.

Maurer, R. E., & Pedersen, S. C. (2004). *Malcolm and me: How to use the Baldrige process to improve your school.* Lanham, MD: Scarecrow Education.

Payne, R. (2001). *A framework for understanding poverty.* Highlands, TX: Aha! Process, Inc.

Schemo, D., & Fessenden, F. (2003, December 3). Gains in Houston schools: How real are they?, *New York Times,* A1, A27.

Weis, L., & Fine, M. (2003). Extraordinary conversations in public schools. In G. Dimitriadis & D. Carlson (Eds.), *Promises to keep* (pp. 95–124). New York: RoutledgeFalmer

Wells, H. G. (1935). *Things to come.* New York: Macmillan.

6

TEACHING AFTER THE MARKET

From Commodity to Cosmopolitan

ALLAN LUKE

INTRODUCTION

Nearly three decades after Apple's *Ideology and Curriculum* (1979), some issues addressed there are still unresolved: schools and teachers struggling to deal with communities that face extreme economic conditions; increasing disparities in wealth and achievement; and school systems unable to come up with policies other than standardization via testing and corporatized curricula that offer "paint by numbers" solutions. But the context of our work has changed, with the coming of globalized political economies, new modes of cultural production and representation, dense and complex new knowledge and discourse, and blended local cultures and identities. This chapter is a historical extension of Michael Apple's critique. It draws upon semiotic, postcolonial, and cultural theory in an attempt to provide new directions for remaking teaching in the face of cultural and economic globalization.

Beginning from curriculum studies, Apple's work laid an analytic path for a generation. Large-scale historical processes of social reproduction and ideological control were by then well documented. These processes had new material grounds in the political economy of postwar corporate capitalism. But we did not fully understand the mechanisms—or "mediations," to use a later theoretical vocabulary—through which these larger patterns of reproduction translated into everyday classroom practice.

Apple's work reminds us that lives in classrooms and staffrooms, boardrooms and playgrounds grind on, and that powerful ideas and analyses, simply put and always fraught with contradiction, still have the chance and responsibility to make a difference. I saw this again recently when I gave an introductory lecture to 400 Singapore graduate students beginning their teacher training. I am well into my third year of work in Singapore, still learning about this place, its histories, and complex cultural and linguistic politics. My lecture notes put aside—I found myself beginning with a narrative introduction to Freire's initial work in Brazil, drawing pictures to explain the banking model, generative themes and key words, monologue and dialogue. I connected the model to work of a Singapore year-1 primary teacher we had been working with. With the Education Ministry's new focus on local, teacher-based curriculum development, she had tossed out the worksheets and replaced them with developmental drama and narrative writing around generative themes from the students' lives. These then were skillfully woven into elements of traditional grammar teaching. The results were primary school student narratives of meaning, sophistication, and power—more linguistically complex and culturally telling than those of many secondary school students we had also been working with.

After I finished the talk, I was approached by several student teachers, some of whom had left successful careers to teach. None had heard or experienced ideas such as this before. There was little of the cynicism that we encounter from sophisticated undergraduates in the North and West, no "just tell me what to do on Monday" vocationalism, no "yes but the system won't allow it" appeals to the status quo, and no learned postgraduate, metatheoretical dismissal—just a refreshing commitment to weigh and explore the ideas further.

Their responses made me recall the powerful impact that Apple's work had on me as a teacher and researcher. I first read his analysis of teacher deskilling in the late 1970s. It was a similar moment, where words jump out of the page or lecture, reframing what you have been seeing and hearing in your classroom, making the familiar at once more accessible and more alienating. It explained to me much of what I was trying to do as a teacher: break away from the narrowly scripted instruction I had been told to use, challenge my students to talk and think, narrate and describe their worlds, all the while trying to envision how this might make a difference.

Apple's work set the grounds for an empirical and interpretive research agenda that continues to guide critical research on teachers and pedagogy. This involves detailed empirical work on: (1) the ideological character of curriculum policies, textbooks, and learning materials; and (2) teachers' and students' face-to-face negotiations of knowledge, power, and capital. But these analyses are incomplete without: (3) the shaping of alternative pedagogies, policies, and, indeed, local political economies that would work toward disrupting and shifting these patterns. Particularly in the context of current debates over what might count as educational research, evidence, and policy—the task remains. The powerful legacy of Apple's work is not what we have achieved in 30 years of critical educational research—but his persistent concern with what is to be done.

CONTEMPORARY CONTEXTS OF TEACHERS' WORK

In a *USA Today* survey on American attitudes toward occupations ("Who Do Americans Trust?" 2002, p. 1), teachers were listed in the top tier of people to have won U.S. "public trust"—alongside small businesspeople, police, and firefighters, but well above politicians, stockbrokers, and, at the bottom of the list, corporate CEOs and priests. In countries governed by opinion polls these are pyrrhic victories at best, particularly in the United States where teachers and their work have been the objects of increasing direct government intervention and management and conservative criticism in the past 5 years. These include efforts to shape and control teacher certification (e.g., NCATE in the United States; teacher registration boards in Canada and Australia) (Cochran-Smith & Dudley-Marling, 2001), large-scale teacher testing (e.g., Darling-Hammond, 2001), the specification of academic curriculum content and pedagogic procedures in teacher education programs by state authorities (e.g., California's reading initiative) (Garan, 2001), and current moves to standardize classroom instruction through mandated curriculum packages following the controversial findings of the U.S. National Reading Panel (Ehri et al., 2001). Variations on these policy moves are under way in the United Kingdom, Australia, New Zealand, Europe, and elsewhere (e.g., Weiner, 2003).

Whatever its empirical or political origins, the U.S. attack on teaching has been aided and abetted by powerful right-wing public interest lobbyists, who have directly funded, supported, and published critiques of teacher education and calls for teacher testing, as part of a larger agenda for the marketization of state schooling (Laitsch, Heilman, & Shaker, 2002). On November 18, 2002, this culminated in a call by Reid Lyon, chief of the Child Development and Behavior Branch of the National Institute of Child Health and Development, advisor to the George W. Bush government and driving force behind the National Reading Panel, to "blow up colleges of education."[1]

In Commonwealth countries, royal commissions, reforms, inquiries, and parliamentary examinations into teachers, teaching, and teacher education are not simply signs of state ministerial and bureaucratic dissatisfaction with teaching and student performance. They have also been motivated by the implications for teachers' work of complex transitions in union/employer relationships, unresolved issues about what to do with new technologies, the increasing diversity of student bodies, and the workload and professional development consequences of what appears to curriculum departments within ministries to be an infinitely expandable and elastic curriculum. At the same time, in many state and regional jurisdictions, teachers constitute the largest single workforce in the economy,[2] potentially a formidable political force but one whose action historically has been focused principally on issues of pay and working conditions.

In *The Logic of Practice*, Pierre Bourdieu (1990, p. 121) argues that trust, reputation, and honor are dependent on a profession's symbolic capital in social fields of value. Bearing in mind the local complexity and political economies within which debates over teachers and professionalism are undertaken—and trying to be sensitive, perhaps overly so, to the degree to which the debates over teachers and teaching themselves have become almost painfully local and parochial from all sides—I begin from a necessarily theoretical question that borrows from Bourdieu: How would we begin to redefine and reframe, rebuild and rework the cultural and social capital of teachers at this particular historical moment? Where and on what programmatic and normative grounds would we begin in a cluttered and confused social field where schooling has become spectator sport—as bureaucrats and senior public servants like Reid Lyon, teachers' unions, professional organizations, policy think tanks, academics, journalists and politicians, and conservative lobby groups conduct a free-for-all over standards, research evidence, claims of decline, market share, and the overall credibility of public schooling? Or to the theoretical point: Is it possible to redefine and "reboundary" the social field of teaching and education?

There are clear patterns in the public debate to date. Teachers and teaching become the objects of scrutiny and critique right at key junctures of social, economic, and cultural change. The common discourse strategy of the political right is a shunting of responsibility for changes in youth culture, community demographics, and employment, and, indeed, moral stance to schooling as cause and concomitant of such changes. Teachers and teaching get blamed for everything from deteriorating physical plants and eroded funding of schools, changing family structure and community social relations, and youth unemployment, to changes in identity and dominant technologies for intellectual formation and cultural expression. The current debates are, at least in part, attributable to larger, unresolved ideological matters as nation-states, institutions, and communities struggle to understand and articulate new and viable narrative accounts of life pathways into and around economies and cultures that are visibly in transition (Luke & Luke, 2001).

But at the same time, the response of many teachers' unions, professional organizations, and teacher educators has often been a critical defense of these self-same systems and practices that themselves are struggling to identify, name, and contend with new material conditions and discourses. Although they are crucial and necessary matters, better pay, smaller class size, improved per capita state funding of teacher education, and better funded professional development in and of themselves will not prepare teachers sufficiently for what are fundamental educational challenges posed by difficult economic conditions, new formations of youth, and new forms of work. The difficulty of the situation is compounded by the tendency of many educational theorists, researchers, and policy makers, across a broad ideological and methodological spectrum, to offer a counterhypothesis: that an adjustment of current educational interventions—whether curricular, instructional, or evaluative—has the potential to redress both residual and emergent structural social and economic inequality. This claim is as theoretically suspect and empirically vulnerable as those made in the Coleman Report (1966). As Apple's (2001, p. 97) recent comments suggest, the failure of progressive and democratic educational constituencies to articulate a forward-looking, strategic alternative to neoliberal governance and teacher deskilling marks a "tragic absence" in public debate and educational activism. But apart from a defense of professionalism versus deskilling, of craft versus proletarianized work, what would such a new positive thesis for teaching and teacher educators look like?

Narrow debates over scientific evidence aside, the breadth of international sociodemographic and social policy data can only lead to the conclusion that we are at a critical moment. The empirical conditions and contexts of schooling, identity, and knowledge formation are changed and changing. Schools, teachers, and students face the accelerated power and contradiction of forces of late and globalized capitalism. The actual community contexts, social, human, and fiscal resources, for schooling are not those of the relatively stable postwar periods, which spawned many of our current educational interventions and policy strategies. Human subjectivities and their varied life narratives and patterns are changing, with shifting and risky life pathways to and through schooling to insecure employment prospects and markets. Schools across national and regional jurisdictions are still struggling to contend with cultural and linguistic diversity, and, now are attempting to deal with the epistemological diversity affiliated with popular media, world youth cultures, and new technologies. Although these are still taken as classic signs of deficit in many staff rooms, boardrooms, and among particular research communities, shifting family shapes, mobile communities, and new, for many teachers unrecognizable, forms of identity will not go away. Quite the contrary, they seem to morph and shift even as traditional educational approaches, methods, and structures struggle to respond to them.

The structural conditions for supporting educational institutions also have been in transition. In the case of Australian education, despite the levels of funding of state and nonstate education holding steady at around a quarter of state budgets, an increasing burden of overall expenditures has been shifted from taxation bases to fees. This has been abetted by changes in allocative formulae that effectively have increased the federal subsidy of private and religious schools. In many ways, the truly radical alternative to the assumption that educational reform must occur either in a zero-sum public funding environment or through privatization was proposed by the Labor Party in the run-up to the 2000 Australian federal election: a flat taxation levy for education to recommit a significant percentage of public spending, bringing Australia's spending back up toward the Organisation for Economic Co-operation and Development (OECD) comparable levels or those of educationally focused nations like Singapore.

In an object lesson for U.S. researchers studying vouchers and charter schools as forms of marketization, the process of privatization of Australian state schooling has been ongoing, taking various guises, with around 30% of Australian students attending taxpayer-subsidized nongovernment schooling, some of it not covered by any educational credentialing or regulatory systems beyond the licensing of basic health and physical plant standards. In such a context, to argue that marketization and technocratic commodification are responsible and viable educational responses to new conditions is contestable, empirically questionable (cf. Luke, 2003a, 2003b; Darling-Hammond, 2004), and, from a policy perspective, tautological; that is, there is an implicit claim that the rules of the market will shake out structural educational deficiencies and problems that, arguably are exacerbated if not caused by the market. At the same time, I agree with Apple that to maintain a defense of an industrial system of schooling and particular version of the teacher and teaching tied to a progressive response to modernity and industrialism may be equally risky, both empirically problematic and strategically naive.

Australian schools, and their U.S., British, Canadian, and New Zealand counterparts, now have in place two decades of conservative, neoliberal governance and managerial reforms. Taken together, these reforms include the following:

- devolved school management and a business model of education at the local level, monitored through new standards for institutional performativity; gauged through
- universal standardized norm-referenced achievement testing; accompanied by
- expanding and often untrained usage of other standardized measures in schools and classrooms; and,
- a rapid and ad hoc proliferation of compensatory pull-out programs for dealing with the aforementioned cultural, linguistic, and epistemological diversity; relatedly,
- a universal and growing expenditure on behavior management programs; in the context of
- the slow-cycle implementation of outcomes-based curricula, with voluminous print-based documentation and infrastructure in place in all states; one affiliated total effect of which is
- increased usage of packaged and commodified instruction, reinforcing worksheet pedagogic practices.

In sum, the response to the new configurations of student diversity and affiliated differential patterns of achievement has been marketization and an agglomerative approach to compensatory programs that range from classical remediation to mainstreaming, each with specific tied funding and powerful constituency lobby support (e.g., special education, behavior management, speech pathology, English as second language programs, reading recovery, counseling, and educational psychology). At the same time, there are moves to further standardize and tighten curriculum to deal with variation.

Regardless of where any of us might stand vis-à-vis any particular educational analysis of the ideological bases or educational consequences of such developments, the change achieved over a decade by both Coalition and Labor federal and state governments in Australia (and in the United Kingdom, Canada, and New Zealand) has been dramatic. Market ideology has been infused into different levels of the educational system in less than two decades. Its extent would almost certainly qualify Australia for International Monetary Fund structural adjustment funding if it had developing-nation status, as countries throughout Asia, the Americas, Africa, and the Middle East are being required to emulate many of these managerial models in the modernization of their educational systems (e.g., Nozaki, Openshaw, & Luke, 2005). At the same time, any NGO (i.e., nongovernment organization of the sort that both in the United States and internationally increasingly influences and drives public policy making) suggesting that neoliberal reform is the solution to a paradigm crisis in educational governance and practice would have had to have been elsewhere in the past decade.

What is missing here is any attempt to radically reenvision or reinvent pedagogic practice. Conceptually and politically, these are tactical rather than strategic fixes. That is, they are attempts to modify the existing system, to somehow keep it on the road in the face of difficult and unprecedented conditions, without doing the practical policy and development work required by the radical reconstruction of student epistemology and ontology, new forms of knowledge, power, and practice, and changing social fields and attendant forms of life.

Taken together, current reforms are demonstrably and visibly struggling to increase the ostensive efficacy of schooling, even as they attempt to redefine the criteria of efficacy in, from the perspective of the social and educational history of assessment and measurement (Shepard, 2000), somewhat anachronistic terms. Suffice to say that these efforts do not align with the lofty goals of systems' attempts to embrace knowledge economies and global connectivity. Following initial effects and impacts, test scores have stalled in many states (e.g., Calfee, 2003), and how improved numbers actually flow through to expand educational participation, improve life pathways, employability and mobility, civic decency, and ethical business remains, at best, empirically and conceptually unclear.

Quite the contrary, the largest classroom-based study in Australian education (Lingard et al., 2002) found emergent evidence that the ideological combination of a basic skills curriculum model and local school management as business ethos have the potential at least to exacerbate disparities in educational achievement. In that study, many teachers reported that the testing, basic skills, and accountability push had encouraged a narrowing of the curriculum. This is apparently affiliated with the study's other key finding: a shaving off of higher order and critical thinking and a lowering of cognitive demand and intellectual depth (cf. Newmann et al., 1996).

To refocus on teachers and teaching, what is most interesting are not the most overt aspects of such reforms—the change in systems-level administration and school management to fit mercantile practices and new age metaphors—but rather the ways in which teaching has increasingly been appropriated both by curriculum and instructional commodities and the extent to which teachers have moved toward consumer-like behavior.

As for teachers' work, there are two immediate impacts of the suite of reforms noted above: first, near universal work intensification, as teachers struggle to keep systems designed for a different era operating with a veneer of educational efficacy and public credibility. Much of the intensification focuses on the management of diversity, through the planning of multiple lessons and materials, and classroom and behavior management issues, and on the paper and systems compliance activities required by systems accountability and school-based management systems.

Second is a retrograde recommodification of knowledge, as systems and teachers increasingly turn or return to an industrial model of teaching, with packages, tests, and standardized pedagogic sequences seen as enabling both compliance to new criteria for performativity and, more to the point, simple occupational survival in a work environment of proliferating curricular and administrative bids for time. As I argued previously, the attempts at reform, of variable educational ideology and quality, share an overall agglomerative approach, which, if unattended to, can create an avalanche of systems compliance requirements at all levels. This leads not only to change fatigue and cynicism in the workplace, but it also signals an ostensible difficulty in prioritizing change and coordinating reform at senior levels of bureaucracy and government (Luke, 2005b). For teachers, the result is a volatile cocktail of accountability, compliance, and work intensification that increases the allure of commodity. The effect, I argue here, is to turn teaching into a neoclassical form of commodity fetishism.

Our response as a profession in Australia, and as an intellectual/academic community, has been to reassert the principles of democratic, state education, and egalitarianism—in effect reassembling the dialectics of Dewey's (1966) seminal response to the industrial nation-state,

Democracy and Education, while recovering and defending what from the 1970s on had been a key element in the modernization of Australian institutional and economic life. This agenda turns on an assertion of Australian egalitarianism, about the need for a fair attempt, about the right and entitlement to education for all, the necessity of a common curriculum, preparation for democratic citizenship (which, in relation to digital and globalized civic spaces, geopolitical secular, and nonsecular conflict, we do not fully understand yet), and the demand for a system that brings together in common experience and cause an increasingly culturally and linguistically diverse community. Analytically, as in various critical projects elsewhere, its sustainability depends on a reconnoitering of Dewey's neo-Hegelian dialectics: to balance the skilling of a population for gainful and productive labor within a late capitalism that continually warrants critique, while we try to find productive and agentive pathways through, around, within, and against it for ourselves and our students, and struggle to build and maintain a strong, equitable civic sphere and ongoing radical social transformation. Yet as powerful as these arguments should and must be, the profession, whatever it has become, whatever and whomever it entails, wherever it exists, and whomever it actually is, has yet to articulate a powerful, new strategic vision of teachers and teaching for new times. Here I want to argue for a vision of teaching as cosmopolitan work and profession in critical and contingent relation to the flows, contexts, and consequences of cultural and economic globalization. This is the conversation we need to have—not a parochial or national one about teacher testing, licensing, or local needs of systems for curriculum implementers or school-based managers, but a whole-scale reenvisioning of teachers and teaching across time and space, beyond narrow regional parochialism, state regulation, and ethnonational epistemology.

What if we considered teaching not as a profession, not as a kind of reified, universal phenomenon the characteristics of which we struggle to map onto competency scales and teacher education outcomes statements, teacher education curriculum, and industrial agreements, but rather as dynamic social field (Grenfell & James, 1998)? By such an account, we could refigure teaching as a complex set of relational exchanges between heterogeneous and differentially positioned human subjects, as a form of dialogic intersubjectivity that occurs within the constraints of dynamic institutions, instead of the traditional subject/object relations presupposed in the current U.S. push for objective evidence for schooling. Such an approach to teaching also might deparochialize it, without universalizing it, looking for confluences, similarities, and points of overlap between teachers working in very different national and political economic contexts.

We could accordingly view the teacher not as psychological composite or sociological ideal type, which so much of the literature on teaching and teacher education does, but rather as situated within and in relationship to institutional fields of regional and national governance, and the capital production of goods and texts, but also in relation to the emergence of larger transnational economies and their affiliated cultures and identities. We could also expand existing sociological definitions by arguing for the necessity not just of teachers' cultural capital per se (that is, their internalized and evidenced skills, knowledges, bodily dispositions, intuitions, capacities, and so forth), but rather as requiring forms of intercultural capital, that is, the capacity to engage in acts of knowledge, power, and exchange across time/space divides and social geographies, across diverse communities, populations, and epistemic stances. Accordingly, the questions around teachers and teacher education could become: How would we reenvision democratic education in the conditions of later globalized capitalism? And, accordingly, how would we want to reshape and rework the symbolic, cultural, and social capital of teachers for these new conditions? Or, what could teaching beyond but within the nation be?

What follows, then, is an attempt to move beyond the critique of the neoliberal redefinition and reorganization of teachers' work and toward a new positive thesis. Here I want to ask how we can reconceptualize teaching and teachers in terms of capital, in terms of their particular baskets or portfolios of capital, in relation to how, where, and to what ends such capital might be deployed in new times, with an explicitly normative agenda about the deployment of that capital in relation to an educational agenda that is transnational and cosmopolitan. What if we envisioned as part of our rethinking of democratic education a reconstruction of teachers and students as world citizens, thinkers, intellectuals, and critics, and within *this* context, as national and community-based subjects?

TEACHING AND COMMODITY FETISHISM

William James's (1899/2001) prototypical modern treatise on education, *Talks to Teachers on Psychology*, claimed pedagogy as the "art and science of teaching." It is this tension that aptly defines the current push for objectivist, positivist sciences of education (in the service of what is called evidence-based policy) versus an insistent humanist defense of teaching as meaningful intersubjective action. It is worthwhile to recall that at the point of the founding of educational psychology, James, Harvard's first self-professed psychologist with an appointment in philosophy, was offering psychological science as a balance to the domination of pedagogy and teaching by a nonsecular moral/philosophic/aesthetic discipline. That is, the earliest scientization of pedagogy was a response and reaction to a 19th-century educational amalgam that was very much a blend of Protestant moral discipline and colonialism.

Drawing from preindustrial economies, we can of course define teaching as craft (e.g., Calderhead, 1988). Craft work entails an artisan eye and skill, design, and execution. The power and currency of the metaphor of teaching as craft is that it suits well notions of teaching as master/apprentice relationship, complementary as well to current sociocultural psychology and the focus on communities of practice in the educational change and reform literature. But there are many further applications of the metaphor here. Among them, we could ask whether the teacher as craftsperson is actually engaged in mentoring and apprenticing children into transformative cultural practices, signifying systems, participation in economic fields, and agentive participation in civic life. Or does the craftsperson reproduce craft, as in a master/apprentice relationship? To what degree, where, and how does the craft metaphor enable innovation of design, as well as execution of task? Analytically, the craft metaphor invokes a dialectic of the local reproduction and disciplining of skill, and of the provision of space within that training for design, redesign, innovation, and extrapolation (cf. New London Group, 1996).

Further, as a model of preindustrial work, craft implies a degree of extrainstitutional autonomy (e.g., in relation to the guild, but often in cottage industry or unsurveilled settings) that teachers might once have had and probably retain only in rural and isolated one- or two-room schools. For those who taught up country or in the bush, pedagogical autonomy and the need to work in multiage settings is a key aspect of teaching in rural and remote schools. The metaphor of craft implies one's right to select and work with materials, to combine and modify these material resources, to have autonomy in design, in envisioning and shaping the ultimate artifacts that are created, and in making varied rather than uniform products given available resources. But it is important to bear in mind that historically the craftsperson also was tied to productive exchange in an emergent mercantile economy. The craftsperson also was wholly dependent on the exchange value of the goods produced. While the ideal of connecting conception with execution might indeed be Braverman's (1976) ideal of unalienated labor, no such singular autonomy has existed in teaching *qua* institutionally governed waged labor for over a century, not incidentally, since the remodeling and expansion of mass state schooling for industrial, urban economies.

Teaching remains tool and semiotic code work, entailing the organization of intersubjective and intrapsychological discourse work with cognitve, aesthetic, and semiotic artifacts. It is nonetheless intrinsically and intimately institutional in character. What this means is that whatever scaffolding and pedagogical orchestration of intersubjective relations we undertake (via direct instruction, authentic pedagogies, or whatever) in the classroom, it is situated within a political economy, a division of pedagogic/discourse labor, and within larger material relations between spatially located and discursively positioned classes of human subjects. That is, whatever craft and aesthetic work remains in teaching, and however ostensibly pure its constructivist aspirations, local task or invention necessarily is within and indexes broader social and economic relations. As Yrjo Engestrom's updating of Leontev's sociocultural activity theory argues, tool use and skill acquisition, mentoring and scaffolding, necessarily produce and reproduce divisions of labor (cf. Cole, Engestrom, & Vasquez, 1997).

As a result, the crass objectivism and economism of the technocratic and market-oriented educational reforms described above have a self-fulfilling social and economic facticity about them. Hence their commonsense appeal: that the principal purpose of teaching is the seamless reproduction of job skills, needed by the economy, nation, and, the prospective worker/citizen. Not the least of this is a training and disciplining of students into how to recognize what counts as teaching and, in many instances, to aspire to participate in what is an increasingly pedagogized civic and commercial sphere, where everyone and everybody, from infotainment stars to home shopping, from news readers to Oprah, from politicians to salesmen are involved in overt pedagogic acts. As social fields, the public pedagogies (Luke, 1998) of everyday life overlap and inform teaching and schooling, but at the same time can look extremely school-like in their generic shapes and linguistic registers.

That calculable institutional systems can be reorganized for the optimal, efficient production of that worker/citizen *qua* raw material turned into usable capital should surprise nobody. No one could accuse the current versions of the human capital rationale of subtlety or deception about the aims and processes of education that they presuppose. And in the evacuation from grand narratives about the moral and civic purposes of education pre-September 11, 2001 (Luke, 2005a), the sanctity and orthodoxy of the human capital model stand apart, dominant as a new form of common sense among bureaucrats, politicians, corporate and business leaders, and parents and students.

But what is so interesting is the degree to which human capital-based educational policy, while it professes to be the relevant and powerful response to new economic and social contingencies, seems blatantly to have missed the point about the new work order (Gee, Hull, & Lankshear, 1998). On the one hand, most state educational policies have begun to profess the systemic necessities of new service and semiotic work, networked and globalized regional economies,[3] while on the other hand the most advanced systems such as the United States and the United Kingdom appear to have adopted industrial/pedagogic strategies for remaking the teacher and teachers' work that have their genesis in the early 20th-century behaviorism of Watson and Taylor, Thorndike and Skinner. Simply, the attempt to move toward setting in place the conditions for the production or even the imagining of the new teacher has lagged even further behind attempts via curriculum reform to address new economies. The fundamental trappings of pre-service and in-service training, practica within industrial-era physical plants, and the management of teachers to optimize curriculum compliance and test score production, the focus on teacher outcome competency/skill taxonomies, and the proliferation of teacher testing, the moves toward a more systematic managerial calculus for the production of the teacher and teaching are simply products of another political economy, another epistemological universe, another institutional era. Notably, to simply add information technology requirements and standards or, for that matter, token commentary on linguistic minority or special needs clientele to generic teaching standards underlines the poverty of current teacher education debates.

The story of how this came about is, of course, well rehearsed in the history and folklore of U.S. education. The long tradition of the industrialization of teaching as work began in earnest with the application of Fordist and Taylorist principles to school architectural design, school administration, curriculum design, testing, and funding in the first two decades of the past century (Callahan, 1962). The aim of a comprehensive teacher-proofed package of textbook, student workbook, and teacher guidebook materials long predates 1970s' calls for a technology of teaching by Skinnerians. It can be traced to their intellectual forbearer E. L. Thorndike, whose vision of educational progressivism was that of an objectivist behaviorism, which led to philosophic and practical clashes with John and Edith Dewey at Teachers College. As early as the 1920s, Thorndike envisioned a textbook and teachers' guidebook that would, in effect, micromanage teacher behavior to maximize the efficiency of teaching, and at the same time devise the prototypes and principles for standardized, norm-referenced achievement testing as the quality-control device to assess that efficacy (Luke, 1988).

Given all the current enthusiasm for postmodern theories of knowledge and for post-Fordist models of work both within and outside of schools, it is almost ironic that the terms of our debate over teachers and teaching is a reiteration, almost a century later, of the Thorndike/Dewey debate, shunting between an objectivist, scientific technicist and child-centered progressive humanism, between what James (2001) called "science" and "art." Now as then both justify themselves as committed to reform, as viable structural responses to new economic and social conditions, and as the most powerful responses to educational inequality.

It was Apple's (1981) landmark work of the late 1970s that applied Braverman's analysis of the industrial deskilling of work to a critique of the Thorndike/Skinner model of teachers' work. This led to studies of how teachers use commoditized curriculum packages as part of a larger political economy of textbooks and knowledge construction. More recent work continues to follow this argument, extending it into the study of teachers as consumers of multinational products, with media comarketing. Most recently, the U.S. federal government tied Title I funding to the use of scientifically proven curriculum materials in No Child Left Behind. This has amounted to a de facto endorsement of Open Court Readers and other phonics-based reading series nationally, in effect both shifting and reshaping the multibillion dollar multinational textbook market toward particular basic skills orientations to literacy (Allington, 2002). In this regard, while the emergent commodification and marketing industry targets early childhood through a range of cross-media products, and while publishers like McGraw-Hill have begun to provide digital products as adjuncts to print classics like SRA Reading Packages (Luke, Carrington, & Kapitzke, 2004)—the old industrial/print political economy of textbooks has reconsolidated itself in conjunction with the neoliberal reform I have described here. Programs like Open Court become de facto national mandates, with parallels in the mandated literacy materials in Australia and the United Kingdom.

This process of commodification has several profound educational effects (Decastell, Luke, & Luke, 1989). First, it has translated educational practice into a form of commodity fetishism. That is, it predicates the efficacy of educational policy, the practice of teaching, and particular versions of student outcomes on product use. The operational assumptions are that the right method, textually encoded into a particular commodity and then decoded and remediated into a normalized set of behaviors around the text/commodity, constitutes an optimal educational practice and experience. This translates teachers' work into what Marx (1976, p. 711) termed productive consumption. Marx distinguished "final production" and "productive consumption" from the "individual consumption" undertaken by human subjects as market consumers outside of their waged labor (Fine, 2002, p. 64). However, in postmodern semiotic economies more generally, the relationships between productive and individual consumption have become blurred. To return to our model of craft, for the preindustrial craft or for industrial production alike, workers principally were involved in the consumption of raw materials to produce goods with exchange or market value. In the case of semiotic and postindustrial work like teaching, teachers actually become the consumers of marketed commodities that are themselves semiotic production. As teaching is necessarily text/discourse work, teachers become the handlers, recyclers, and potential remediators of textual products. They may act as ciphers and ventriloquists for the already written and coded messages of packaged curriculum. In this regard, marketized pedagogy involves a coequation of teachers' work and teachers' consumption.

What I am outlining here is something more than economism and marketization, broadly described. It involves an historical convergence of:

- neoliberal management and administration;
- a reassertion of early 20th-century logical positivism as the official science underpinning testing/assessment to curriculum;
- a huge national and regional multimillion dollar state/statutory enterprise in the production, specification and construction, enforcement of grids of outcomes, however contested and subverted, for students and teachers;
- a reinvigorated political economy that brings together policy production and textbook production, the latter a multibillion dollar industry dominated by transnational knowledge and media corporations; with
- a redefinition of educational research as market commodity *qua* objective product testing and market research; leading to
- the reframing of educational policy as commodity testing, purchase, and endorsement.

In terms of teaching, this represents a new synthesis of the technocratic/industrial model of education, with huge potential for large-scale deskilling and deprofessionalization of yet another generation of teachers. Since the powerful critique mounted by the new sociology of education in the 1970s and 1980s, this seems to be hardly news, either theoretically or empirically. But the dimension I have focused on here is the recasting of teachers themselves as commodity fetishists—as lacking, wanting, and desiring consumers—and the reframing of pedagogy not simply as enacting a deskilled script, which Apple explained in his original 1981 analysis, but moreover of pedagogy as a relationship between consumer and product, with the semiotic re/presentation and redeployment of this to a third party, the student, in the scaffolded social and discourse milieu of the classroom. In this way, the subject/object, teacher/commodity dualism I referred to earlier has been repunctuated. The curricular commodity is discourse-producing subject and the teacher is constituent object of these discourses. At once, the teacher is the desiring subject and object of the market, with the curricular commodity as the object of desire. At the same time, this move has transformed educational research, driven by universities desperate to substitute commercial activities and contract research for the same public disinvestment in education noted at the onset of this chapter, into a kind of market research in the service of these new forms of commodity fetishism. Hence, the recent important and lively internal debate among the members of the editorial board of *Reading Research Quarterly* on the ethics and publication protocols for research on commercial products developed, endorsed, or sponsored by the researchers.

The response to this kind of model in critical policy debates and among teacher educators has been to reassert a model of teacher as professional, implying models of self-governance, autonomy, self-surveillance, and trusted management of the self. There are, of course, extensive and contending definitions of what counts as a professional. But to return to Bourdieu's metaphor of trust and honor, the professional gains ostensible autonomy and trust that accompany autonomy, through demonstration in the habitus of having internalized an epistemological self-surveillance. That is, the symbolic capital requisite for a professional is that of trustworthiness, having acquired the demonstrable self-discipline to profess, an act that, Derrida (2002) recently argued, is more about an evocation, a ritual doing and performing of education than the constantive claim of having or transmitting knowledge. Accordingly, to *do* education implies just that, the capacity to publicly and performatively stand for and on behalf of a particular form of life, rather than knowing something or having specific skills per se.

This in an environment where to be a teacher may entail the visible possession and manipulation of commodity, whether that be textbook or software, worksheet or package.

Credentialing, the deeming of institutional capital, is a key component for verifying that the professional in question has embodied the normative practices, discourses, and disciplines required to be able to operate *in loco parentis*, without overt and direct surveillance either by parents, by governments, and so on. But increasingly the accountability functions of educational governance suggest that the teacher also operates *in loco politicus*, as a stand-in for bureaucratic governance. In each case, specialized discourses—the law, medicine—are deemed as requiring specialized knowledge that laypeople and clients in and of themselves cannot sit directly or daily in judgment, both from lack of access to specialized cant and also because it would impinge on the daily flow of work and the specialists' capacity to do the work.

The reassertion of professionalism by teachers thus is an ironic move in the forms of solidarity and class consciousness that it signals, given the encroachment of the aforementioned accountability, standardized commodity, and testing on industrial wage and status conditions. The defense of teaching as profession versus industrial work is progressively less tenable, as we move increasingly toward a new dialectics of surveillance and self-surveillance across professions. One of the most interesting moves is the degree to which doctors, priests, lawyers, and CEOs, as they drop down the most trusted opinion polls, now face stricter regulatory regimes, direct inspection, and surveillance (one could imagine a competency grid for priests, or an Educational Testing Service credentialing benchmark for CEOs and stockbrokers but I am certain they have been considered). Consider also recent debates over the relationships between medical practitioners and the pharmaceutical multinationals. Here issues have arisen about the patterns of corporate sponsorship, marketing, and product endorsement and the degree to which these mark out a new terrain of the general practitioner as paid or sponsored commodity endorser, user, and dispenser.

As with the craft model, the actual working contexts on which the concept of professionalism was founded have been destabilized and historically superseded. I would argue that the concept of professionalism has in fact become a regulative rather than constitutive principle of teachers' work, attempting to reassert a de facto model of autonomy and independence as a defense against the encroachment of commodity fetishism. But in and of itself this does not provide sufficiently clear normative grounds for the actual kinds of capital—cultural, social, and symbolic—that might be necessary to rebuild teaching as work in a reenvisioned model of democratic education. I conclude with some preliminary notes on that task.

BEYOND NATION AND NATIONALITY:
TEACHER AS COSMOPOLITAN

Where to after the "pedagogical juggernaut" (Ong, 1958) of corporate, marketized, and rationalized texts and education? To critique the commodity fetishism of textbook products and the production of performance indicators as an assault on the democratic ideals of universal state education is hardly novel or clever, here or in educational sociology and philosophy more generally. Such critiques remain necessary analytic and political moves. But they do not suffice for a new positive thesis about teaching as work and as social field in relation to the configurations of state and capital, culture, and community.

Teaching and schooling historically have been developed as technologies of nation, nationality, and nationalism. This means that they have been juridically territorialized. That is, teaching and schooling have been defined, regulated, and, quite literally, fenced in by powerful statutory responsibilities to the local. Deans and program directors are constantly reminded of this by the restrictions on practicum placements and by increasing direct pressure by local employing authorities and state bureaucracies to gain control over content of curriculum methods courses (e.g., the push in California to inspect and monitor curriculum content in reading courses in the state universities' teacher education programs). In many international sites teacher education is increasingly becoming a narrow training in how to do a particular educational jurisdiction's curriculum and how to work its particular assessment grids and systems. Its craft-like apprenticeships are conducted in local sites, allowing a production and reproduction of the parochial, however inexact that initiation into the regulative behaviors, interactional norms, discourses, and forms of discipline might be. In this regard, the teacher *qua* professional is prepared and entitled to profess the local, regional, and national. Although our critical analyses might argue for new forms of democratic education, we rarely question this structural isomorphism that defines and constrains a priori the epistemological parameters of teachers and teaching: that teachers are trained, however explicitly or implicitly, as advocates of the nation-state, and to varying degrees, the region, province, and local district. Teachers are licensed to practice locally, and the vast majority of them stay within the territories and jurisdictions where they were trained.

There are several interesting historical contradictions at work here, particularly as these school systems attempt to shift human capital production in response to transnational information/service economies. First, educational systems of the North and West have begun to move to produce world kids with GATT-transportable, generic skills, knowledge, and competences. As the ongoing EU credentialing negotiations have shown, the transportability of professional degrees, credentials, and registration is a substantive free trade/tariff/boundary issue (cf. Marginson & Considine, 2000). That is, one response to new conditions is to construct an educated human subject who has transportable and generic characteristics rather than those that solely entitle and enable participation in a relatively static local employment market.[4] At the same time, there has been a subordination of moral and ethical training to the production of job skills.

A second, further knowledge effect of the local regulation of teacher education and teachers' work is to limit the hybridization and blending of forms of professional habitus by delimiting the social fields that count as legitimate for teaching practice. That is, teacher training, practica, and local statutory regulations on licensing have the effect of circumscribing the social fields for training and thereby limiting the kinds of cultural and social capital that will count as entitling one to profess, teach, and educate. In many teacher training programs, this means that curricular content and field experience are narrowly local or regional in character, with all that this might imply in terms of the setting of epistemological horizons and engagement with other life worlds of teaching and learning. The regionalism and localism, further, is often aided and abetted by pleas for local relevance and connectedness as motivational tools and curricular goals (Luke & Carrington, 2001).

Explanations of the broader dialectics of globalization are characterized in the literature in terms of local/global, push/pull effects, whereby global flows are remediated and recontextualized by local communities and regions in less than readily predictable ways (Burbules & Torres, 2000). My point is that the structural relationships of teacher education and neoliberal educational reform that I have described here have a contradictory territorializing effect. At once, they push the construction of the generic teacher as accountable and compliant consumer across national and regional boundaries; at the same time, they define the production and disciplining of the teacher as local and regional activities. This is occurring precisely at a time when both the ethical and moral demands on education, as well as the changed conditions of human capital production I have described here, are requiring broader critical engagements with globalization, with

cross- and trans-cultural knowledges, and with the complex syner-
gies between geopolitical, economic, and local events and knowledges.
Simply, while new economic and geopolitical conditions require new
teachers to have critical capacities for dealing with the transnational
and the global, current policies have turned teachers into a generic
consumer of multinational products with a narrowly local, regional,
and national epistemic standpoint.

What is needed is nothing short of the reenvisioning of a transcul-
tural and cosmopolitan teacher: a teacher with the capacity to shunt
between the local and the global, to explicate and engage with the broad
flows of knowledge and information, technologies and populations,
artifacts and practices that characterize the present historical moment.
What is needed is a new community of teachers that could and would
work, communicate, and exchange—physically and virtually—across
national and regional boundaries with each other, with educational
researchers, teacher educators, curriculum developers, and, indeed,
senior educational bureaucrats. What is needed is a teacher whose very
stock and trade is to deal educationally with cultural "others," with
the kinds of transnational and local diversity that is now a matter of
course (Chua, 2004).

The term cosmopolitan is attributed to Immanual Kant's essay
To Eternal Peace (1795/2001). Like most of his contemporaries, Kant
would scarcely have traveled beyond his village, much less national
and regional boundaries. Writing at the point of the emergence of the
European nation-state and empire, when Prussia and France were con-
cluding the Peace of Basel, Kant attempted to define a transnational,
worldly citizenry. In his "third definitive article of the eternal peace"
he talks about the necessity of "Cosmopolitan or World law," which
would depend upon a "universal hospitality" (p. 448). At the same
time, he critiques colonialism, describing the "inhospitable conduct
of the civilized, especially of the trading nations of our continent, the
injustice which they display ... to foreign countries goes terribly far"
(p. 449).

In the 18th and 19th centuries, travelers across national borders
were a curious mix of active agents of empire and its discontents
(e.g., soldiers, bureaucrats, but equally priests and missionaries, scientists and teachers), and those who were its unwilling diasporic victims,
slaves, guest workers, scientific objects, and refugees. In transnational,
late capitalism, that mix has become more a complex blend, with an
increasing proportion of the world's population on the move at any
given time, whether willingly or not, in search of work, better forms of
life, more stable and safer political conditions, and so forth. Hence, we

are increasingly part of what anthropologist James Clifford (1997) has termed traveling cultures, with economic and social conditions for the cultural, linguistic, and epistemological diversification and, potentially, hybridization of the very educational institutions in which we work.

To rebuild teaching as a cosmopolitan form of work requires a major rethinking of teacher education. It would entail an exploration and articulation of the ethical and moral dimensions of teaching as work in relation to globalized flows and economics. The task is in part a matter of honor, of rebuilding and maintaining the status of the profession in the face of reductionist attempts to remove any remnants of industrial and intellectual autonomy from teachers:

> The interest at stake in the conducts of honour is one for which economism has no name and which has to be called symbolic. ... Just as there are professions, like law and medicine, whose practitioners must be "above all suspicion," so a family has a vital interest in keeping its capital of honour, its credit of honourability, safe from suspicion. The hypersensitivity to the slightest slur or innuendo, ... and the multiplicity of strategies designed to belie or avert them, can be explained by the fact that symbolic capital is less easily measured and counted than land or livestock. (Bourdieu, 1990, p. 191)

It is indeed difficult, if not impossible, to reduce teachers and teaching to crude measures. For us to recover, reframe, and rebuild teaching as work in postmodern democratic education may indeed require a reassertion of strong vision of what is distinctive about each of our nation's education systems, arguing for a new version of democratic entitlement and new visions of what schooling can enable. But to simply argue that teachers should become more activist is to beg a prior question: Such activism requires a strong normative analysis of the limits of teaching as national and regional project. My sense is that calls for professionalism and activism may not be enough to restore the honor and symbolic capital of the community of teachers in a time of major economic and cultural change. Without a cosmopolitan, intercultural vision and new (local *and* regional, national *and* transnational) social contracts around issues of cultural reconciliation and cohesion, immigration, and, indeed, geopolitical responsibility and ethics, such moves risk reclaiming, however unintentionally, a parochial nationalism and a restorationist industrial strategy.

The educational contract argued for in *Democracy and Education* (1966) was Dewey's attempt at a pragmatic Hegelianism. It was built around an educational model that both committed to the advancement of industrial capital, and therefore for American economic empire, but also for transformative models of democratic citizenship through the extension of universal educational rights to independent and critical thought, to social engagement, enfranchisement. However naive such a position might have been, Dewey hoped this would generate the kinds of active citizenship to sustain social transformation, without claiming a priori what such a transformation might entail.

Bourdieu (1990) goes on to warn that the defense of reputation and symbolic capital in the face of new material conditions "can lead to 'economically' ruinous conduct." Analyzing patrimonial and matrimonial family ties to land, he argues that the modes of "symbolic capital" are "inseparable from tacit adherence ... to the axiomatics objectively inscribed in the regularities of the (in the broad sense) economic order" (p. 121). The professional reputation, status, and position that teachers strive to protect and restore are tied in some ways to the regularities of industrial, modernist capital. I have here argued that the tying of teachers into the expansion of capital principally has entailed two retrograde and self-annulling moves: a model of performativity that positions them as commodity fetishists as well as the implicated production and reproduction of what appear to be increasingly outdated forms of human capital in the face of new economic, social, and cultural dynamics. My case here is that the rebuilding of symbolic capital of teachers and teaching requires an engagement with and redefinition of new material and economic conditions.

The task of self-redefinition of teaching needs to be part of a transnational strategy for democracy and education, which directly takes up challenges of globalization, geopolitical instability, and multinational capitalism. We would have to begin exploring the conditions for intercultural and global intersubjectivity by both teachers and students, an engagement in "glocalized" analyses that continually situate and resituate learners and teachers, their local conditions, social relations, and communities, in critical analyses of the directions, impact, and consequences of global flows of capital, bodies, and discourse. This constitutes a kind of teachers' intercultural capital—that is, a distinctive species of cultural capital that is not a simple restatement of the parochial and restricted, national or regional cultural capital that we see produced and reproduced in outcome competences and skill taxonomies (which, ironically, begin to all look alike after a while) and deemed in our current systems of credentials. Rather it would be an attempt to push continually the boundaries of the social field of teaching. It would aim to constitute the kinds of embodied skills, competences, and knowledges that are requisite for modeling for students an agentive engagement in flows across cultures, geography, and sites. This might be the beginning of learning to teach and learn beyond the nation.

ACKNOWLEDGMENTS

I wish to thank Donna Alvermann, Naomi Silverman, Peter Freebody, and Pat Thomson for comments. This chapter is reprinted from: *Teachers College Record* (2004) *10b*(2), 1422-1443.

NOTES

1. The comments were made in a fifteen-minute talk by Lyon at the Council for Excellence in Education–sponsored meeting, "Evidence Based Education Forum with Secretary Paige." The incident was widely reported in the educational press and corroborated in a later apology by Lyon to an International Reading Association forum at Rutgers in 2003. See accounts by Susan Ohanian at www.substancenews.com/janO3/threats.html; by Kenneth Goodman at tlc.ousd.kll2.ca.us/~acody/Goodman.html; and Lyon's apology reported in the International Reading Association's newsletter *Reading Today* at www.reading.org/publications/rty/0308_urban.html.

2. In Queensland, where I worked as deputy director general of education and chief educational advisor to the minister (Luke, 2005b), the teaching workforce for state schools is well over 30,000, with an additional 10,000 employed by private and religious schools. This would make public education the largest single employer in the state. Similar workforce scale exists in many other U.S. and Australian states.

3. See, for example, strategic policy statements on web pages of the OECD, most Australian state ministries, and policy statements on the websites of many countries and provinces, including Canada, India, Hong Kong, and Singapore.

4. The emergence of the English as a second language teacher as a transnational and postcolonial guest worker with international certification and credentials (e.g., Cambridge language certification) is a case in point (Pennycook, 1994).

REFERENCES

Allington, R. (2002). *Big brother and the national reading curriculum: How ideology trumped evidence.* New York: Heineman.

Apple, M. (1979). *Ideology and curriculum.* New York: Routledge.

Apple, M. W. (1981). *Education and power.* London: Routledge.

Apple, M. W. (2001). *Educating the "right" way: Markets, standards, God, and inequality.* London: Routledge.

Bourdieu, P. (1990). *The logic of practice* (R. Nice, Trans.). Oxford, UK: Polity Press.

Braverman, H. (1976). *Labor and monopoly capital.* New York: Monthly Review Press.

Burbules, N., & Torres, C. A. (Eds.). (2000). *Globalization and education.* New York: Routledge.

Calderhead, J. (1988). *Teacher professionalism.* Basingstoke, UK: Falmer Press.

Calfee, R. (2003, May). *Introduction to the state of reading in California.* Paper presented at the Conference of the University of California Literacy Consortium, Berkeley, CA.

Callahan, R. B. (1962). *Education and the cult of efficiency.* Chicago: University of Chicago Press.

Chua, B. H. (April, 2004). *The cost of citizenship: Diaspora, ethnicity and class.* Paper presented at the Workshop on Identities, Nations and Cosmopolitan Practice, Asia Research Institute, Singapore.

Clifford, J. (1997). *Routes: Travel and translation in the late twentieth century.* Cambridge, MA: Harvard University Press.

Cochran-Smith, M., & Dudley-Marling, C. (2001). The flunk heard round the world. *Teaching Education, 12*(1), 45–63.

Cole, M., Engestrom, Y., & Vasquez, O. (Eds.). (1997). *Mind, culture and activity.* Cambridge, UK: Cambridge University Press.

Coleman, J., Campbell, E., Hobson, C., McPartland, J., Weinfeld, F., and York, R. (1966). *Equality of educational opportunity.* Washington, DC: U.S. Government Printing Office.

Darling-Hammond, L. (2001). Teacher testing and the improvement of practice. *Teaching Education, 12*(1), 11–34.

Darling-Hammond, L. (2004). Standards, assessments, and school reform.. *Teachers College Record 106*(6), 1047–1085.

Decastell, S. C., Luke, A., & Luke, C. (Eds.). (1989). *Language, authority and critics.* London: Falmer Press.

Derrida, J. (2002). *Without alibi.* Palo Alto, CA: Stanford University Press.

Dewey, J. (1966). *Democracy and education.* New York: Free Press.

Ehri, L. C., Nunes, S. R., Willows, D. M., Sinister, B. V., Yaghoub-Zadeh, Z., & Shanahan, T. (2001). Phonemic awareness instruction helps children learn to read: Evidence from the National Reading Panel's meta-analysis. *Reading Research Quarterly, 36*(3), 250–287.

Fine, B. (2002). *The world of consumption: The material and cultural revisited* (2nd ed.). London: Routledge.

Garan, E. (2001). Beyond the smoke and mirrors: A critique of the National Reading Panel's findings on phonics. *Phi Delta Kappan, 82*(7), 500–506.

Gee, J. P., Hull, G., & Lankshear, C. (1998). *The new work order.* Boulder, CO: Westview Press.

Grenfell, M., & James, D. (1998). *Bourdieu and education.* Basingstoke, UK: Taylor and Francis.

James, W. (2001). *Talks to teachers on psychology and to students on some of life's ideals.* New York: Dover Press (Original work published 1899).

Kant, I. (2001). *To eternal peace* (C. J. Freidrich, Trans.). In A. W. Wood (Ed.), *Basic writings of Kant* (pp. 433–476). New York: Modern Library (Original work published 1795).

Laitsch, D., Heilman, E. E., & Shaker, P. (2002). Teacher education, pro-market policy and advocacy reform. *Teaching Education, 13*(3), 251–271.

Lingard, R., Ladwig, J., Mills, M., Hayes, D., Bahr, M., Chant, D. et al. (2002). *Queensland School Longitudinal Restructuring Study.* Brisbane, UK: Education Queensland.

Luke, A. (1988). *Literacy, textbooks and ideology.* London: Falmer.

Luke, C. (Ed). (1998). *Feminisms and the pedagogies of everyday life.* Albany: State University of New York Press.

Luke, A. (2003a). After the marketplace: Evidence, social science and educational research. *Australian Educational Researcher, 9*(3), 43–78.

Luke, A. (2003b). Literacy and the other: A sociological approach to literacy policy and research in multilingual societies. *Reading Research Quarterly, 38*(1), 134–141.

Luke, A. (2005a). Curriculum, ethics, metanarrative: Teaching and learning beyond the nation. In Y. Nozaki, R. Openshaw, & A. Luke (Eds.), *Struggles over difference: Curriculum, texts, and pedagogy in the Asia-Pacific* (pp. 11-24). Albany: State University of New York Press.

Luke, A. (2005b). Evidence-based state literacy policy: A critical alternative. In N. Bascia, A. Cumming, K. Leithwood, & D. Livingstone (Eds.), *International handbook of educational policy* (pp. 661-677). Dordrecht: Springer.

Luke, A., & Carrington, V. (2001). Globalisation, literacy, curriculum practice. In R. Fisher, M. Lewis, & G. Brooks (Eds.), *Language and literacy in action* (pp. 231-250). London/New York: RoutledgeFalmer.

Luke, A., Carrington, V., & Kapitzke, C. (2004). Textbooks and early childhood literacy. In J. Marsh, J. Larson, & N. Hall (Eds.), *Handbook of research in early childhood literacy* (pp. 249-258). London: Sage.

Luke, A., & Luke, C. (2001). Adolescence lost/childhood regained. On early intervention and the emergence of the techno-subject. *Journal of Early Childhood Literacy, 1*(1), 91–120.

Marginson, S., & Considine, M. (2000). *The enterprise university.* Cambridge, UK: Cambridge University Press.

Marx, K. (1976). *Theories of surplus value: Part I.* London: Lawrence & Wishart.

New London Group. (1996). A pedagogy of multiliteracies. *Harvard Educational Review, 66*(1), 60–92.

Newmann, F., & Associates. (1996). *Authentic achievement: Restructuring schools for intellectual quality.* San Francisco: Jossey-Bass.

Nozaki, Y., Openshaw, R., & Luke, A. (Eds.). (2005). *Struggles over difference: Curriculum, texts, and pedagogy in the Asia-Pacific.* Albany: State University of New York Press.

Ong, W. (1958). *Ramus: Method and the decay of discourse.* Cambridge, MA: Harvard University Press.

Pennycook, A. (1994). *The cultural politics of English as an international language.* London: Longman.

Shepard, L. A. (2000). The role of assessment in a learning culture. *Educational Researcher, 29*(7), 4–14.

Weiner, G. (2003). Uniquely similar or similarly unique: Education and the development of teachers in Europe. *Teaching Education, 13*(3), 273–285.

Who do Americans trust? (2002, June 7). *USA Today,* 1.

III

On Spaces of Possibility

7

CONTESTING RESEARCH
REARTICULATION AND "THICK DEMOCRACY"
AS POLITICAL PROJECTS OF METHOD

MICHELLE FINE

"Now I'd like you to look at the suspension data, and notice that black males in high schools were twice as likely as white males to be suspended, and there are almost no differences between black males and black females. But for whites, males are three times more likely to be suspended than females: 22% of black males, 19% of black females, 11% of white males, and 4% of white females." Kareem, an African American student attending a desegregated high school, detailed the racialized patterns of school suspensions to his largely white teaching faculty. Despite the arms crossed in the audience, he continued: "You know me, I spend a lot of time in the discipline room. It's really almost all black males." Hesitant nods were followed by immediate explanations about how in June "it gets whiter," and "sometimes there are white kids, maybe when you're not there." Kareem turned to the charts projected on the screen, "You don't have to believe me, but I speak for the hundreds of black males who filled out this survey. We have to do something about it."

Contesting the commonsense belief that discipline problems are wholly generated by students, and the hegemonic belief that disciplinary practices are race-neutral, Kareem tried to rearticulate the "problem" of suspensions to his teachers as relational and indeed racial. He invited the faculty to collaborate with him on research to investigate these patterns. Once it was clear that the faculty was not likely to take him up on his offer, Kareem took up the persona of the social researcher, reporting the aggregate evidence as a call for action. He explained, calmly, that while the educators might choose to ignore his particular case, they would nevertheless have to contend with hundreds of African American boys who completed the survey and told us the same. He tried to articulate that this is not an individual problem, not race-neutral, and not separable from the larger school culture. He provided evidence that tore at the ideological representation of the school as integrated and fair. Kareem came to see this school context as ossified, as Franz Fanon has written: "[a] society that ossifies itself in determined form … a closed society where it is not good to be alive, where the air is rotten, where ideas and people are corrupt" (1967, pp. 182, 224–225). The school was refusing to hear; the air was rotten.

Kareem was engaged in what I am calling *contesting research*—critical research designed to challenge standard, inequitable educational practices and rearticulate what could be. As if enacting Gramsci's project of *rearticulation*, Kareem understood that

> [The objective of ideological struggle is not to reject the system and all its elements but to rearticulate it, to break it down to its basic elements and then to sift through past conceptions to see which ones, with some changes of content, can serve to express the new situation. (Gramsci, interpreted by Mouffe, 1979, p. 192)

In the spring of 2003, Kareem was asking his faculty for nothing less than educational justice. As a youth researcher on our large-scale Participatory Action Research project interrogating youth perspectives on racial and class (in)justice in public schools, Kareem developed and then taught other youths the skills of research, collaboration, and organization.

Kendra, a young white student, was a junior attending another public desegregated high school. During the summer of 2003, Kendra joined a dozen youth, spoken word artists, dancers, educators, lawyers, historians, and activists from the New York metropolitan area to study the history of the *Brown v. Board of Education* decision and the racial inequities that persist to date in public education. Having immersed herself in the history and contemporary struggles for racial justice in education, Kendra created a spoken word piece on the classroom-based racial imbalances that loiter within her desegregated high school. To an audience of almost 800 educators, activists, youth, policy makers, and civil rights organizers, Kendra bridged history and the present:

and in the classrooms, the imbalance is subtle,
undercurrents in hallways.
AP classes on the top floor, special ed. in the basement.
and although over half the faces in the yearbook
are darker than mine,
on the third floor, everyone looks like me.
so it seems glass ceilings are often concrete.
so let's stay quiet, ride this pseudo-underground railroad,
this free ticket to funding from the board of ed.
racism is only our problem if it makes the front page.
although brown faces fill the hallways,
administrators don't know their names,
they are just the free ticket to funding,
and this is not their school. (Kendra Urdang)

Dissecting hegemonic beliefs about desegregation and privilege, Kendra exposed racial inequities in her school, as she challenged the widely held belief that privileged students do not care about injustices from which they benefit.

Kareem and Kendra represent activist scholars of the next generation. Revealing the fault lines of inequity that hold their desegregated schools together, and at the same time, rendering them vulnerable, these young people have witnessed injustice in schools, researched the policies, practices, and consequences of inequity, disarticulated hegemonic beliefs, and worked hard to reimagine schools of justice. Kendra was relatively advantaged and Kareem relatively disadvantaged by equivalent systems. Yet both were stimulated toward critical scholarship to interrupt the "everydayness" of educational injustice.

Taking a lead from Michael Apple's writings on political action, democracy, and education, and his trenchant analysis of Porto Alegre, I am interested in the project of social research as a process of critical and collective rearticulation, designed through what Apple calls thick democracy "a practice that is based in the control of decisions about production, distribution and consumption in the hands of the majority of working people in this country, one that is not limited to the political sphere but to, say, economics and critically, gender relations" (1995, p. 155). I am interested in stretching Apple's conceptions of resistance and thick democracy into the field of epistemology and methodology; to think through projects of collective action in which social research plays a pivotal, counter-hegemonic role, by revealing the fault lines of injustice, engaging in democratic practices, or accompanying activists in global/local struggle. In this chapter I want to think aloud about how we situate critical research within larger struggles for social justice and how we design critical research projects that are at once provocative and democratic; rich in theory and activism, analytically wide and locally deep.

ECHOES OF BROWN: YOUTH DOCUMENTING AND PERFORMING THE LEGACY OF *BROWN V. BOARD OF EDUCATION*

We must contest a particular assumption—that of passivity. (Apple, 2003, p. 87)

Over the past decade, in sites as varied as prisons, the South Bronx Mothers on the Move (MOM), community-based organizations, and suburban and urban public and private schools, we have taken up projects of participatory action research with youth (this includes a broad cast of researchers, including Janice Bloom, April Burns, Lori Chajet, Monique Guishard, Yasser Payne, Rosemarie A. Roberts, Maria Torre, and a number of youth, educators, and organizers). In these spaces, youth critique has attached to educational studies and harnessed to sustained struggle. Youth critique and research have risen to collective challenge and action—in schools, communities, prisons, court rooms, and on the theater stage. Sometimes heard, but often not. And so we begin to address Michael Apple's question: "How can we interrupt dominance in education?" (2003, p. 19).

To ground our conversation about methods for collective resistance and thick democracy, I introduce a multisite project of participatory action research (PAR) launched with youth—street and suburban, Advanced Placement (AP), and special education, African American, Latina(o), Asian American, immigrant, and white American, wealthy and poor—to map the political economy and social psychology of educational injustice in the United States today. Organized as *doubled resistance*, the Opportunity Gap Project was designed to reveal the presence of deep, historic, and sustained injustice in schools, as well as the clever, creative, and exhausting ways that youth of poverty—and privilege—everyday resist and negotiate these injustices. Further, this project was designed to provoke action, in discrete and linked sites. (For another example of activist research with youth see Fine, Burns,

Payne, and Torre [2004], on *Williams v. California*, a class action lawsuit in which poor and working-class youth, as a class, sued the state of California for inadequate schools, undercertified educators, insufficient books and materials, decaying buildings, and less than sufficient intellectual preparation for college.)

In the fall of 2001, a group of suburban school superintendents of desegregated districts gathered to discuss the disaggregated achievement gap data provided by the states of New Jersey and New York. As is true nationally, in these desegregated districts, the test score gaps between Asian American, white American, African American, and Latina(o) students were disturbing. Eager to understand the roots and remedies for the gap, Superintendent Sherry King of Mamaroneck, New York, invited researchers from the Graduate Center of the City University to join the research team. We agreed under the condition that we could collaborate with a broad range of students from suburban and urban schools to research for our multiyear participatory action research project.

Over the course of three years of youth inquiry, through a series of "research camps," more than 100 youth from urban and suburban high schools in New York and New Jersey joined researchers from the Graduate Center to study youth perspectives on racial and class-based (in)justice in schools and the nation. We worked in the schools long enough to help identify a core of youth drawn from all corners of the school to serve as youth researchers—from special education, English as second language (ESL), the gay/straight alliances, discipline rooms, student councils, and AP classes. We designed a multigenerational, multidistrict, urban-suburban database of youth and elder experiences, tracing the history of struggle for desegregation from *Brown* to present day and social science evidence of contemporary educational opportunities and inequities analyzed by race, ethnicity, and class (see Fine, Bloom et al., 2005).

The research was all the richer because it had deep local roots in particular youth research collectives tied and committed to real spaces—the streets of Paterson, the desegregated schools in New York and New Jersey, MOM in the South Bronx, and small schools in New York City—and because we facilitated cross-site theorizing and inquiry to deepen the cartography of inequity we were crafting. Thus, as if a friendly amendment, we took seriously Apple's call for *thick, local democracy* and then added research and organization that would enable *wide, cross-site analysis*. By blending deep local work with relatively homogeneous collectives, with critical, cross-site analysis, we were able to create what Mary Louise Pratt (1991) calls a *contact zone*, in which we could chart critically the uneven distribution of finances, cultural capital, opportunities, hope, despair, and resistance. Documenting inequity through youth research we were also nurturing the tools of critical resistance broadly and deeply in this next generation.

At our first session with close to fifty youth from six suburban high schools and three urban schools, the students immediately challenged/ disarticulated the frame of the research: "When you call it an achievement gap, that means it's our fault. The real problem is an opportunity gap—let's place the responsibility where it belongs—in society and in the schools." With democratic challenge stirring, we—including the embarrassed adults—quickly changed the name to the Opportunity Gap Project, sheepishly remembering Friere's words:

> [T]he silenced are not just incidental to the curiosity of the researcher but are the masters of inquiry into the underlying causes of the events in their world. In this context research becomes a means of moving them beyond silence into a quest to proclaim the world. (Freire, 1982, pp. 30-31).

Students met as research collectives within their local spaces, and they also participated in a series of cross-site "research camps," each held for two days at a time in community or university settings. Immersed in methods training and social justice theory, spoken word, and hip hop music, film, and *Boondocks* cartoons, the camps were design to explore how to conduct interviews, focus groups, and participant observations, design surveys, and organize archival analyses. We worked with historians, lawyers, and activists who discussed the history of race and class struggles in public education, the history of the *Brown* decision, civil rights movements, and struggles for educational justice for students with disabilities, second language learners, and lesbian/gay/bi/trans and queer youth.[1]

In our early sessions, the agenda and questions were set—in pencil—by the adults. We had determined that we would study the "gap"—quickly reframed by the youth. At the first retreat, we brought in a "wrong draft" of the survey, which the young people quickly trashed, revised, and radically transformed, and we set much of the skills-building agenda. Over the course of that first weekend, we redesigned the survey to assess high school students' views of race and class (in)justice in schools and the nation. Over the next few months, we translated the survey into Spanish, French-Creole, and Braille and distributed it to 9th and 12th graders in 13 urban and suburban districts. At the second and third camps, another group of youth researchers from the same schools (with some overlap) analyzed the qualitative and quantitative data from 9,174 surveys, 24 focus groups, and 32 individual interviews with youths.

After that first session, however, the local research collectives began to take up their local work. Within individual schools, community-based organizations, and neighborhoods, the youth research teams determined, with adults, the questions they would study, what they would read, who they would interview, the music they would listen to, and the methods they would deploy to investigate questions of justice and consciousness. The "street life" collective of young men who work the streets in Paterson, New Jersey, facilitated by Yasser Payne, read together a number of excerpts on how scholars represent the "streets" and then culled from contemporary hip hop music how they would choose to represent themselves, as they set up focus group interviews for young men working the streets. The MOM youth researchers group, facilitated by Monique Guishard, read "everything I was reading in my graduate methods course" (personal communication) and brought in articles from youth magazines, contemporary music, and spoken word to develop their theorizing of critical consciousness. In the suburbs, the youth researchers working with April Burns and Maria Torre determined the methods, samples, and "spots" for interviews and participant observations in order to capture the full story of desegregated schooling, including the untold stories of internal segregation. And in the small urban schools, where Janice Bloom and Lori Chajet taught youth research courses as senior year internships, students collectively determined the questions to be investigated, the methods, readings, the persons to be interviewed, and the products to be generated (see Acosta et al., 2003).

Across the three years, across these varied settings, we studied the history of *Brown*, Emmett Till, Ella Baker, Bayard Rustin, finance inequity, tracking, battles over buses, and bilingualism, the unprecedented academic success of the small schools movement, new schools for lesbian/gay/bisexual/transgender students, the joys, the dangers, and "not-yets" of integration. We researched the growth of the prison industrial complex at the expense of public education, and we reviewed how, systematically, federal policy has left so many poor and working-class children behind.

We collected and analyzed data from the large-scale, broad-based survey moving across suburban and urban schools, and also rich, local material from the site-specific research projects. Designed to dig deep, these local projects included an in-depth study of the causes and consequences of finance inequity; an oral history of a South Bronx MOM organization, in which founding members were interviewed by their children and grandchildren; a systematic investigation of the racialized tracking of students in middle school mathematics; cross-school visits, interviews, and senior transcript analysis to document differential access to AP courses; and suspension rates by race/ethnicity and track in suburban schools (e.g., the extent to which "test scores" differentially predict enrollment in AP classes by race/ethnicity, see also Fine, Bloom et al 2005).

Together we created a topographical map of the racial, ethnic, and class (in)justices in secondary public schools. We documented structures and policies that produce inequity, the ideologies and youth beliefs that justify the gap, and those spaces within schools and communities in which educators and youth have joined to create extraordinary collaborations to contest the "gap." We wrote scholarly and popular articles, delivered professional and neighborhood talks. We traveled the nation to gather insights, listen to young people, and to provoke policy, practice, and change with our research.

Our research, conducted across some of the wealthiest and poorest schools in the nation, confirms what others have found: a series of well-established policies and practices ensure and deepen the gap. The more separate America's schools are racially and economically, the more stratified they become in achievement. In our empirical reports on these data we refer to these ongoing sites of policy struggle as "Six Degrees of Segregation":

- urban/suburban finance inequity,
- the systematic dismantling of desegregation,
- the racially coded academic tracking that organizes most desegregated schools,
- students' differential experiences of respect and supports in schools,
- the class-, race-, and ethnicity-based consequences of high-stakes testing, or
- the remarkably disparate patterns of suspensions and disciplinary actions (see Fine, Roberts, et al., 2004 for details).

Buoyed by our research findings and participatory process, during 2003 we conducted many feedback sessions in schools (like the chapter-opening scene with Kareem) and communities throughout the suburban communities circling New York City, and within the city. We presented our material to groups of educators and policy makers throughout the country. As we traveled with the stories of our findings, we worried, however, about the limits of talk. We saw most audiences nod in solidarity, but met far too many adults who refused to listen to young people's complex renderings of *Brown*'s victories and continuing struggles. We sat inside schools where it was clear that the "achievement" gap—the latest face of segregation—was built fundamentally into the structures, ideologies, and practices of these schools; too heavy to move; too thick to interrupt. The state apparatus was well oiled and justified. We were caught in the waves of what Gramsci and Mouffe have called the passive revolution:

> The category of "passive revolution" … qualify[ies] the most usual form of hegemony of the bourgeoisie involving a model of articulation whose aim is to neutralize the other social forces … enlarging the state whereby the interests of the dominant class are articulated with the needs, desires, interests of subordinated groups. (Mouffe, 1979, p. 192)

We found ourselves trapped by obsessive questions pointing to poor youth and youth of color—*What's wrong with them? Even in the same school building, we have a gap? But if we stop tracking how else can we teach students at their "natural" levels?* We grew weary of the volley of youth interruption followed by adult denial—critical research presented and refused.

And so, in the summer of 2003, with the anniversary of *Brown* approaching, we decided to move our critical scholarship to performance. We extended our social justice and social research camps into a Social Justice and Arts Institute. We brought together a diverse group of young people aged 13–21, recruited from the same schools and beyond, with community elders, social scientists, spoken word artists, dancers, choreographers, and a video crew to collectively pore through data from the Educational Opportunity Gap Project (Fine, Roberts et al., 2004), to learn about the legal, social, and political history of segregation and integration of public schools and to create *Echoes,* a performance of poetry and movement to contribute to the commemoratory conversation of the 50th anniversary of *Brown v. Board of Education of Topeka, Kansas.*[2]

In a scholarly and aesthetic experiment that challenged the boundaries of time, geography, generation, and discipline, we braided political history, personal experience, research, and knowledge gathered from a generation living in the long shadow of *Brown* with performance. Across the generations of our research collective, we produced a performance for 800 on May 17, 2004. We also published a DVD/book of the work, including all the elder interviews, a video of the Social Justice and

Arts Institute, youth spoken word, detailed commentary by the adult and youth researchers and educators working on educational justice in desegregated schools, lectures on high-stakes testing, tracking, and the everyday politics of racism—*Echoes: Youth Documenting and Performing the Legacy of Brown v. Board of Education.* (Fine, Roberts et al., 2004).

To give you a sense of how we worked, witness an afternoon session during the summer institute, with feminist lawyer Carol Tracy who was helping the youth researchers/performers historicize the impact of the *Brown* decision on civil rights, feminism, disability rights, and the gay/lesbian movement. Tracy explicated how the *Brown* decision opened doors for girls across racial/ethnic groups, students with disabilities, and gay/lesbian/bi/trans students. Her talk was punctuated by student writing sessions and questions seasoned by the students' original research.

A hot conversation ensued about the new Harvey Milk School—a new small school in New York City designed to support gay/lesbian/bisexual and transgender students. The students in the institute started pressing Carol, "Is this progress … a school for lesbian and gay students? Or is this a step backward into segregation again?" The debate was lively. Most of the young women agreed that all schools should be working on issues of homophobia and that segregating gay and lesbian students would simply be a throw back to the days of segregation.

But then Amir spoke. An African American youth researcher who attends a desegregated suburban school, Amir had shared his deep disappointment with the unmet promises of his desegregated high school. But at this point in the conversation, Amir was inspired to "come out" as a former special education student.

> When we were talking about the dancer [Kathryn Dunham] and how she walked off the stage in the South during the 1940s because blacks were in the balcony, I realized that happens today, with me and my friends—at my high school they put the special education kids in the balcony, away from the "normal kids." They (meaning gay/lesbian students) may need a separate school just to be free of the taunting. Putting people in the same building doesn't automatically take care of the problem.

Amir's poem, "Classification" reveals the connections he made from history, and with the lesbian/gay/trans students at the Milk school:

> Possessing this label they gave me,
> I swallowed the stigma and felt the pain of being seen in a room with six people.

Yeah, it fell upon me and the pain was like stones raining down on
  me.
From the day where school assemblies seemed segregated
and I had to watch my girl Krystal from balconies …
Away from the "normal" kids
to the days where I found myself fulfilling self-fulfilled prophecies.
See I received the label of "special education"
and it sat on my back like a mountain being lifted by an ant—it just
  can't happen.
It was my mind's master.
It told me I was dumb, I didn't know how to act in a normal class.
I needed two teachers to fully grasp the concepts touched upon in
  class,
and my classification will never allow me to exceed track two.
So what is it that I do—
so many occasions when the classification caused me to break into
  tears?
It was my frustration.
My reaction to teachers speaking down to me saying I was classified
and it was all my fault.
Had me truly believing that inferiority was my classification.
Cause I still didn't know, and the pain WAS DEEP. The pain—OH
  GOD! THE PAIN!
The ridicule, the constant taunting, laughing when they passed me
  by.

Amir had been working with us for more than a year, as a youth
researcher in his high school and then as a spoken word artist and per-
former in the institute. He had never told us about his special education
status until that moment. In writing this piece, Amir drew on his experiences as an African American student in a desegregated school, having spent too many years within special education classes. He pulled
from our cross-site research findings on rigor/respect/belonging, the
history of *Brown* and what he had learned about the dancer Kathryn
Dunham. With all these strings in hand and mind, Amir argued for a
separate school for gay/lesbian/bisexual and transgendered youth in a
climate where the price of integration is paid in taunting and physical
abuse. In this context of thick critical inquiry, Amir's voice, experience, and rage were embroidered into historic patterns of domination
and exclusion, contemporary evidence of youth of color yearning for
rigor, respect, and belonging.

Since the performance, these youth researchers have published, lectured, and brought their skills to other social movements for educational justice. Some have gone on to participate in the Campaign for Fiscal Equity, researching and organizing for finance equity in public schools in the state of New York. Others have testified in state legislature for the Performance Assessment Consortium, arguing for multiple forms of assessment in New York State, rather than the single, high-stakes testing regime that has spiked the dropout rates for poor and working-class African American and Latina(o) students. Those still in high school have brought their concerns about lack of respect, computers, gym, and college-application support back to their schools, communities, peers, and organizations of educational professionals and organizers. White suburban students have launched campaigns for detracking and a serious look at racial inequities in their schools. Together, the collective has presented their research and spoken word pieces at the National Coalition for Educational Activists, the Public Education Network, and the Cross Cultural Roundtable. These youth have learned the skills of thick democracy—to reveal and provoke. And they understand that their fame and performance means nothing if they stand alone. For in the end, all came to Amir's conclusion, "I had to speak for the others because the silence, oh the silence, is just as bad."

CONTESTING RESEARCH:
DEMOCRATIC THEORY, PRACTICE AND PROVOCATION

Echoes is but a puddle in a sea of global youth resistance movements (Harris, 2004). Fueled by the critical knowledge of youth, the work has been electrified by their ability to chronicle injustice across zip codes, racial and ethnic lines, and the borders of social class. The research and performance were propelled into collective action as the youth joined other social movements, in new sites, with allied struggles. As Luís Armando Gandin and Michael Apple argue in their analysis of Porto Alegre, from the critical rearticulation of a democratic educational space can emerge a radically reconceptualized history that denaturalizes "what is," a sharp-edged challenge to dominant discourses about race, class, ethnicity, and education and a range of allied projects.

I turn now to sketch a program of contesting research projects that have been or could be undertaken by those of us concerned with educational injustice. These are impossibly hard times to see the signature or imprint of critical thinkers and yet we turn to history and the future to understand the conditions under which social critics, intellectuals, and journalists have punctured the hermetic seal of dominant discourse.

Daniel Ellsberg speaks of the crucial role of the "leaker":

> Leakers are often accused of being partisan and undoubtedly many of them are. But the measure of their patriotism should be the accuracy and the importance of the information they reveal. It would be a great public service to reveal a true picture of the administration's plans for Iraq. ... In 1964 it hadn't occurred to me to break my vow of secrecy. Though I knew that the war was a mistake, my loyalties then were to the secretary of defense and the president. It took five years of war before I recognized the higher loyalty all officials owe to the Constitution, the rule of law, the soldiers in harm's way or their fellow citizens. ... The personal risks of making disclosures embarrassing to your superiors are real. If you are identified as the source, your career will be over; the friendships will be lost; you may even be prosecuted. But some 140,000 Americans are risking their lives every day in Iraq. Our nation is in urgent need of comparable moral courage from its public officials. (2004, p. A25)

As Ellsberg suggests, public intellectuals pay for silence and pay for speaking. The stakes for collusion in war, like (mis)education, can be severe. But in the case of (mis)education (see Woodson, 1977), the collateral damage accumulates slowly over time, seeping into communities and across generations. The remainder of this chapter takes up varied projects that we might engage in the contestation of educational and social injustice: bearing witness, finding cracks in the hegemonic cement, documenting the distortions, and linking critical studies and social movements of resistance.

Bearing Witness

[T]he imperative to tell—the vital urge not to forget—is driven by the imperative to transmit; to the "awakening of others." (Apfelbaum, 2001, p. 30)

Critical researchers have documented, theoretically and empirically, the perverse consequences of neoliberal reform on bodies, souls, families, communities, and the democratic fabric of the nation. As Apfelbaum suggests, these writers are compelled to resuscitate collective memories, to tell stories long buried, to provoke the collective imagination. Lois Weis (2004) in *Class Reunion*, like Mindi Fullilove (2004) in *Root Shock*, traces with painful eloquence and precision, the damage wrought by a nation that has undermined the working-class economy and struggling urban communities. These two writers bear witness with and for those whose trajectories are being erased. They connect lives and experiences to the histories and structures of oppression so deep and often so invisible. They chronicle, theoretically and graphically, the apocalypse as it consumes our young, poor, and working-class adults.

Both Weis and Fullilove bear witness for readers who may be living at such distance from poor and working-class communities that they have forgotten, or grown autistic to, the cries. Both writers remind readers that fates are joined at the knotty nexus of class relations—in labor, schools, on the streets, and ultimately in crime. Weis concludes her text with an eloquent statement of the radical project of "engaging respectfully with the lives of 'others' so as to understand what is happening to individuals and communities inside the new world order" (2004, p. 191). *Class Reunion*, Weis reminds us, "represents a form of 'working the hyphen'—a traveling between the lives of people and larger social structures with a deep commitment to social justice" (p. 192).

In *The State and the Politics of Knowledge*, Gandin and Apple write on the Citizen School, designed

> Through the collective creation of goals and mechanisms that generate active involvement of the communities, [that] so far seems to be a genuinely transformative experience. The Citizen School has broken with the separation between the ones who "know" and will "educate" … and the ones who "don't know" and need to be "educated." A new form of thinking not only about education but also about the whole society seems to be in gestation. … The epistemological rupture that plays such a major role in the experiment also allows for optimism. (2003, p. 211)

A second task for critical scholars is to find those places where democratic structures and practices thrive; cracks in the hegemonic cement. The documentation of transformative sites offers a critical mirroring back to society. The Citizen School created a space, a legacy, and an infrastructure to support thick democratic work. In *Echoes*, we worked across sites, with youth, organizers, policy makers, and educators to craft a diaspora of critical research and organizing. We produced a sprawling community of democratic inquiry, a narrative of critique and possibility, and a product—book, DVD, scholarly writings, white papers—that demands recognition by policy makers, youth, organizers, educators, and community.

Telling stories of the Citizen School or the small schools in New York City does the work of denaturalizing oppression, revealing simply that it does not have to be this way. In the absence of counter-stories, we are left, tragically, with a *false consensus*, believing that what is must be; that present conditions are inevitable and natural; that things have always been the same; and that most everyone else believes it is just fine. *Echoes* was indeed a grand collection of counter-stories of resistance, imagination, desire, and yearning for what must be, in a nation that has walked away from educational dreams for children of color and poverty.

Finding Cracks in Cement/Telling Counter-Stories

[If we lose these examples] we have lost our own history of socialist education and, in essence, are faced with starting anew. Alternative pedagogies and curricular models need to be developed in an atmosphere that fosters such a process ... the articulation and construction of serious democratic socialist alternatives is not to be taken lightly. As long as such a clear alternative does NOT exist, each segment of the working population will remain unlinked to the others in terms of its vision of education. (Apple, 1995, pp. 114–115)[3]

Linking Critical Studies to Movements of Possibility

A third form of resistance project involves linking critical studies to movements of social action and possibility. This work entails what Michael Omi and Howard Winant (1994) consider a "strategy of *war of position* [that] can only be predicated on political struggle—on the existence of diverse institutional and cultural terrains upon which oppositional political projects can be mounted and upon which the racial state can be confronted" (p. 81). The Cross City Campaign has done this by bringing together youth activists from across the country; WhatKidsCanDo.com by displaying a virtual site for youth activist researchers; Rethinking Schools by connecting a movement of educational activists deeply embedded within their local communities.

Radical geographer Cindi Katz (2004) offers a method for documenting simultaneously the local roots and global reach of our work. In her book, *Growing Up Global*, Katz traces the long arm of globalization as it compares growing up in the Sudan and in Harlem, New York. With a fine ethnographic eye that penetrates deeply within each site, Katz calls for social analyzes that trace globally, and dig locally, through a "spatialized understanding of problems." She argues that any effective politics challenging a capital inspired globalization must have similar global sensitivities, even as its grounds are necessarily local. This is different from a place-based politics. "Built on the critical triangulation of local topographies, countertopographies provide exactly these kinds of abstractions interwoven with local specificities and the impulse for insurgent change" (2001, p. 1235).

Apple calls for the academy to take up such cross-site analytic work in his calls for linking social analyses to social movements.

> Unlike, say Karl Mannheim's view of the unattached intelligentsia where the relative classlessness of free floating intellectuals enables them to stand aside from the political and ideological struggles of the larger society and to look at the "interest of the whole" ... I believe that we are already deeply positioned. We must attach our criticism to identifiable social movements that expressly aim to challenge the relations of exploitation and domination of the larger society. (Apple, 2003, p. 222)

Recently, for instance, Julio Cammarota and Shawn Ginwright (Ginwright, 2004; Ginwright & Cammarota, 2002) brought together researchers working with activist collectives of youth researchers nationwide, on campaigns ranging from finance equity to HIV/AIDS, abolition of juvenile prison facilities, queer youth rights, and immigrant labor struggles. The gathering was a serious interrogation of methods for research, organizing, generating audiences, and an opportunity for young people to meet peers engaged in a similar conversion of outrage to research and organizing. The connections established between African American, Muslim, white, and Puerto Rican youth in New York City and Chicano youth from Arizona were stunning. There was the devastating recognition that "your special ed kids are in the basement too?" and the more empowering recognition that "we're involved, together, in a national movement for youth justice in public education." These links are as treacherous and delicate as they are critical and inspiring. These youth are the carriers of knowledge, networks, and skills to be brought to the next generation of political struggles, and these are not skills they are likely to be learning in school.

Documenting the Distortions

An important, and typically overlooked, piece of resistance work involves documenting the distortions that erupt, with regularity, because the rhythms of oppression have overdetermined alternative endings. Thus, for instance, Thea Abu El-Haj wrote about how U.S. schools deal with "Palestinian-Jewish" tensions as if it were simply an issue of youth discipline, rather than an opportunity to educate about global conflict. In the powerful stories she tells, we can hear how global tensions circulate within peer relations in U.S. schools, and how schools deflect:

> At a multicultural fair earlier in the year, Palestinian students had performed a traditional folk dance—the debke for the school. They had, however, been explicitly forbidden to display a Palestinian flag during the performance because it was perceived as too controversial. At the subsequent multicultural fair … the Palestinian students were confronted with a large Israeli flag at the Israel table. An argument ensued, in which, according to the disciplinary report, one Arab student said, "fuck, that's not Israel. That's Palestine." Several days later there was another argument in which a Palestinian boy was reported to have cursed at Jewish students, "fuck the Jewish kids." These incidents were written up as racial/ethnic harassment, a level two disciplinary offense. The students were suspended and recommended for transfer to disciplinary schools. School administrators argued that there were no underlying ethnic/racial tensions … this action was in keeping with the school's "zero tolerance for intolerance" policy.

> Rather than denying the embedded racial/ethnic and religious tensions, the ongoing conflicts between Jewish and Arab students might have been viewed as ripe educational opportunities to explore the different experiences and narratives to each community. We must be willing to traverse uncomfortable territory … building curriculum that can addresses seemingly intractable inter-ethnic conflicts … rather than retreat behind the gloss of a discourse on intolerance. (Abu El-Haj, 2004, p. 208)

Like Apple's (2001) analysis of African American families organizing for vouchers in Milwaukee, it is critical to trace the well-ironed corduroy lines through which dissent and despair will flow unless resisted or interrupted. Once we can assess the nature of the predictable flow of resistance, we can begin to rearticulate how to interrupt it so that an alternative, counter-hegemonic story can unfold.

Rearticulations

When we can't dream any longer we die. (Goldman, 1977)

Gramsci speaks of the project of disarticulation and rearticulation. For our work, we consider these essentially intertwined. Indeed, disarticulation involves findings the fractures, the outliers, and connecting them; shedding the hegemonic robes that deny and distort, revealing the costs of what is. But rearticulation, as Maxine Greene (1988) would argue, insists that we help people reimagine—dream, for Emma Goldman—of what could be, public, democratic, and collective. Across sites of youth research, including *Echoes* as performed, we crafted a series of resistance projects to document not only the enormous costs of what is and youth discomfort with contemporary inequities, but also to theorize educational actions toward justice.

Arjun Appadurai (2004) offers an image of rearticulation when he reports on the "Toilet Festivals" sponsored by the Slum/Shackdwellers International Alliance in Mumbia, Western India, building the capacity to aspire through resistance, he argues, with actions defined by "a spirit of transgression and bawdiness, expressed in body language, speech styles and public address" (p. 78).

> The Toilet Festivals (sandas melas) organized by the Alliance, which enact what may be called the politics of shit. Human waste management, as it is euphemistically described in policy circles, is perhaps the key arena where every problem of the urban poor arrives at a single point of extrusion. ... Shitting in the absence of good sewage systems, ventilation and running water ... is a humiliating practice that is intimately connected to conditions under which waterborne diseases take hold, creating live threatening disease conditions. ... The Toilet Festivals organized by the Alliance in many cities of India are a brilliant effort to turn this humiliating and privatized suffering into scenes of technical innovation, collective celebration, and carnivalesque play with officials from the state, World Bank and middle class officialdom ... these toilet festivals involve the exhibition and inauguration not of models but of real public toilets, by and for the poor, exercises in technical initiative and self dignification. This is a politics of recognition from below. (pp. 78-79)

The Toilet Festivals, like *Echoes*, our participatory study of college in a women's prison (www.changingminds.ws), and Charles Payne's (1995) history of the Freedom Schools of the South, dare to tell a story that must be told, from a small, hot space in hell, about possibility. Sites of resistance can shrivel from loneliness. Without these stories, we have good reason to believe that dissent will hollow to despair and degenerate from there to violence, anger, or simply smooth exit—as the voucher movement has so masterfully demonstrated. But with these stories, with critical images, research, and organizing dedicated to resuscitating a democratic public sphere, we find that dissent can ride on the wings of hope to create a very different tomorrow.

CONCLUSION

Michael Apple has contributed in so many ways to a theory of contesting research: critical educational studies that speak against domination, toward contestation, and through "thick democracy." He has offered critical scholars a counter-story, of theory and method, so that we might be able to craft resistance projects for a very different tomorrow. The challenge today is that financing for critical research is evaporating; federal grants are dedicated toward a much more conservative set of questions, true experimental designs, and often privatization of the funding. The corporatization of the academy poses a serious threat to intellectual freedom, activist research, and to what remains of democracy.

The radical and rapid sweeps to the Right have not only dramatically altered economic and political relations, they have propelled a deep and pervasive sense of despair, hopelessness, and the naturalizing of inequality. Progressive scholars must labor today to create evidence of resistance and possibility so that we can remind the next generation of what a democratic public sphere did or could look like. For without a sense of possibility, as Apple and others have found, critique—distributed so pervasively among poor and working-class youth—can metastasize to retreat, despair, or exit. "The articulation and construction of serious democratic socialist alternatives is not to be taken lightly. As long as such a clear alternative does not exist, each segment of the working population will propose disparate plans and demands" (Apple, 1995, p. 115). And so we study and organize, wedged into a space between what is and what should be, buoyed in no small way by the writings of Michael Apple.

NOTES

1. Many students received high school credits (when a course on participatory research was offered in their schools) and 42 received college credit for their research work.

2. The 13 youth were drawn from wealthy and economically depressed communities in the suburbs surrounding New York City and within the city; representing the kind of wisdom borne in advanced placement classes and the kind borne in special education classrooms. We joined Christians, Jews, Muslims, and youth with no religious affiliation; those of European, African, Caribbean, Palestinian, Latina(o), and blended ancestries; young people headed for the Ivy League and some who have spent time in juvenile facilities; some who enjoy two homes, and some who have spent nights without a home. We recruited youth interested in writing, performing, or social justice from youth groups and public schools in the greater New York metropolitan area including northern New Jersey. We gathered together an intentionally diverse group of young people—by gender, race, ethnicity, class, sexuality, (dis)ability, "track"; by experiences with racism, sexism, homophobia, school administrators, social service agencies, "the law"; by (dis)comfort with their bodies, dance, poetry, groups; etc. Their real names are used only when their poetry is used. Otherwise, pseudonyms are used.

3. As Hank Levin (2004) has written on workplace democracies, "we need 'existence proofs' that can be disseminated widely so people have images of a set of workplace relations so at variance with their traditional work" (p. 24).

REFERENCES

Abu El-Haj, T. (2004). Global politics, dissent, and Palestinian-American identities. In L. Weis & M. Fine (Eds.), *Beyond silenced voices: Class, race, and gender in United States shools,* (2nd ed., pp. 199-215). Albany: SUNY Press.

Acosta, N., Castillo, J., DeJesus, C., Geneo, E., Jones, M., Kellman, S. W. et al. (2003, Fall). Urban students tackle research on inequality: What you thought we didn't know. *Rethinking Schools, 18*(1), 31–32.

Apfelbaum, E. (2001). The dread. An essay on communication across cultural boundaries. *International Journal of Critical Psychology, 4,* 19–34.

Appadurai, A. (2004). Capacity to aspire: Culture and the terms of recognition. In R. Vijayendra & M. Walton (Eds.), *Culture and public action* (pp. 59-84). Stanford, CA: Stanford University Press.

Apple, M. (1995). *Education and power.* New York: Routledge.

Apple, M. (2001). *Educating the "right" way.* New York: RoutledgeFalmer.

Apple, M. (2003). *The state and the politics of knowledge.* New York: RoutledgeFalmer.

Ellsberg, Daniel. (2004, September 28). Truths worth telling. *New York Times*, A25.

Fanon, F. (1967). *Black skin, white masks.* New York: Grove Press.

Fine, M. (1994). *Framing dropouts.* Albany: SUNY Press.

Fine, M., Bloom, J., Burns, A., Chajet, L., Guishard, M., Payne, Y. et al. (2005). Dear Zora: A letter to Zora Neal Hurston fifty years after Brown. *Teachers College Record, 107*(3): 496-528.

Fine, M., Burns, A., Payne, Y., & Torre, M. (2004). Civics lessons: The color and class of betrayal. *Teachers College Record, 106*(11): 2193-2223.

Fine, M., Roberts, R., Torre, M., Bloom, J., Burns, A., Chajet, L., et al. (2004). *Echoes of Brown: Youth documenting and performing the legacy of Brown v. Board of Education.* New York: Teachers College Press.

Freire, P. (1982). Creating alternative research methods: Learning to do it by doing it. In B. Hall, A. Gillette, & R. Tandon (Eds.), *Creating knowledge: A monopoly* (pp. 29–37). New Delhi: Society for Participatory Research in Asia.

Fullilove, M. (2004). *Root shock.* New York: Ballantine.

Gandin, L., & Apple, M. (2003). Educating the state, democratizing knowledge: The Citizen School Project in Porto Alegre, Brazil. In M. Apple (Ed.), *The state and the politics of knowledge.* New York: RoutledgeFalmer.

Ginwright, S. (2004). *Black in school.* New York: Teachers College Press.

Ginwright, S., & Cammarota, J. (2002). New terrain in youth development: The promise of a social justice approach. *Social Justice, 29*(4), 82–96.

Goldman, E. (1977). *Love and marriage, anarchism and other essays.* New York: Dover. (Original publication in 1911)

Greene, M. (1988). *Dialectic of freedom.* New York: Teachers College Press.

Harris, A. (2004). Future girl: Young women in the 21st century. New York: Routledge.

Katz C. On the grounds of globalization: A topography for feminist political engagement. 2001 SIGNS vol. 26(4): 1213–34

Katz, C. (2004). *Growing up global: Economic restructuring and children's everyday lives.* Minneapolis: University of Minnesota Press.

Levin, H. (2004). Workplace democracies. Retrieved on November 29, 2005 from http://www.iosj.com.

Mouffe, C. (1979). *Gramsci and Marxist theory.* London: Routledge and Kegan Paul.

Omi, M., & Winant, H. (1994). *Racial formation in the United States: From the 1960s to the 1990s* (2nd ed.). New York: Routledge.

Payne, C. (1995). I've got the light of freedom: The organizing tradition and the Mississippi freedom struggle. Los Angeles: University of California Press.

Pratt, M. L. (1991). Arts of the contact zone. Modern Language Association. *Profession*, pp. 33–40.

Weis, L. (2004). *Class reunion.* New York: Routledge.

Woodson, C. G. (1977). *The mis-education of the Negro.* New York: AMS Press.

8

(RE)VISIONING KNOWLEDGE, POLITICS, AND CHANGE

Educational Poetics

ANDREW GITLIN

Michael Apple, who for over three decades has illuminated and challenged the oppressive relations between schools and capitalist America, noted in the preface of his second edition of *Ideology and Curriculum* (1990) that "one of the most fundamental questions we should ask about the schooling process is what knowledge is of most worth" (p. vii). By posing this query, Apple was not simply adjusting the educational terrain but rather (re)visioning the nature of educational studies. Before the writing of the first edition of *Ideology and Curriculum* (1979), educational scholars directed their attention primarily on how to produce objective scientific findings that could filter down to teachers and other educators, thus impacting the way they thought and taught (Schubert, 1986). The question Apple posed, in contrast, redirected epistemological debates about knowledge and encouraged a rethinking of the relation between politics, knowledge, and change. Whereas educational change was often thought of as a process where experts, researchers of one type or another, produced knowledge that teachers could use (e.g., Dunkin & Biddle, 1974), within Apple's view, the process was intimately and inherently political. According to Apple, schooling was infused with a type of politics that had its roots in the economy and the ideologies that emerged from that materialist base. This politic influences students, the curriculum, and the work of teachers (Apple, 1982). Understanding the ideological and material politics of schooling as a way for educators to become critical subjects (Freire, 1970) that acted on inequities is a central aspect of Apple's project. By encouraging educators to become critical subjects, Apple (1990) shifted the educational terrain toward a focus on commonsense. He states:

> To challenge the use of systems management procedures and the like means that one must also raise questions about the categories we employ to organize our thinking and action in cultural ... economic institutions like schools. ... [T]herefore I shall examine how these commonsense categories we use to think through the very basis of what we are about and the modes of amelioration which stem from them are also aspects of the larger hegemonic configuration of an effective dominant culture. (p. 124)

By looking at commonsense, Apple was suggesting that indeed there was a hidden curriculum that needed to be attended to and challenged. Part of that challenge involved examining a set of school structures (e.g., tracking) and ideological categories (e.g., conflict) and their link to the materialist base of the economy that circulated both locally and more broadly and shaped debates, practices, and even the types of questions one could and should ask.

Apple's project has captivated me for years. For much of that time, I viewed this project as truth or at least having the outline of truth. In many ways, I still do. However, when I returned to some of the writings of the Frankfort school and the later more humanist writings of Marx, an alternative epistemology, educational poetics, started to emerge that both builds on Apple's central insights about knowledge, politics, and change but also takes a somewhat different approach. What follows is an account of my journey to this place I call educational poetics and its implications for epistemology, politics, and change—a process I refer to as innovative necessity.

KNOWLEDGE, POLITICS, AND CHANGE

As noted, underlying Apple's focus on knowledge and change is an articulation of the intimate relation between politics and schooling. I too have tried to tie epistemological considerations to a political understanding of schooling. However, as opposed to a type of politics that tries to work out the complex and often contradictory aspects of group identities such as class, race, and gender and their relation to schooling, the politics I am trying to develop, a politic fundamentally rooted in the scholarship of the Frankfort school, focuses on a form of political humanism where teachers and other educators create some separation from alienated relations (Blauner, 1964) to enter into relations of freedom. And it is within the fabric of freedom that a new politics is born—what I refer to as a deep politic. This politic attempts to recover, uncover, and enhance our ability to foresee—to consider "ought" questions without those questions being totally seduced by commonsense and the categories of this sense that direct our attention. In a phrase, the politics I am thinking of concerns the quest to use imagination and creativity—our human potential—to inform and revision traditional types of knowledge production that, as Apple notes, are unlikely to make a difference in terms of the sweeping goal of social justice. In many ways, this project moves back to the Frankfort school with its emphasis on aesthetics, image, politics, and social justice (Adorno, 1997) and forward to a poststructuralism where there is more uncertainty and possibilities for new epistemological considerations. By switching back and forth, I am attempting to address Apple's question of what knowledge is of most worth from an alternative perspective that does not lie comfortably in either a strict structuralism (e.g., Marxism) or a relativist poststructuralism. So what is this alternative epistemological approach that I call educational poetics?

EDUCATIONAL POETICS

I am using the word poetics to describe an epistemological approach that moves between inspiration and traditional views of knowledge such that reflection on experience is a process emerging from the mind/body as well as the soul (Bachelard, 1969, p. xvii). This mind/body/soul linkage is reflective of the ancient *Nahuas* who understood that mind/body/soul refers to the speaking of words and the doing of deeds. Taken together, mind/body/soul refers to the process of "inventing oneself" (Anzaldua, 1990, p. xvi). When the mind/body/soul becomes involved in the knowledge process, there can be an awakening of sorts that moves beyond the press of the everyday (of commonsense) such that a new image, a new creation of sorts, may come forth that is not predictable or knowable in advance. And it is this imaginative process, which cannot be codified or put into some causal relation, that is linked to relations of freedom. As Bachelard (1969) suggests:

✳ What delight the poetic imagination takes in making a game of
censors! [or, in my terms, commonsense] Time was when the
poetic arts codified the licenses to be permitted. Contemporary
poetry, however, has introduced freedom in the very body of
the language. As a result, poetry appears as a phenomenon of
freedom. (p. xxiii)

As a form of poetics, freedom is linked to the creation of an image.
In the institution of schooling, the image, what the teacher or other
educator sees when they view students, is related to our lens, the perspective we use to view the educational world. This lens is usually based
on the known—our collective experiences. However, it is still possible
to look upon the world in ways that transcend some of the premises of
sensibility or commonsense. When the premises of sensibility do not
totally saturate our lens, we exploit the human potential to be free—to
imagine. Imagination is an important quality of human nature because
it can help us look to the future without that view being totally structured by the past and the current realities. "Imagination separate[s] us
from the past as well as reality [the ongoing commonsense]; it faces the
future. ... If we cannot imagine we cannot foresee" (Bachelard, 1969,
p. xxx).

Looking to the future without being overly determined by the past
and present, a type of foreseeing, is one of the possibilities of the form
of inquiry I call educational poetics. Although the past is worthy of
all sorts of accolades, as humans we have the potential to see anew,
to look through and beyond the past in thinking about acting on the
future. And it is this foreseeing that holds the potential for an educational poetic, an alternative epistemology, to contemplate new, unforeseen directions that, at times, can create a different, *more expansive
or multidimensional* commonsense that can be argued to represent a
form of progress.

These unforeseen directions, this epistemological process of foreseeing, are, in large measure, linked to the marriage of two processes
that in practice are somewhat contradictory—education and poetics.
Although institutional education is often a process of socialization,
part of a system of accommodation and control aimed at producing
conformity of one type or another, poetics is typically about the punc-
ture of socialization, the common way of being or understanding the
world. As Marcuse (1967) states:

Since the thirties we see the intensified and methodological
search for a new language, for a poetic language as a revolu-

tionary language, for an artistic language as a revolutionary language. This implies the concept of imagination, as a cognitive faculty, capable of transcending and breaking the spell of the Establishment. (p. 55)

Instead of seeing this "difference" between institutional education and poetics as a threat to the concept of educational poetics, I view this difference between education and poetics as an engine of sorts that can help create a new terrain, or space for inquiry, belonging to neither tradition. And it is upon this terrain that the pull toward socialization and the push toward the unforeseen can be played out within this approach to inquiry.

Commonsense as a Directive for Inquiry

This alternative form of inquiry begins with Apple's fundamental insight about commonsense. However, whereas Apple's focus on commonsense is centered on understanding and challenging the limiting efforts of this "sense" as it relates to both structural and ideological assumptions of schooling that reflect dominant interests, educational poetics focuses more narrowly on challenges to commonsense that utilize our imagination and creativity to see anew in ways that are more expansive or multidimensional. It is not simply a critique of commonsense that educational poetics is after, but an escape from the seduction of the everyday (Smith, 1987). Put more directly, where Apple utilizes a view of politics that emerges from a critique of commonsense, educational poetics and other political humanist epistemologies combine critique, a looking out at the social world, with a looking in at the lens we utilize to form our perceptions. *where he is coming from*

Apple and there is no alternative, can no longer imagine

Because I am using commonsense in a unique way, and this concept is so central to the epistemology I call educational poetics, it might be helpful to say a few more words about how this term is used. Commonsense, in my view, is a catchall phrase that refers to dominant discourses, the broad-based circulating value systems that often move across multiple contexts and local discourses, the specific contextual normative systems found in a particular local. Commonsense, however, is not a free-floating "sense," but a sense or normative account that is directly tied to context or contexts. In this sense, educational poetics has a materialist base, although not strictly an economic one. When I use the word context, I am referring to architectures such as economic systems, the influence of the state, institutional rules and organizations, and even the layout of a particular space, among a variety of contextual "structures." Marcuse (1958) illuminates this link between sense, in this case a form of commonsense, and context in his discussion of the commonalities of Soviet and U.S. social control mechanisms in the 1950s:

> Both systems show common features of late industrial civilization—centralization and regimentation supercede [*sic*] individual enterprise and autonomy; competition is organized and rationalized; there is a joint rule of economic and political bureaucracies; people are coordinated through the "mass media" of communication, entertainment, industry, education. (p. 66)

What I hear Marcuse saying is that while some think of Soviet and U.S. contexts, at this time, as quite different, these contexts have certain common features or structures. These structures, if you will, reflect the desirability to "coordinate" individuals and cultural groups. This coordination function has the effect of helping to produce a commonsense, in this case an unnamed conformism to the structural priorities becomes the watchword of a secular faith, a faith that suffocates the exploration of cultural needs and interests, and relations that are defined by economics, bureaucracies, and mass media (Reitz, 2003, p. 162). Now, this unnamed conformism is not guaranteed, rather it is a contextual priority that requires cultural participation. Commonsense emerges, in large measure, from the interaction of contextual priorities and cultural participation.

Commonsense, however, does not simply operate on the wide planes of governmental systems; it is also in our homes and communities and moves back and forth between these broad boundaries and local contexts. An example closer to our educational homes might clarify this point. If a teacher is going to produce knowledge (i.e., reflect on her experience) as part of her attempt to develop a sixth-grade social studies curriculum, the knowledge she produces is likely to be influenced by a dominant discourse found in many, if not most, schools that education functions, in part, to sort students from best to worst. Further, it is also possible that at a particular school, or even a department in the school, there is a local discourse about how we should understand U.S. history. It might be that this local discourse encourages teachers to focus the curricular content on historical accomplishments, not points of controversy. As a result, it is "common" at this school that the sections in the U.S. history text on the protests against the Vietnam War are either deemphasized or left out altogether. In this case, it is not as if each teacher thinks about this decision in any depth, it is something that, at this local level, has become normative and taken for granted as the "way we do things here." Finally, this teacher's knowledge of curriculum development is likely to be bounded by certain aspects of the context of school including the relation between the school district, administration, and teacher decision making (Gitlin, 2001) because this teacher is unlikely to even investigate an issue if that issue appears to reside outside of her decision-making authority. Put more directly, if the context of schooling makes it difficult for teachers to teach against the grain (Cochran-Smith, 1991) such that these practitioners are neither rewarded nor recognized for teaching in this way, then the context makes it likely that sustained actions over time will not occur in this particular direction (against the grain). Teachers' thinking and action, therefore, are not simply an individual choice, but rather part of local and dominant discourses and contextual influences that motivate and influence teachers, even though the teacher is not likely to see a good many of the influences and motivations we categorize as commonsense.

The commonsense of schooling that I refer to in the above example moves back and forth between the classroom and the school district and of course wider forms of commonsense found at the governmental level to focus attention on competition, producing hierarchies (this is the sorting function), minimizing controversies and protest-oriented histories, and staying within role boundaries. Now you might be saying to yourself, "So what? What is the problem here?" The problem, from my point of view, is not that competition is inherently evil or that history should focus solely on controversies or protests, or that the teacher role is fundamentally flawed. Instead, my "problem" is that all these aspects of commonsense direct our attention to the "is," the way things are, and encourage conformity to that social reality. As such, the educational commonsense I mention stands in opposition to freedom, the "unquestioned ethical and political value to social nonconformism" (Marcuse, 1978, pp. 55–56). To build on Marcuse's (1964) language, cultural commonsense has made us *one dimensional*, and part of becoming multidimensional is to emerge, in part, from the saturating aspects of commonsense that deny us the ability to perceive and act beyond the known of everyday life and normative considerations. This view of commonsense, then, fosters a type of politics that not only looks out at social injustices but also inward at "our" participation in conformity to normative aspects of culture that stand in the way of freedom. As used within educational poetics, commonsense, as an object of inquiry, attempts to combine critique with a freedom

wed his humanist vision with Apple's political urgency

quest that is based on utilizing our creativity and imagination to produce a political understanding of schooling.]

This focus on commonsense may appear strange because "sense" is
usually associated with what is commonly thought to be right, desirable, and the way to live one's life. However, commonsense can also
be seen as a facade, a constraint that we often drape over ourselves to
appear desirable in one way or another. Understood in this way, commonsense stands in the way of madness, when madness is seen as our
ability to move beyond the everyday and see the world anew, unencum-
bered with the norms of what is supposed to be desirable and right. As
opposed to fearing this madness, my focus on commonsense suggests
we might embrace this non-sense to become ourselves—to escape the
alienated relations, discourses, and contextual factors that try to define
who we are. Although this is an odd way to think about the relation
between commonsense and our cultural selves (How many essays
include a plea for madness?), this type of examination of commonsense has been expressed for almost a century in the field of poetics.

> All who have given any real thought to art or beauty have rec-
> ognized this essential truth—seeing in the poet's madness not
> something for the physician to diagnose, but fancy's eternal con-
> trast with the commonsense of the practical world. ... For the
> madness of poets is nothing more than unhampered freedom of
> expression—expression of the *real self*, and not of mere eccen-
> tricity or whim. (Springard, 1917, pp. 95–96, emphasis added)

This is not to say that we want to throw out commonsense understandings at every opportunity. Rather, within the alternative epistemological form I call educational poetics, I want to create some space
between the suffocating aspects of commonsense that limit identity
formation and the making of history, in order to use our imagination
and vision to experiment beyond the current limiting cultural boundaries. When this is the case, one can enter into a political humanist
form of knowledge production that attempts to further relations of
freedom, by having commonsense become the directive of inquiry
forms such as educational poetics.

In this way, educational poetics can move educators toward new
political understandings that challenge the affirming aspects of culture
—the macro societal understandings that seep into local cultural communities and begin to recify cultural traditions thereby stopping or
slowing down their evolution. (Affirmative culture includes: reason
as the only way to progress, authoritarianism, a sole focus on "is" as

opposed to both "is" and "ought," pacification of resistance to established ways of being and knowing, alienation from the human potential to [re]vision what is possible and desirable. Instead of determining where to draw the line in terms of what knowledge forms are legitimate or not, an educational poetic works the borderland spaces between communities (the educational and the aesthetic or poetic) to rethink what is possible and desirable. In a way, educational poetics tries to rescue aspects of culture and humanity that are lost when affirmative aspects of culture become culture itself. Affirmative culture and educational poetics are alternative poles of a common process to shape and influence the bounds of culture and human potential. If affirmative culture focuses solely on the "is," the status quo, and the archaic influences of history, educational poetics is a struggle to link "is" to the "ought," to see the status quo as a construction, to know that reality that can be made and remade, and to view historical/futures such that humanity (culture and commonsense) is no longer concealed from itself. In part, the struggle is to consider the aesthetic, the imaginative, as aspects of knowledge, change, and progress. As Marcuse (1955) states:

> [I]magination sustains the claim of the whole individual, in union with the genius and with the archaic past. ... Like imagination, which is its constitutive mental faculty, the realm of aesthetics is essentially "unrealistic"; it has retained its freedom from the reality principle at the price of being ineffective in the reality. ... Before the court of theoretical and practical reason, which has shaped the world of the performance principle, the aesthetic existence stands condemned. (pp. 140–141, 172)

And it is this very condemnation by the powers of commonsense that allows aesthetics to act as a movement toward freedom, the freedom to exploit and utilize the "whole" genius of human life. And it is this freedom quest that identifies educational poetics as an alternative epistemology—an epistemology that searches for a deep politic.

The Search for a Deep Politic

Again, building on Apple's insight about the way schooling is infused with politics, educational poetics also tries to foster a political understanding of schooling but does so from an alternative key. One unique aspect of the politics educational poetics tries to foster is that it focuses in part on images—the metaphoric perceptions that tie our understandings, actions, and relationships to the status quo. In this regard Malcolm X taught me much about the relation between images and a deep politic. In a speech given at the Harvard Law School in 1964, Malcolm X made the following comments:

> When you let yourself be influenced by images created by others, you'll find that oftentimes the one who creates those images can use them to mislead you and misuse you. A good example: A couple of weeks ago I was on a plane with a couple of Americans. ... We were in the same row and had a nice conversation for about thirty-five to forty minutes. Finally, the lady looked at my briefcase and said, "I would like to ask you a personal question," and I knew what was coming. She said, "What kind of last name could you have that begins with X?" I said, "Malcolm." Ten minutes went by and she turned to me and said, "Your not Malcolm X?" You see, we had a nice conversation going, just three human beings, but she was soon looking at the image created by the press. She said so: "I just wouldn't believe that you were that man," she said. ... [After several similar examples Malcolm X continues]

> Now I have taken time to discuss images because one of the sciences used and misused today is this science of [image making]. The power structure uses it at the local level, at the national level, at the international level. And oftentimes when you and I feel we've come to a conclusion on our own, the conclusion is something that someone has invented for us through the images he has created (Malcolm X, 1970, p. 299)

What I see in this passage is a man trying to tell me about *a priori* commitments—everyday politics. He is suggesting that these everyday politics shape how we see people, our relations with those different from ourselves, and the conclusions we draw about those relationships. Further, and this is critical for me, he is noting that these everyday politics not only influence others but also Malcolm X himself, as he states: "And oftentimes when you and I feel we've come to a conclusion on our own, the conclusion is something that someone has invented for us through the images he [*sic*] has created." I take this to say that everyday politics is so seductive, that even one aware of its influence can be taken in. And if this is the case, what needs to occur at a fundamental level to confront oppression and move toward any form of social justice is to make everyday politics the *object of inquiry*, and if we do, we may come to a new level of politics, a deep politic that many times underlies everyday *a priori* commitments. And how does one move toward this deep politic? Malcolm X again begins to provide an answer.

Malcolm X talks about Americans, Muslims, Africans, and most importantly racists. In all these examples, he talks of groups and their contexts and then moves from this understanding to make proposals to confront racism. The most foundational proposal that emerges from his talk is captured in the following few lines: "Victims of racism are created in the image of racists. When the victims struggle vigorously to protect themselves from violence of others, they are made to appear in the image of criminals, as the criminal image is projected onto the victim" (1970, p. 300). From this perspective a deep politic, as a central part of educational poetics, requires a moving out beyond individuals and an a-contextual analysis to interrogate how the "victims of racism [to use one powerful example] are created in the image of racists."

This is our human potential to see anew in ways that are not totally saturated with the known, and it is this human potential, often not utilized, that is at the core of a particular type of freedom, a freedom that is linked to a deep politic and the alternative epistemology I speak of—educational poetics. As always, this deep politic ensures nothing except that one does not *have to* repeat commonsense cultural history. And it is this imaginative process that sparks our quest for a deep politics that at a fundamental level (re)imagines cultural relations that have become *the* way to think and act. We can see part of this (re)imagining process and its link to a deep politic in a segment of Langston Hughes's (1994) poem "Let America Be America Again."

In this poem Hughes creates a tension between a looking forward and a looking back. As Hughes looks forward beyond the present he sees a land of freedom. However, as we transition to the line between stanzas he states that this "land of freedom was never America to me." I take this to mean that the question before us, the reader, is not one of just recapturing the glorious past, but rather examining that past in order to dream anew, dream of a land where everyone is free. In the second stanza, Hughes goes on to talk about what should be examined if we are to move out and dream beyond the everyday circumstances where some are not free. In part, that examination is about hierarchies, privilege, and the possibility of one man being able to crush another. Dreaming is linked to the examination of what America has become. In the third stanza, Hughes develops further the tension between the myth and the reality of America by focusing on opportunity, equality, and freedom (the myth) and then stating this is not so for me.

In looking at the stanzas of this poem, they speak to a confrontation with a myth—that America is a land of freedom, love, equality, and

liberty. Why is this a myth? Because for some cultural groups freedom is an illusion. So why does the myth persist? The myth persists
because those who reside in the center not only have a different set of
experiences, which closely matches the myth, but they have the power
to make that myth, that illusion, that image stick as a form of commonsense. In this sense, Hughes is urging the commonsense view of
America, to be seen as that—a view emerging from a particular location—the center—that does not apply to all. If we are to dream, to see
anew, we must, according to Hughes, look, examine, and reconsider
the commonsense myth of what we see as America. If we do so, we can
dream in ways less structured by commonsense and consider the possibilities of having "equality in the air we breathe." In my view, Hughes
is suggesting that it is not enough to simply critique society nor is it
enough to dream—the two are attached in important ways. The politics that emerges from dream/critique utilizes critique, imagination,
and creativity to foster a deep politic and is a central part of the epistemology called educational poetics.

KNOWLEDGE PRODUCTION AND CHANGE: THE QUEST FOR INNOVATIVE NECESSITY

To this point, I have tried to provide a brief overview of educational
poetics, and suggest its relationship with the project that Apple began
over two decades ago. However, in doing so, I have glossed over the
issue of change. What I would like to do now is focus the discussion on
change as it applies to the development of a political humanist epistemology—educational poetics—and then make links to Apple's view of
change.

Langston Hughes speaks to the relation between knowledge and
change when he points to the failure of U.S. society in 1926 to move in
a direction that supports basic human values:

> America has never been—a land where men are free to grow
> in spirit and in humanness, to love and know they are loved
> because they are human beings who have the gift of life to share,
> a place where the entire design of society is aimed at enabling
> people to share the laughter and tears and joys of this existence
> in ever more creative ways. (1994, p. 162)

What I take Hughes to be saying is that equal opportunity, to enter
the center, is in some ways limited unless primary respect and value is
placed on all humans and done so in creative ways. After reading this

statement several times, I asked myself, if we focus on the words of this great writer and the standard of creative approaches to humanness and assessed the past 80-some-odd years, would it be accurate to say that the more things change the more they remain the same? Has anything changed progressively in terms of spirit, relations across differences, and the sharing of existence in creative ways? I think not.

If things have not changed in terms of the standards Hughes proposes, then we might want to think about the roots of change in alternative ways, such as that of innovative necessity. If we are to move in this direction, a direction I associate with social justice and the development of political humanist epistemologies such as educational poetics, then is could be that it is important to have commonsense and affirmative aspects of culture be the objects of inquiry at the same time that a more specific focus is directed at the notion of margin and center itself. One commonsense influence in this regard is the seeming universal appeal of inclusion as an end-point for change. To overcome the limits of focusing change only on inclusion, I want to suggest that we think of change and its relation to educational poetics as a process that requires a double move. The first move is likely to be based on inclusion. However, at the same time, efforts should be made to rethink the necessity of having a center and a margin, especially a center that defines margin. One way of doing so is to not only move toward inclusion, but at the same time move conceptually out of the center, or the margin for that matter, to a borderland between this hierarchical scaffold in order to see, examine, and possibly (re)imagine the new improved commonsense being formed at the center. Put differently, what this means is that educational poetics and the notions of change embedded within this epistemology do not emerge necessarily from within a particular cultural community (e.g., working class) but rather from the borderlands between cultural communities that allow us to look out at the social world and injustices and back at our own communities and their influences on our perception and imagination and creativity.

In attempting to do so, educational poetics tries to (re)imagine the everyday world. Because the word (re)imagine has a specific meaning, it is important that I spend a few minutes clarifying this term before returning to the relation between (re)imagining, "centered" forms of commonsense, innovative necessity, and its relation to educational poetics.

One way to understand (re)imagining is to contrast it with (re)searching. Most research is about being reflective, engaging in a cognitive process to make an informed judgment about a particular problem or issue (Cates, 1985; Elliott, 1991). By (re)searching, looking again, research has the possibility of linking what we know without any great amount of reflection, with what we can know when we take the time to study, contemplate, and reflect on an issue in some depth. In a way, therefore, reflection connects the known with the known—it provides access to our own knowledge and allows our knowledge to be communicated to others (Schon, 1987). In contrast, (re)imagining connects the known to the unknown, by first engaging with centered commonsense and then (re)imagining center/margin. (Re)imagining is a bridge that brings together the human potential to see the world anew with the contemplative and active moments of knowledge production. To (re)imagine is to link the body with the mind and the soul, not primarily to think more clearly about a topic or to eliminate bias, but rather to use our human potential to see anew. A (re)imagining process links affect with cognition (Eisner, 1998) and creativity with imagination. In this sense, (re)imagining is about moving beyond the status quo, it is not simply about doing something again, but rather is a process of reclaiming a human potential to strike out beyond the inclusive/exclusionary matrix that is and has been a feature of U.S. society since the formation of this nation-state (Popkewitz, 1998).

With this understanding of (re)imagining in mind, let's return to the question of centered forms of commonsense and innovative necessity. One reason to emphasize centered forms of commonsense in terms of thinking about innovative necessity is that no matter how inclusive the population in the decision-making group, commonsense will be conservative; it will reflect a construction that moves almost to the present but rarely gets there. As such, the center represents a form of commonsense that is conservative and will continue to define the margin in exclusionary ways unless efforts are directed at getting into the center and at the same time challenging the commonsense found in the center. But making the double move to be inclusive and also to focus on centered forms of commonsense, innovative necessity in this case, is a specific type of advancement that is directed at the conservative nature of the inclusive/exclusionary matrix and a particular ambition of educational poetics. Because the intent of the double move is to (re)imagine center and margin, innovative necessity is an advancement based on the social justice principle that we can move beyond allowing people into the club and instead more directly and fundamentally work on and reconfigure the inherent hierarchy that is part of the club mentality.

In many ways, educational poetics is an attempt to make the double move that informs innovative necessity. I want to suggest, for example, that teachers and other actors who have been excluded from the

incorporate everyone

knowledge-production process need to be included in this process. I also want to argue, that along with this inclusive move, teachers and others should look back at the "legitimate" knowledge they produce to examine new forms of commonsense that inherently will be embedded in their knowledge production process. With this examination in place, teachers and others are in a position to (re)imagine these centered (centered where teachers and others are seen as legitimate knowledge producers) forms of commonsense.

In sum, innovative necessary differs from some other approaches to change, such as those inferred by Apple, in several ways. Primarily, innovative necessity not only has a goal of inclusion for disenfranchised groups, as is true of many critical forms of knowledge production that has an embedded politics, but it just as importantly also focuses on the actual hierarchy itself—margin/center. Educational poetics directs us to make a double move. For example, if change is bottom-up or top-down or some combination, a question to ask might be how does this process of exclusion (top-down) or inclusion (bottom-up) address the commonsense position that hierarchies are a natural and inevitable part of social life? Is there a way to think about change that does more than rethink who is allowed into the club—the center? Second, innovative necessity suggests that to both look outward at social justice and inward at our perceptions, it is important to do so from a location on the borderlands, not so much within a particular community. It is from this borderland position that the looking out and looking back is becoming more likely. Finally, while critical perspectives, such as those endorsed by Apple, have often pointed to educators, policy makers, and institutions as the focus for change, less attention has been paid to academics or researchers themselves. Within an educational poetic, educational change—innovative necessity—requires a looking back by researchers at their perceptions, images, understandings, contexts, behaviors, and relationships to move beyond the categories, images, and forms of commonsense that tie our insights to the status quo. By doing do, it is my hope that change as innovative necessity (re)imagines the world in ways that escape, even if ever so slightly, the commonsense view of change that has made the statement "the more things change the more they stay the same" a watchword of our educational community.

SWITCHBACKS

In this chapter I have tried to articulate an alternative epistemology and its relation to politics and change. This "project" if you will, owes much to the important work of Michael Apple and his question of what knowledge is of most worth. In particular, his focus on politics and schooling, his use and critique of commonsense, and his move to a type of change that challenges the hidden curriculum, provided a space for me to attempt to take these now well-established conceptions in alternate directions.

Although there are important differences between Apple's position and the one found in this chapter, what is of importance to me is the way Apple's question continues to reverberate in ways that are generative. That reverberation has led me to ask a series of questions that extend those posed by Apple. On a conceptual level, I hope it is clear that I am following up on Apple's question concerning what knowledge is of most worth and the relation between politics and schooling by considering the possibilities of an epistemological form of political humanism. I am asking how a deep politic might differ from the more typical politics that *only* follow the mantra of race, class, and gender. There is an attempt to move to a humanistic politics that looks out at social injustices and inward at the perceptions that bound us to the tried and true and limit a freedom quest to use imagination and creativity to move beyond the everyday normative forms of commonsense. In turn, this deep politic informs not only an alternative epistemology, educational poetics, but a type of change that is not so much based on the standpoint of a group or groups but rather tries to make a double move that challenges the inclusive/exclusive matrix that is so much a part of the establishment of margin and center and the lens we use to develop our perceptions. To do so, the place from which knowledge is produced is less about a particular cultural location but rather a borderland between cultural communities such that the inquirer can look out at the world and back at the community that forms commonsense and normative perceptions that become part of that cultural life. Furthermore, this chapter also questions the legitimacy of epistemological hierarchies implicit in Apple's question about what knowledge is of most worth. Where Apple focuses on confronting some of the limiting ways we understand the legitimacy of certain types of knowledge, such as scientism, this chapter asks how all sorts of research may be participating in a "research form of commonsense" (e.g., the quest for authority and expert status) that limits the way knowledge forms push against the status quo.

These extensions to Apple's query are not meant to determine who is right or wrong (the central issue should not be about us), but rather to create a space for you (the reader) to enter the text and continue the process of reinventing educational studies, epistemological alternatives, the politics of schooling and change in ways that challenge dominant forms of commonsense that have limited our perspectives and reinforced cultural hierarchies and social disenfranchisement.

If you and I move toward the creation of such an open text (Hejinian, 2000) that encourages critical/dreaming on Apple's important query, we will have initiated a freedom quest. In part, that freedom quest is centrally educative, for education comes from the Latin *educare*, which means to *lead out*. Apple has started us on this educative process of leading out by asking the question of what knowledge is of most worth. I ask you to not delay and participate in the leading out of education so that freedom and education form a type of alchemy that bonds the two processes together as education becomes seen and practiced as an act of freedom.

REFERENCES

Adorno, T. (1997). *Aesthetic theory* (R. Hullot-Kentor, Trans.). Minneapolis: University of Minnesota Press.

Anzaldua, G. (1990). *Making face, making soul: Creative and critical perspectives by feminists of color.* San Francisco: Aunt Lute Books.

Apple, M. (1982). *Education and power.* Boston: Routledge and Kegan Paul.

Apple, M. (1990). *Ideology and curriculum* (2nd ed.). New York: Routledge.

Bachelard, G. (1969). *The poetics of space* (M. Jolas, Trans.). Boston: Beacon Press.

Blauner, R. (1964). *Alienation and freedom.* Chicago: University of Chicago Press.

Cates, W. (1985). *A practical guide to educational research.* Englewood Cliffs, NJ: Prentice Hall.

Cochran-Smith, M. (1991). Learning to teach against the grain. *Harvard Educational Review, 61,* 279–310.

Dunkin, M., & Biddle, B. (1974). *The study of teaching.* New York: Holt, Rinehart and Winston.

Eisner, E. (1998). *The enlightened eye: Qualitative inquiry and the enhancement of educational practice.* Upper Saddle River, NJ: Merrill.

Elliott, J. (1991). *Action research for educational change.* Milton Keynes: Open University Press.

Freire, P. (1970). *Pedagogy of the oppressed.* New York: Continuum.

Gitlin, A. (2001). Bounding teacher decision making: The threat of intensification. *Educational Policy, 15*(2), 227–258.

Hejinian, L (2000). *The language of inquiry.* Berkeley: University of California Press.

Hughes, L. (1994). Let America be America again. In A. Ramsersad (Ed.), *The collected poems of Langston Hughes* (p. 189). New York: Vintage Books.

Malcolm X. (1970). Speech at the Harvard law school forum of December 16, 1964. In G. Ducus & C. Van Doren (Eds.), *Great documents in black American history* (pp. 296-306). New York: Praeger.

Marcuse, H. (1955). *Eros and civilization: A philosophical inquiry into Freud.* Boston: Beacon.

Marcuse, H. (1958). *Soviet Marxism: A critical analysis.* New York: Vintage.

Marcuse, H. (1964). *One-dimensional man: Studies in the ideology of advanced industrial society.* Boston: Beacon.

Marcuse, H. (1967). Art in a one-dimensional society. In L. Baxeball (Ed.), *Radical perspectives in the arts* (pp. 53-67). Baltimore: Penguin.

Marcuse, H. (1978). Theory and politics: A discussion with Herbert Marcuse, Jurgen Habermas, Heinz Lubasz, and Tilman Spengler. *Telos* (38).

Popkewitz, T. (1998). *Struggling for the soul: The politics of schooling and the construction of the teacher.* New York: Teachers College Press.

Reitz, C. (2003). *Art, alienation and the humanities: A critical engagement with Herbert Marcuse.* New York: State University of New York Press.

Schon, D. (1987). *Educating the reflective practitioner.* San Francisco: Jossey-Bass.

Schubert, W. (1986). *Curriculum: Perspectives, paradigm and possibility.* New York: Macmillan.

Smith D. (1987). *The everyday world as problematic: A feminist sociology.* Boston: Northeastern University Press.

Springard, J. (1917). *Creative criticism and other essays.* New York: Harcourt, Brace.

Marnina, Gonick B/w Femininities: Ambivalence, Identity and the Edu. of Girls

Carrie Paechter Educating the Other: Gender, Power, Schooling

9

SITUATING EDUCATION

Michael Apple's Scholarship and Political
Commitment in the Brazilian Context

LUÍS ARMANDO GANDIN

This chapter will highlight the impact that Michael Apple's scholarship and political commitment have had in the Brazilian education environment (particularly in the city of Porto Alegre) and outline some of the key contributions of his already classic *Ideology and Curriculum* and following books to critical scholarship in education. It is important to say at the beginning that I do not intend to extensively map out Apple's influence in the educational field in Brazil. Although this would be of great interest and importance, it would require much more space than I have in this chapter. Instead, I will show how Apple's theory and his constant support to social movements around education in Brazil have reinforced an already politicized view of education present in the educational community of that country.

APPLE'S WORK IN BRAZIL

Apple's work has had a strong influence in the scholarship of education in Brazil. Part of the reason for this influence—apart from the sophistication of his theoretical analysis—has to do with his neo-Marxist roots. Let me explain this claim. When Apple's work was first made available in Portuguese in the Brazilian context, there was already a thrust toward discussing reproduction using culture not as central or as an epiphenomenon. In the late 1970s and early 1980s this movement was highly influenced by the work of Pierre Bourdieu and his book *Reproduction in Education, Society and Culture* (published with J. C. Passeron and released in Brazil in 1975). Although Bourdieu opened the doors for those not convinced by the very strict economic explanations of certain Marxist approaches, he closed other doors for those who were not ready to abandon Marxism altogether. The work of Apple represented an answer for these scholars and educators: it was an educational theory capable of incorporating gender, race, and cultural issues to the analysis of education without disregarding class and economic analyses. Apple's neo-Marxism was the answer many education activists and scholars were looking for.

Furthermore, Apple's heavy reliance on Gramsci's theorization resonated with the progressive educational community that was already using Gramsci as a Marxist way into culture and education. Gramsci's work was already well known in Brazil, mainly through the work of Paolo Nosella, who was already publishing articles in the early 1980s (for example, Nosella, 1983) showing the relevance of Gramsci to the field of education. When Apple's texts arrived in Brazil they resonated with a group of intellectuals who were also developing a complex theory of hegemony.

Brazilian educational space was already, on average, much more critical than the one in Apple's native country. The study of Freire and Bourdieu (at least in the work of his Brazilian interpreters), together with a leftist militancy among large contingents of teachers, had helped to create a fertile soil for Apple's conceptions to grow. In fact Brazil—and in particular the state of Rio Grande do Sul—had a recent history of strong influence on progressive educational movements and academic communities.

To understand this context it is central to evaluate the impact that Apple's concepts and ideas have had in Porto Alegre. In terms of teachers movements, history is full of examples that serve to illustrate why Apple's theory was so well received. In 1978, the teachers union (at that moment technically not a union, because civil servants were prohibited by law to organize unions, but clearly operating as one), the CPERS (Rio Grande do Sul Teachers' Center), gathered 15,000 teachers in a meeting to call for a strike. The power of a union can be measured by the number of teachers who belong to it. In 1991, 70% of all teachers of state schools were members of the CPERS, making it the largest teachers union in Brazil, with 78,000 members (Bulhões & Abreu, 1992, pp. 13–14). Between 1979 and 1991, the state teachers of Rio Grande do Sul organized nine strikes. The economic gains of the strikes were significant, but the economic situation of the country, marked by high inflation, ended up drastically reducing many of the gains. However, there was an important gain that is not emphasized enough at times in the literature about teachers' struggles. Through its mobilizations, which overcame the corporatist causes and were directed at the defense of public school and democratic management inside schools, the CPERS was able to resist much of the conservative reforms that governments tried to introduce in the state schools, including the kinds of "intensification processes" that Apple talks about, such as higher pay for better grades and total quality management (TQM). As Hypolito (1999) says:

> All the conservative proposals initiated in Rio Grande do Sul by the last governments could not be implemented. Even the ones that had a pedagogical character did not even reach the classrooms. … The actions of the union and teachers, sometimes with strikes, manifestations, and protests—when the measures demanded a contestation of the official policy and struggle for better work conditions, sometimes with silence—when the government was trying to impose some pedagogical orientation, were crucial to stop the consolidation of an explicit conservative educational project. (p. 95)

This resistance of the organized teachers movement has been crucial to public education and it has influenced the educational policy initiatives in Brazil and the general arena of education in the country. This is the context where Apple's ideas are received. His history as a former teachers union president allows him to connect very strongly with the ones who are facing intensification and are fighting against it.

In terms of the academic community, it is important to stress that the early 1980s was a period when a strong resistance to the more technocratic tendencies in education were taking place. The dominant groups highly influenced by liberal ideologies of development through education encountered a fierce criticism from the ones identified with Freirian and Marxist traditions. In a truly revolutionary way, the latter group gained hegemony in the Brazilian educational academia within a few years. The struggles to overcome the 1960s and 1970s dictatorship had created an organized and disciplined resistance that was striving for participation, democracy, and an educational theory that was connected with social justice objectives. At the Federal University of Rio Grande do Sul (UFRGS) in Porto Alegre, in the early 1980s, the progressives were occupying key positions in the School of Education and using the journal *Educação e Realidade* (Education and Reality), a highly respected academic publication, to make Apple's work known in the Brazilian educational community.

This is the context in which Apple was received in the early 1980s. But there would be no simple and pacific reception for Apple's first book. *Ideology and Curriculum* was published in Brazil in 1982. The publisher (Editora Brasiliense) released a relatively small number of copies and the book was very soon hard to find. The immediate impact of the book was not a widespread acceptance. This happened in part because the publisher—a leftist publishing house—did not have at the time a critical mass of educational publications that could form a community around it. But perhaps the main reasons are the ones described by Moreira (1990). Trying to explain why, in the critical environment of 1980s Brazilian education, Apple's ideas[1] were not fully incorporated by leftist educators, Moreira claims first that Apple was seen as a strict specialist in curriculum and at that time curriculum specialists were still concentrated in other U.S. influences, such as Tyler and Taba. The ones dealing with larger issues in education were not using Apple's book because of his label as a curriculum expert, and those who specialized in curriculum theory were too influenced by technocratic paradigms to adopt Apple's ideas. Second, the more orthodox Brazilian educational Marxists saw Apple's use of diverse intellectual sources as eclecticism and therefore distrusted his work. Third, the period of redemocratization after the long dictatorship represented a moment of rejection of U.S. influences (in contrast with the blind incorporation of anything that came from the United States that some had had during the dictatorship), and Apple's work suffered from this generalization. And fourth, the sharp difference between the Brazilian and the U.S. contexts and the fact that Brazilian educators were trying to understand and critique the Brazilian educational reality also helped to block Apple's immediate influence.

Even those who realized that Apple represented a breakthrough in curriculum theory were somewhat reluctant to use his work with students. Moreira (1988), in a thorough review of the intellectual influences in curriculum and programs courses in universities of the state of Rio de Janeiro, shows that in 1988, *Ideology and Curriculum* was recommended in every syllabus. In interviews with professors, however, he found that many were not directly using Apple's book with students. Some of them considered Apple's writing too difficult for students, and some claimed that his thinking was important but did not provide the kind of answers students were looking for in their practice as teachers.

Despite this initial cold reception, some progressive scholars understood Apple's importance and contribution and helped to spread his work in the universities. Antonio Flavio Barbosa Moreira was one of those key professors. In 1989, Moreira published an article in a very prestigious academic publication at the time titled "Michael Apple's Contribution to the Development of a Critical Curriculum Theory in Brazil." In that article the author (a former Ph.D. student of Michael Young in London and one of the most respected scholars in the field of curriculum in Brazil) examined Apple's trajectory and helped to make Apple's work better known to the academic audience.

But certainly it was the work done by Tomaz Tadeu da Silva (a Stanford graduate), as scholar, editor of the journal *Educação e Realidade* (Education and Reality) and the series titled *Educação: Teoria e Crítica* (Education: Theory and Critique) for a Porto Alegre publisher (Artes Médicas), and translator, who made Apple's work widely available in Brazil and helped situate his work within the tradition of local progressive educators. Silva was central in forming a community where Apple's ideas were well received and understood in their full critical potentiality. It was in Porto Alegre where Apple's work started to gain real importance in the Brazilian context and began to be widely used by professors in their courses and by teacher activists in their militancy.

It is very easy to prove the claim that it was through the work of Silva and his colleagues at the School of Education of the Federal University of Rio Grande do Sul in Porto Alegre that Michael Apple's texts started to really have an impact in the educational arena in Brazil. In 1982, when *Ideology and Curriculum* was only available in Portuguese in Brazil, the School of Education's Graduate Program brought Apple to Porto Alegre to participate in the International Seminar on Teaching. During that visit, Apple gave a talk, spoke to professors and students, and gave an interview to Silva and Nilton Bueno Fischer (another Stanford graduate) who introduced his work to many readers who did not have access to the Brazilian edition of *Ideology and Curriculum* (Fischer, Silva, & Apple, 1986). In the interview for the journal *Educação e Realidade*, Apple talked about his work since *Ideology and Curriculum* and how he had only dealt with ideology as dominance and not as a field of struggle in that book. The interview represented the first effort that Silva and his colleagues made to make Apple's work (and the work of critical scholars from the English-speaking world, such as Paul Willis, Henry Giroux, and Peter McLaren) better known in Brazil, and its impact was certainly strong. The interview was published in *Educação e Realidade* in 1986, and in that same year, Apple's piece (with Lois Weis) "Seeing Education Relationally: The Stratification of Culture and People in the Sociology of School Knowledge" was also published. Therefore, in a period of one year, Apple lectured, had an interview and an article published, all in Porto Alegre. In following years this trend would continue.

In 1989, Apple's *Education and Power* was the first book to be published in Tomaz Tadeu da Silva's series "Education: Theory and Critique" with Artes Médicas. In that same year, Apple's "Social Crisis and Curriculum Accords" (first published in the journal *Educational Theory* and published in Brazil with the title "Currículo e Poder") was published in *Educação e Realidade*. By then, there was already a critical community that understood Apple's contribution to education in Brazil and was ready to do what Silva already defended in his introduction to Apple's article in 1986: to overcome the generalization of resisting every theorist that came from the United States and to understand Apple's contribution to emphasizing both reproduction and the production of alternatives.

Since the early 1990s Apple has had a constant presence in the Brazilian educational debate. One could write several articles extensively mapping out all his publications and visits to Brazil, a task that I cannot pursue in this chapter. Nevertheless there are some trips that Michael Apple made to Porto Alegre that are crucial to understanding not only the impact of his scholarship in Brazil but also the critical support he has given to creating alternatives in education. Apple has always insisted that his theory is not isolated from his opinions but rather strictly connected to his political beliefs. His trips to Brazil since his first one in 1985 show this to be true. But there are two visits that are most significant.

The first visit consisted of two separate trips to participate in the third (1996) and seventh (2000) editions of the International Seminar of Curriculum Restructuring. Porto Alegre's Municipal Department of Education (SMED) promoted[2] this seminar annually and this event was part of the larger radical reform known as the Citizen School Project. This is a project that Michael Apple deeply cares about and he has cited it as a real alternative to neoliberal and neoconservative reforms in education. Along with me, Apple has written (Gandin & Apple, 2002, 2003) about the real advances of this initiative in constructing an educational system that radically democratizes access, knowledge, and governance. But Michael Apple not only writes about the project, he is so deeply committed to it that he is the only well-known international scholar that was invited twice to participate in the International Seminar. Every time he is in Porto Alegre he is asked to visit schools and meet with teachers.[3] He is always willing to lend his name to democratic educational causes and understands the impact that this gesture has.

There was a second significant visit in 2004 to Porto Alegre. Apple was invited to be one of the keynote speakers in the World Education Forum. More than 22,000 people from 47 countries participated in the third World Education Forum, a space created to discuss and exchange democratic and progressive initiatives in education around the world. Apple's conference "Knowledge, Power, and Emancipation" had an audience of more than 10,000. In the conference he showed the dangers of marketizing education and emphasized the fact that teachers from Porto Alegre can be the teachers of the world in terms of how to build a democratic and inclusive reform. His willingness to support events such as the World Education Forum (without receiving any honoraries) offers a concrete example of his political commitment, something increasingly rare these days.

These two examples clearly show that the real impact of Apple's work in Brazil is not circumscribed to academia; in fact, Brazilian social movements and those involved in progressive educational reforms know they can count on his support and his time to think through tough political decisions.

SITUATING EDUCATION

But what impact has Apple's scholarship produced for those involved with education? Perhaps a good example is the influence Apple's "cheap French fries" article (1997) has had on my second-semester student teachers.

When they start the second semester they had already had courses on sociology, philosophy, history, and research in education, had read Marx and Freire, and were increasingly aware of the need to "situate" education (as Apple had put it in *Ideology and Curriculum*). But it is when they read Apple's "Consuming the Other" (1996b) that they indeed understood the meaning of situating education and all social life, for that matter. In that text, Apple tells the story of his trip to an Asian country and the fact that the fields he passed on the way to his meetings were all potato plantations for a famous fast-food chain. I never ceased to be amazed by the glow in my students' eyes when we start discussing the connection between the demand for cheap French fries and the lack of schools for the people in that region. They are particularly struck by the words of Apple's interlocutor in the dialogue: "Michael, these fields are the reason there're no schools in my city. There're no schools because so many folks like cheap French fries" (Apple, 1997, p. 4). For my students this is a clear example of what Apple means by the need to situate education. Suddenly all the theory we had been studying made sense to them; they learned to do what Apple calls for, and that was an invaluable lesson for them. In a way that elegantly combines political conscientization and theoretical competency, Apple offers a text that speaks to the needs of teachers and the ones involved in education in general. It is not a pragmatic (in the sense that is preoccupied only with "what can be used tomorrow") scholarship, but it is equally not an abstract exercise.

As Gentili (1995) would say, in this text Apple shows a remarkable ability to revisit the concepts that are central to him, since *Ideology and Curriculum*, such as hegemony, class, and commonsense, and to resignify them. Rather than sticking to concepts because of some fixed content, Apple, in this text, shows us the real meaning of using theory to understand the complexity of reality rather than to simplify it. Examining otherness and connecting issues of race to class, Apple shows the real usefulness of complex theories to the work of understanding domination in several layers and of resisting and creating alternatives.

This is why my students like this text so much and why they do not find it complicated or inaccessible: Apple is able to speak with theory rather than speaking of it. The text demands that we situate education and that is precisely what Michael Apple does throughout that piece. This is something he has done since *Ideology and Curriculum*, and his contribution to developing a complex theory of how education is connected to larger social relations is invaluable.

Since *Ideology and Curriculum* Apple has shown us that education (and more specifically the field of curriculum) had been dealing only with the question *how*. What Apple does is encourage us to ask the questions *why*, *to whom*, and *whose knowledge*. He made us think about ideology, about conflict and different class interests in *Ideology and Curriculum*. He was one of the first to introduce a Marxist analysis that did not oversimplify the relationship between ideology and the dominant classes.

Apple's use of hegemony and his distancing from ideology as simply a "false consciousness" represent a great advance for those interested in social transformation. It greatly sophisticated social theory to account for agents who are not merely going through the motions, but are deeply immersed in hegemonic struggles.

Apple wrote *Ideology and Curriculum* in a context in which ideology had a particular meaning to the Marxist traditions of research in education. Without abandoning Marxism as a strong reference, Apple lays out the arguments for a neo-Marxist approach, in which ideology plays a central concept.

The early use of the concept of ideology in education was connected only with the interests of the dominant class and had a deterministic approach.[4] Works based on Althusser's conception of the ideological state apparatuses (ISAs) portrayed the schools solely as reproductive sites, as places where the dominant ideology is perpetuated. The insistence of Althusser that the school was the ISA "in the dominant position" (Althusser, 1971, p. 152) was a strong influence in studies of education.

In Althusser's theory, for the most part, actors seem to be merely playing a detailed prearranged script. His theory ends up giving space to the accusations of being another example of a historic "structuralism." Criticizing his theory as one that conceives economy and the other spheres of the social as pregiven empty places to be filled by agents with the right ideologies, Willis points out that, in Althusser:

> [F]ar from being the result of contestation and struggle over meaning and definition … , structure is an hypostasized given in a quite unsocial world. The absolute given contours of "places" are to be filled by agents who share no collective principles of variation or continuity of their own (Willis, 1981, p. 52)

Althusser does not seem to consider the historical characteristic of economic and cultural relations. As Williams—a strong influence on Apple's arguments in *Ideology and Curriculum* and in his subsequent books—shows:

> [It is only when we realize that "the base" … is itself a dynamic and internally contradictory process … that we can begin to free ourselves from the notion of an "area" or a "category" with certain fixed properties for deduction to the variable processes of a "superstructure." (1977, p. 82)

Although Althusser has the great merit of having shown us that ideology has a material existence, not only existing in the world of ideas, but also constituting concrete realities and constraints, his concept of ideology is much too monolithic. In Althusser's work, ideology does not have history; instead, it is something that "always-already" interpellates individuals. It is an all-encompassing concept and there is little room for agency inside this omnipresence of dominant ideology. According to Althusser (1971), "ideology has the function … of 'constituting' concrete individuals as subjects" (p. 171). This is a very innovative approach to ideology, one that tries to show that individuals operate within ideology. However, I think it fails to offer a refined and satisfactory explication of the relation between education and ideology, as I will explain below.

This conception theorizes ideology "in singular": ideology appears to be always composed solely of the ideas of the dominant class, something that does not capture the contradictions always present in the process of dominance. This notion of ideology does not allow space to understand what is central in Apple's work and can be represented by Hall's words: "there is never any one, single, unified and coherent 'dominant ideology' which pervades everything" (1996, p. 433). Furthermore, there seems to be no space here for any resistance or alternative creation because ideology "has" agency, not the agents. Structure and ideology are the entities that "act," not people.

Against that conception of ideology, Apple offers—already in *Ideology and Curriculum*, but more explicitly in 1982's *Education and Power*—a different understanding, one that invites us to always focus on "contradictions, conflicts, mediations, and especially resistance, as well as reproduction" (Apple, 1995, p. 21). He is particularly interested in showing that ideology is

> [N]ot a form of false consciousness "imposed" by an economy. Rather, it [is] part of a lived culture that [is] the result of the material conditions of one's day to day practices. It [is] a set of meanings and practices that indeed did have elements of good sense as well as reproductive elements within it. (p. 25)

Apple gives space here for the concept of commonsense and the elements of good sense inside it. This is an important shift. The traditional Marxist perspective would say that commonsense, in a given society, is always either filled with dominant ideas or is too "naive" to even be considered in the counter-hegemonic struggles and, therefore, would dismiss it as an irrelevant concept. However, following a Gramscian characterization, Apple treats commonsense as a central concept where hegemonic and possibly counter-hegemonic articulations are forged.

The ideas that form commonsense are not there because they were forced in, but because they make sense to people, based on their own everyday experiences. Commonsense is formed by different ideologies; however, these ideologies are not "false images" of reality or a product of a "false consciousness," but of particular classed, gendered, or raced views of the reality. As Apple says:

> [T]he first thing to ask about an ideology is not what is false about it, but what is true. What are its connections to lived experience? Ideologies, properly conceived, do not dupe people. To be effective they must connect to real problems, real experiences. (Apple, 1993, p. 20)

Commonsense is formed mainly (but not exclusively) by hegemonic ideologies, because the dominant class (or race or gender) is able to present its ideas as the natural way of understanding society. The hegemonic discourse is accepted, in part, because it is able to anchor itself in previous understandings present in commonsense.

Apple helps us to understand that this is a process of constant movement, where the hegemonic groups must struggle to maintain leadership. This is not automatically guaranteed by the fact that those groups have the economic power (especially because groups without economic power could be brought inside the dominant alliance). Through this analysis, we can identify a permanent process of struggle from the dominant groups to maintain their dominance. This is hegemony: "a process in which dominant groups in society come together to form a bloc and sustain leadership over subordinate groups" (Apple, 1996, p. 14). However, this must be settled inside the hegemonic bloc as well. In order to form a bloc, an alliance, the dominant classes constantly build bridges between the different, and sometimes conflicting, interests. So, the process of guaranteeing hegemony is not just a matter of conquering (and maintaining) ideological leadership over the social formation where the bloc operates, but also keeping the bloc together.

Therefore, hegemony is neither guaranteed from the start nor everlasting once it has been achieved. To build leadership, the hegemonic bloc has to connect its discourse to practical life in each society. This is the cultural work that the hegemonic bloc is constantly doing: establishing its discourse as the one that "makes sense," one that is not regarded as dominant discourse, but as the natural way of thinking and doing things.

There is an important connection of this idea of "making sense," of producing "naturalized" ways of conceptualizing the social relations with the concept of commonsense that Apple offers us. No ideology becomes dominant if it is not at least partially linked to the commonsense of each historic period. So what the dominant ideology promotes is not a totally strange idea to the public, neither a totally "false" reality.[5] An important part of hegemony is achieved when the dominant discourse turns itself into the knowledge that becomes known as commonsense, when this dominant discourse is able to articulate itself with the elements of "good sense" (Apple, 1996, 1999a; Gramsci, 1997) within commonsense. This is a historic construction, and commonsense is never totally converted into the dominant discourse. In fact, although commonsense has historically been the object of the "work" of the dominant discourses, it has preserved its basic characteristics: it is still fragmented and contradictory, filled with different ideologies. The hegemonic "organization" of commonsense is not stable or permanent. Because commonsense is "fluid" and because it is the knowledge that orients everyday life, hegemony is only maintained if there is a constant process of production and reproduction of its content inside commonsense. And because of that, commonsense is an arena of ideological struggle.

Apple's use of hegemony also helps us to understand the complex politics of hegemonic alliances. His more recent use of Gramsci's notion of hegemonic bloc helps us to understand the heavy lifting involved in constructing and maintaining an alliance. Through his clear examination of these alliances we see that the simplified notions of hegemony and counter-hegemony are more complicated than some simplistic Marxist trends want us to believe. Dominated groups show us that Apple can be drawn to the hegemonic alliance, and not only class issues play a role in this positioning. Since *Ideology and Curriculum*, where the analysis is still reluctant, and more directly in later works, Apple has been showing that issues of race and gender are central to the analysis of these alliances and its maintenance.

Although Apple's work has been groundbreaking in several aspects, as I showed above, his theory has been subjected to criticism. One constant critique of Apple's work by educational scholars in Brazil is the fact that it stresses too much the reproduction aspects and only minimally the production of alternatives (this critique is already present in Moreira, 1989). I tend to generally agree with the critique, especially in relation to Apple's emphasis, in his core works, in studying the New Right and only marginally in analyzing progressive and transformative projects and alternatives. I side with those who would like to see an entire Michael Apple book, with the sophisticated level of analysis we have come to expect from him, fully dedicated to the analysis of resistance and proactive construction of counter-hegemonic proposals. Nevertheless, I would urge that we not rush to conclusions regarding this matter. The fact that Apple does not have a core work dedicated to the left in education does not mean he is not actively involved in supporting and helping to improve such projects.[6] Those who know Apple can testify that he travels around the world, several times a year, to lecture and work with activists and teachers (who, most of the time are also activists) and offer his solidarity and lend his name to their cause.

But this was also true even with his first book. Even though it is true that *Ideology and Curriculum* does not analyze ideology as a "battle field" (as Apple himself stated in his first interview to Brazilian scholars in 1985), we should not forget that the final chapter of that book is titled "Beyond Ideological Reproduction." In that chapter, Apple clearly (but perhaps not as emphatically as one would expect and not as pronounced as in his later works) states:

> The notion of reproduction can lead to an assumption that there is (and perhaps can be) no significant resistance to such power. This is not the case. The continuing struggle for democratic and economic rights by workers, the poor, women, Blacks, Native Americans, Latinos, and others serves as a potent reminder of the possibility and actuality of concrete action. (Apple, 1990, p. 160)

Sure this quote is in the last chapter and not part of the central argument of the book. However, this quote shows that Apple was cautious not to close the door to the possibility of transformation. This preoccupation can certainly help to explain the impact of his work in the Brazilian context, where the notion of reproduction was building a sense of impossibility to social activism.

Another aspect that should be highlighted is the fact that there is a difference between broadening the notion of reproduction to include culture and gender/race relations—something that Apple clearly does—and discussing and analyzing the production of the new—something that many claim to be one of Apple's shortfalls. Even when Apple sophisticates his understanding of hegemony and adds gender and race as central categories to understanding the complex matrix of subordination, he does it to enhance the notion of reproduction. Now reproduction is not only a class phenomenon; it is also related to core race and gender relations. But one should not confuse Apple's (and McCarthy's) nonsynchronous parallelist position with one that opens space for understanding and theorizing transformation. The fact that Apple greatly enhances the strength of his theory to understand the complexities of education, ideology, hegemony, politics, and power, should not be confused with a theorization of change, something that would be a great addition to Apple's powerful scholarship. It is important to add, nonetheless, that Apple's theory has the strength necessary to allow the construction of this detailed examination of transformation. Apple reminds us that no scholar alone can do the work of constructing an all-encompassing social theory. Perhaps this is another of his great lessons: we should keep adding new facets to his sociological analysis of education, because he has made the building blocks available.

Finally, I should say a word about Apple's relation to Freire. Apple had many contacts with Paulo Freire. They interacted many times and Freire respected Apple immensely, as it is clear in the praise he wrote for the back cover of Apple's *Official Knowledge* (1993): "Michael Apple is among the most distinguished scholars in the world who are involved in the struggle to build a critical and democratic education." Despite this close connection, Apple always resisted the temptation of using his personal contacts to present himself as Freire's voice in the United States. Being an admirer and a follower of Freire's insights, Apple was always (and still has been) careful not to treat Freire's work as final and untouchable, a direction some scholars in Brazil, as well as the United States and elsewhere, took. In many texts, but more specifically in two (Apple, 1999b, 2003), Apple discusses the importance of Freire's ideas but also insists that we "extend his struggles into [new terrains] as well" (Apple, 2003, p. 116). His intellectual attitude toward Freire is exactly what Freire always recommended to those in education: constant discipline to construct better knowledge about social life and to build new social structures that are nonoppressive. Apple's position of pushing Freire forward and demanding that he included race and gender is not an empty intellectual dispute, but a gesture of someone who understands that only a community of scholars, committed to complementing each other's work, can generate the theoretical and political precision necessary to challenge the ever more complex issues facing education today.

CONCLUSION

In this conclusion I want to go back to the theme of situating education, something that Apple urges us to do in *Ideology and Curriculum*, and the clearer example of how this can be done in the elegant "cheap French fries" piece. One can see the development of an articulated theory of how education and curriculum are strictly connected to struggles around issues of class, race, and gender throughout Apple's work. As I have shown above, even when the presence of gender and race was not central, Apple never closed the door to their importance, not even in his most economicist phase.

The most important aspect of Apple's coherent history is perhaps the consistency of his political commitment to social justice. His work is a concrete example of the possibility of, in the social sciences, not speaking *about* theory but *with* theory. While constructing his theory he never lost track of the real goal: enhancing our understanding of how domination and power work and by doing so, generating tools, together with activists and teachers, to create more just relations in education. Apple's theory of how knowledge is produced, how it circulates, and how it is consumed makes sense when we compare it to his personal history of political engagement. This is certainly what made him so popular in Brazil, in particular among teachers who flock to catch his latest talk every time he is here. His constant attention to teachers' work and social and educational transformation, his coherence, and his cautionary notes about not being romantic about transformations are rare qualities these days in international intellectuals, and it is what causes teachers and social activists to continue expecting more from Apple's scholarship.

Ideology and Curriculum has been out-of-print in Brazil since the late 1980s. Now, the new third edition will be translated and published in 2006, giving back the opportunity to all educators and scholars the chance to revisit (or get to know) this education classic. In the year we celebrate 26 years of *Ideology and Curriculum* and the 20th anniversary of Apple's first visit to Brazil, it is important to remember that we should continue pushing Michael Apple to give us more of the sophisticated theory connected with his political commitment. In sum, I argue we should follow the lesson that he taught us about how to honor the work of Paulo Freire:

> We, too, must take Paulo Freire in, with all of his work's complexities and contradictions, rework him in the light of new and emerging historical circumstances and stand on his shoulders. We must recapture him from the grasp of those who would make him of only academic or theoretical interest, at the very same time as we continue on the theoretical, political, and pedagogic paths he forged. (Apple, 1997, p. 18)

In order to honor Apple's contributions we also should make sure we never forget that Apple's political commitments are the ones that drive him to enhance his theory and scholarship. There is an important lesson to learn from this.

NOTES

1. Moreira also examines the influence of Henry Giroux in this text. For the purpose of this chapter, I only deal with Michael Apple's influence.
2. After the event of the World Education Forum, also taking place in Porto Alegre, the International Seminar gave space to the Forum.
3. As a matter of fact, every time Apple comes to Brazil he asks to gather with teachers and visit schools. That is what he did in June 2004 when he was invited to give a keynote at a national educational conference. He traveled two hours to visit one of the poorest regions and its schools. There he met teachers and listened to them and answered their questions.
4. It is a fact that this interpretation of ideology is still in use, but not as predominantly as in the 1970s and 1980s.
5. So people are not simply being "duped." This idea of ideology as something that is "false" was discussed above.
6. Although Apple has done this partially in *Democratic Schools* (Apple & Beane, 1998), a great collection of alternative-creation experiences, I would argue that the book does not represent a coordinated effort from Apple to construct a theory of change.

REFERENCES

Althusser, L. (1971). *Lenin and philosophy.* New York: Monthly Review Press.

Apple, M. W. (1979). *Ideology and curriculum.* London: Routledge and Kegan Paul.

Apple, M. W. (1982). *Education and power.* London: Routledge and Kegan Paul.

Apple, M. W. (1982). *Ideologia e Currículo.* São Paulo, Brazil: Brasiliense.

Apple, M. W. (1989a). *Educação e Poder.* Porto Alegre, Brazil: Artes Médicas.

Apple, M. W. (1989b). Currículo e Poder. *Educação e Realidade, 14*(2), 46–57.

Apple, M. W. (1990). *Ideology and curriculum* (2nd ed.). New York: Routledge.

Apple, M. W. (1993). *Official knowledge: Democratic education in a conservative age.* New York: Routledge.

Apple, M. W. (1995). *Education and power* (2nd ed.). New York: Routledge.

Apple, M. W. (1996). *Cultural politics and education.* New York: Teachers College Press.

Apple, M. W. (1997). Consuming the other: Whiteness, education, and cheap French fries. In M. Fine (Ed.), *Off white: Readings on race, power, and society* (pp. 121–128). New York: Routledge.

Apple, M. W. (1999a). *Power, meaning, and identity.* New York: Peter Lang.

Apple, M. W. (1999b). Freire, neo-liberalism and education. *Discourse: Studies in the Cultural Politics of Education, 20*(1), 5–20.

Apple, M. W. (2003). Freire and the politics of race in education. *International Journal of Leadership in Education, 6*(2), 107–118.

Apple, M. W., & Beane, J. A. (Eds.). (1998). *Democratic schools: Lessons from the chalk face.* Buckingham: Open University Press.

Apple, M. W., & Weis, L. (1986a). Seeing education relationally: The stratification of culture and people in the sociology of school knowledge. *Journal of Education, 168*(1), 7–34.

Apple, M. W., & Weis, L. (1986b). Vendo a educação de forma relacional: classe e cultura na sociologia do conhecimento escolar. *Educação e Realidade, 11*(1), 19–33.

Bourdieu, P., & Passeron, J. C. (1975). *A reprodução: elementos para uma teoria do sistema de ensino.* Rio de Janeiro, Brazil: Francisco Alves.

Bulhões, M. G., & Abreu, M. (1992). *A luta dos professores gaúchos de 1979 a 1991: o difícil aprendizado da democracia.* Porto Alegre, Brazil: L&PM.

Fischer, N. B., Silva, T. T., & Apple, M. W. (1986) É impossível entender a escola sem uma teoria da divisão sexual do trabalho. *Educação & Realidade, 11*(2), 57–68.

Gandin, L. A., & Apple, M. W. (2002). Challenging neo-liberalism, building democracy: Creating the citizen school in Porto Alegre, Brazil. *Journal of Education Policy, 17*(2), 259–279.

Gandin, L. A., & Apple, M. W. (2003). Educating the state, democratizing knowledge: The citizen school project in Porto Alegre, Brazil. In M. W. Apple et al. (Eds.), *The state and the politics of knowledge* (pp. 193–219). New York: Routledge.

Gentili, Pablo (1995). A macdonaldização da escola: a propósito de *Consumindo o "outro."* In Marisa V. Costa (Ed.), Escola básica na virada do século: cultura, política e currículo (pp. 21-29). Porto Alegre: FACED/UFRGS.

Gramsci, A. (1997). *Selections from the prison notebooks* (Q. Hoare & G. N. Smith, Eds.). (Reprint, original printing 1971). New York: International Publishers.

Hall, S. (1996). Gramsci's relevance for the study of race and ethnicity. In D. Morley & K. Chen (Eds.), *Stuart Hall—Critical dialogues in cultural studies* (pp. 411–440). London: Routledge.

Hypolito, A. L. M. (1999). Trabalho docente e profissionalização: sonho prometido ou sonho negado? In I. P. A. Veiga & M. I. Cunha (Eds.), *Desmistificando a profissionalização do magistério* (pp. 81–100). Campinas, Brazil: Papirus.

Moreira, A. F. B. (1988). *Towards a reconceptualisation of educational transfer: The case of curriculum studies in Brazil.* Ph.D. Dissertation, Institute of Education, University of London.

Moreira, A. F. B. (1989). A contribuição de Michael Apple para o desenvolvimento de uma teoria curricular crítica no Brasil [Michael Apple's contribution to the development of a critical curriculum theory in Brazil]. *Fórum Educacional, 13*(4), 17–30.

Moreira, A. F. B. (1990). *Currículos e programas no Brasil*. Campinas, Brazil: Papirus.

Nosella, P. (1983). Compromisso político como horizonte da competência técnica. *Educação e Sociedade, 14*, 91–97.

Williams, R. (1977). *Marxism and literature*. Oxford, UK: Oxford University Press.

Willis, P. (1981). Cultural production is different from cultural reproduction is different from social reproduction is different from reproduction. *Interchange on Educational Policy, 12*(2–3), 48–67.

AFTERWORD

Critical Education, Politics, and the Real World

MICHAEL W. APPLE

INTRODUCTION

Since many of my positions are clarified in the interviews included in this book, I shall keep my arguments relatively brief in this afterword. I want to make some general points about the nature of critical scholarship and place myself in that tradition, adding something a bit more personal than the well-done histories found in the other chapters and in the very thoughtful introduction by Greg Dimitriadis, Lois Weis, and Cameron McCarthy. In the process, I will reflect on some of the influences that stood behind my early work as well as the work that followed.

I do not want to recapitulate the arguments that I make in *Ideology and Curriculum*; nor can I go into great detail about how I went further on the path that it originally established. Suffice it to say that, as a number of the authors in this book recognize, this was a path that took me from neo-Marxist analyses of social and cultural reproduction, to an (unromantic) emphasis on agency, to treatments of teachers' work and lives, to an enlargement of political and cultural struggles to complement (but definitely not abandon) my original focus on class, and more recently to sustained critical analyses of how powerful movements and alliances can radically shift the relationship between educational policies and practices and the relations of dominance and subordination in the larger society, but not in a direction that any of us would find ethically or politically justifiable. All of these efforts over the years have been grounded in a sense of the significance of cultural struggles and of the crucial place that schools, curricula, teachers, and communities play in these struggles. I shall be brief because descriptions of this trajectory are available already in the various editions of, say, *Ideology and Curriculum* (see, e.g., Apple, 2004) and in the many other books that followed.

In some ways I am still attempting to deal with the same questions about the relationship between culture and power; about the relationship among the economic, political, and cultural spheres (see Apple & Weis, 1983); and about what all this means for the educational work I started over three decades ago. And I still am trying to answer a question that was put so clearly by George Counts when he asked "Dare the Schools Build a New Social Order?" Counts was a person of his time and the ways he both asked and answered this question were a bit naive. But the tradition of radically interrogating schools, of asking who benefits from their dominant forms of curricula, teaching, and evaluation, of arguing about what they might do differently, and of asking searching questions of what would have to change in order for this to happen—all of this is what has worked through me. I stand on the shoulders of many others who have taken such issues seriously and hope to have contributed both to the recovery of the collective memory of this tradition and to pushing it further along conceptually, historically, empirically, and practically.

Of course, no author does this by her- or himself. This is a collective enterprise. And no one who takes these questions seriously, at least not me, can answer them fully or without contradictions or even wrong turns or mistakes. Because of this, I do find very interesting the continuities and discontinuities that the authors in this book find in my work. It seems to me that many of their points, and their criticisms, are perceptive.

GROUNDING TRADITIONS

But before I turn to the issues surrounding interpreting *Ideology and Curriculum* and the work that followed it, perhaps a little history might be useful. What were the traditions that influenced me early on? Let me list many of them here, knowing that it is almost impossible to put down everything that had an impact on me. Among the most important were:

1. Cultural Marxism and Marxist theory, including especially Antonio Gramsci, Luis Althusser, and Raymond Williams.
2. Phenomenology and in particular the social phenomenology of Alfred Schutz.

3. The sociology of knowledge from Marx, Goldmann, and Mannheim to more recent contributors such as Merton, Gouldner, and Berger and Luckmann.

4. Analytic philosophy inside and outside of education, particularly Wittgenstein, Ryle, Hampshire, Soltis, and Scheffler.

5. Critical theory, in particular Habermas and Marcuse.

6. The philosophy, sociology, and history of science, as seen in the work of Kaplan, Kuhn, Toulmin, Hagstrom, and Lakatos and Musgrave.

7. Aesthetics and the philosophy of art, in particular the work of Suzanne Langer.

8. Political economy and studies of the labor process, such as Braverman.

9. The new sociology of education, including especially Bernstein, Bourdieu, Young, Dale, Whitty, Arnot, and others.

10. The critical and literary traditions within education, most profoundly the work of Huebner, Macdonald, and Greene and the early curricular histories done by Kliebard.

Yet, throughout it all, there was one other crucial set of influences on my work. It is more than a little important to understand that the time I spent teaching in one of the poorest communities in the United States and then in a very conservative rural area acted as a reality check, as did my role as president of a teachers union (see Apple, 1999). The fact that I had grown up poor, but in a strongly politically active family, was significant, as was my activity while still a teenager in anti-racist mobilizations. Added to this were the years I spent working as a printer before and then during part of the period of time I was going to night school for my initial college degree. Theory and research was supposed to *do something* about the conditions I had experienced. Because of this, one should not feel totally comfortable within the academy or with an academic life.

Geoff Whitty (1985) points to this danger in some ways when he speaks to the incorporation of what I and others struggled to make legitimate in the face of immense obstacles into what seems almost like part of the mainstream in educational scholarship. (Would that it actually was. For the "mainstream" is rapidly turning backward as both the funding priorities brought about by the fiscal crisis of the state and a backlash politics—to say nothing of the new managerialism now infecting many universities in his nation and my own—have come to dominate much of what we do.)

Others have similar intellectual biographies and political histories as those I note in the above paragraph, I am sure. Certainly, a number of the authors who have commented on my work in this book share significant parts of this intellectual/political heritage. But you will notice, and perhaps be surprised by, a few of the influences on the more academic list above. One influence that is nicely captured by Geoff Whitty and Madeleine Arnot was indeed social phenomenology (see also Whitty, 1985). In important ways, it was through the influence of social phenomenology that not only myself but a number of left-ist thinkers inside and outside of education were able to better engage with issues of everyday life and lived experience (Eagleton, 2003, p. 32). Hence, many of the intuitions that ultimately led to a move toward cultural studies were very much present a good deal earlier.

Do all of these influences add up to a convenient way of categorizing me and my work? To be honest, I am not one who responds well to labels. I am not simply a "neo-Marxist," a "sociologist," a "critical curriculum scholar," or someone in "critical pedagogy." Nor am I someone whose roots can be traced simply to something like "phenomenology meets Marxism." A commitment to the arts—written, visual, and tactile—and to an embodied and culturally/politically critical aesthetic have formed me in important ways as well. It may be useful to know that the "W" in Michael W. Apple stands for Whitman—the poet of the visceral and the popular, Walt Whitman, who like me came from New Jersey. Furthermore, as a filmmaker (see Apple, 2000) who works with teachers and children to create aesthetically and politically powerful visual forms, this kind of activity provides me with a sense of the importance of the very act of creation, of knowledge being something people can *make*, not simply "learn." This commitment is made visible in Gitlin's chapter as well.

In my most well-known written work—aside from say, the chapter on film-making in *Official Knowledge*—this has not been very visible. But as what Raymond Williams (1977) might call a "structure of feeling," it stands behind my social and cultural criticisms as an absent presence. It provides the sense of alternative (perhaps oppositional is a better word) possibilities in which my work has been grounded as well. But it is the more sociocultural efforts to which most of the authors in this book rightly point, so let me return to this.

As Whitty and Arnot remark, well before the publication of the first edition of *Ideology and Curriculum* in 1979, in the early 1970s, I had begun a series of studies that would ultimately be brought together to form the core of that book. I had read Michael Young's edited book, *Knowledge and Control* (1971), and immediately saw connections between what the contributors in England and France were doing and my own work. I sent copies of the first version of "Common-Sense Categories and Curriculum Thought" to a number of the contributors, including Basil Bernstein and Michael Young. A lively trans-Atlantic conversation ensued between me and Bernstein, Young, Roger Dale, Geoff Whitty, and Madeleine Arnot especially, a conversation that has continued for three decades. As Whitty and Arnot show in their own contributions to this book, these trans-Atlantic connections were—and continue to be—crucial in the development of my work. Later on these were joined by intellectual and political connections in Japan, Korea, and elsewhere in Asia, in Spain, Portugal, Norway, and other nations in Europe, and especially in Latin America—particularly in Mexico and, as Gandin so clearly details, powerfully in Brazil. Thus, the international discussions, debates, and co-teaching, and the academic and political activity in which I engaged in these nations, have always had a powerful impact on me and have led me to develop what I hope are more nuanced understandings both of the ways in which context and history matter and of the multiple kinds and forms of dominance and politics that exist. These relations provide some of the reasons I have argued that the North needs to be taught by the South, with the development of the Citizen School and participatory budgeting in Porto Alegre for example being more than a little significant in this regard (see Apple, 2006; Apple et al., 2003). Similar things could be said about my involvement with the struggles of the once banned but now legal teachers union in Korea.

NEO AND POST

The word "development" in the above section is not unimportant here, since just as there are new developments on the ground, so to speak, as the editors and authors involved in the book show, so too has my thought developed over the years since the initial publication of *Ideology and Curriculum*. It is interesting to me that a number of the chapters such as those by Carlson and Nozaki compare Gramscian-oriented approaches in the study of ideology like my own to Foucault, Guattari, and to various "post" positions. Indeed some chapters see certain post influences in my ongoing work. They are not wrong. Also interestingly, as odd as it may sound, during the late 1980s I was giving a series of lectures in Eastern Europe and—much to my surprise—was introduced as the first postmodernist in education.

My focus on the power of language and how technical discourses circulate and have their own conditions of existence, on the complexities of lived experiences, on contradictory political identities, on anti-essentialist and nonreductive forms of analysis, on the specificities of the local, and similar things—all of this was seen as opening the door to a set of paths that led a number of educational theorists to Foucault and others. As some of you may know, and as Geoff Whitty and others have indicated in their chapters, I have been more than a little cautious about the rush to employ various post positions in educational scholarship, since it is often done rather uncritically and without due recognition of the vital debates within these traditions and over them.

I have also been cautious about their incorporation because much of the post tradition grew in Europe against a backdrop of a history of strong socialist movements and strong recognition that class realities were extremely powerful, if not determinate. Thus, criticisms of such things as "grand narratives," economic and class reductionism, "binaries," and a strong concern for ambiguity and the specificities of the local—to take just a few examples—seemed warranted there. Yet a good deal of the development of these arguments was not based on the experiences of the United States, where, for instance, socialist movements and their accompanying institutional and ideological forms and identities have been much less powerful and where class discourse and critical structural understandings of the economy have been historically much less visible. This was and still is certainly the case within education. Furthermore, the intersection of, say, class and race in every sector of the United States made it much harder to be reductive and essentializing.

Although all of this needs to be said, however, as I have stated elsewhere, we are not in a church, so we should not be worried about heresy. Thus, various postmodern and poststructural positions offer crucial insights that need to be taken seriously. Indeed, it would not be possible to fully understand my work over the past 20 years without recognizing the influences of selected parts of the traditions we usually associate with, say, poststructuralism. However, in my mind, none of these relations can be understood without situating (not reducing) all of these elements in relation to particular political economies at particular historical moments. This also requires a profound understanding not only of the classed, but also the raced and sexed/gendered state and economy, and how all of these dynamics interact in complex and contradictory ways to create both public and privates spheres, something I have taken up in more recent work.

Thus, unlike some others, I did not then and do not now see "post" positions as *replacements* for more structurally oriented approaches or for a Gramscian-inspired examination of the complex and contradictory nexus between the construction of both our commonsense and identities and of the multiple relations of dominance and subordination—and of course to the struggles to interrupt these relations. Rather, both kinds of analysis are essential. My position is that it is where these various epistemological and political tendencies rub against each other, where the sparks fly, that real progress can be made. And here, I join with people such as Stuart Hall who early on recognized the similarities between the Gramscian and some poststructural traditions (Morely & Chen, 1996).

CULTURE AND POLITICS

One of the things that makes this position—one might call it a disciplined radical, but unromantic, openness to new political movements and possibilities (with an insistence that we take class and economic relations seriously in nonreductive ways, and without the relativistic elements that make supposedly pluralistic democratic commitments so "wishy-washy")—seem sensible to me is the fact that I have never been satisfied with "life on the balcony." In my mind there are at least three reasons for doing critical theoretical, historical, and empirical work, each one based on a thoroughgoing and honest appraisal of the nature of this society. The first is what we might call "bearing witness to negativity," publicly uncovering the ways in which current social and educational policies and practices privilege those with economic, social, and cultural capital. This is absolutely critical at a time when our own and so many other societies are characterized by growing and truly destructive levels of inequality.

Yet bearing witness is not enough. The second responsibility is to do one's critical analysis in such a way that existing or possible spaces for resistance and counter-hegemonic work are made visible. This requires what Linda Tuhiwai Smith (1999) calls decolonizing methodologies and what Weis and Fine (2004) label as methods that "reveal sites for possibility." Finally, a major task is to act as the "secretaries" of those who are currently engaged in creating these spaces in real institutions, real schools, real movements, and real communities. This is one of the reasons that James Beane and I published a book like *Democratic Schools* (Apple & Beane, 1995), a volume that has been translated into many languages and has been used by hundreds of thousands of educators to provide a sense of real possibility in a time of conservative modernization. And an attempt to deal with all three of these tasks led me in *Educating the "Right" Way* (Apple 2001/2006) to focus on the damaging policies of rightist alliances, on how this alliance operates to alter our commonsense of what education is for, and on the spaces and movements it opens for building critical and counter-hegemonic alliances and practices.

In doing these things, I have tried to take seriously one simple principle—that all of these tasks require not simply rhetorical commitments, but real participation in these movements. As an educator, not simply a "sociologist" or "critical theorist," I also think that this requires that I be close to the real life of schools, curricula, teachers, tests, and community activists.

Unlike some others within what has come to be called the "critical pedagogy" tradition who seem to feel that academic theorizing is our major goal, a number of the authors in this book understand that I do not think that "getting one's hands dirty" by talking about schools, teachers, curricula, and testing is a form of pollution. Critical approaches are best developed in close contact with the object of one's analysis. As a former elementary and secondary school teacher and past-president of a teachers union, and as someone who has been subject to arrest perhaps a bit too often for acting in defense of dissident policies and practices inside and outside of these institutions (I do not mean to romanticize these instances—they can be quite scary), I make no apologies for this. Indeed, it seems to me that all too much of the critical pedagogy tradition in the United States has become part of a set of conversion strategies in which people attempt to convert cultural capital into social capital and then into economic capital in terms of advancement within the academy. In these strategies, politics becomes rhetorical, few risks are actually taken, and a form of possessive individualism is covered by heavily theorized slogans that receive more value the further removed they are from the world of education. This is immensely damaging when one is constantly faced—as we currently are—with the well-organized and increasingly powerful movements on the Right that increasingly dominate our economic, political, and cultural worlds. These dangerous tendencies are well documented in the chapters by Carlson, Torres, and Luke.

Because of these commitments, one of the struggles I have engaged in with myself and others is to try to be as clear as the subject matter will allow. This has never been easy for me and I know that it is not easy in general. But the effort is worth it. This is especially important now since the Right has an advantage in its attempt to talk in "plain folks Americanism" in my own nation. It is perfectly possible to be difficult (that is to try to deal honestly with the complexities of a subject) without being obscure. "Difficulty is a matter of content, whereas obscurity is a question of how you present that content" (Eagleton,

2003, p. 77). Here I agree with Eagleton when he argues that "There is something particularly scandalous about *radical* cultural theory being so willfully obscure" (p. 77).

Obviously, there are times when new theories and new perspectives absolutely require new and unfamiliar vocabularies that serve as "disclosure models" for interpreting the world in powerful ways. Indeed, this is what I needed to do when I introduced cultural Marxist approaches into U.S. education studies in the early 1970s. However, there is a world of difference between recognizing how essential it is to develop and use new approaches and concepts and employing these tools in such a way that they form new rules of exclusion. And in my mind this is what too much of critical educational theory has done over the past two decades.

As I have said elsewhere, it is hard work not to be sloppy. It is hard work to write in such a way that theoretical and political nuances are not sacrificed on the altar of commonsense, but also in a way that the hard work of reading can actually pay off for the reader her- or himself. And it is hard and time-consuming work to write at multiple levels. But if we do not do it, neoliberals and neoconservatives and the movements they support will (Apple, 2006).

One word in the last paragraph provides an important key to my focus. Like Jean Anyon in her most recent work (2005) and in her chapter in this volume, I have focused most of my attention for the past 15 years on social movements. My attention had been devoted especially to rightist social movements, in books such as *Official Knowledge* (2000), *Cultural Politics and Education* (1996), and *Educating the "Right" Way* (2001/2006). Such a focus is crucial, since whether we like it or not, it is social movements that have been the driving forces behind substantive educational transformations, for both good and bad. Without paying attention to social movements—both progressive and retrogressive—and to the identities they create and to the conflicts over official knowledge that they generate, we cannot deal seriously with the depth and breadth of the political acts we call education.

WHAT HAS CHANGED

A discussion about social movements opens up a crucial arena. Carlos Torres correctly asks the question "What has changed?" In my mind, the most important transformations are related to the growth of what following Roger Dale I have called "conservative modernization." I have argued in an entire series of books over the past decade and a half that if we are interested in understanding how to change education and its relationship with the larger society, study those groups and movements who have been and are *successful* in doing that. Thus, as I noted above, I have focused much of my attention on rightist mobilizations and on the processes that they have employed to move an entire society, as well as education, in strikingly conservative directions (Apple, 1996, 2000, 2006; Apple et al., 2003). (Think about education in the United States such as the "naming and shaming" but underfunded legislation No Child Left Behind, the battles over reading and mathematics curricula, over evolution and "intelligent design," the massive defunding of schools and the entire public sector, things that a number of chapters point to in this book.) The Right has engaged in a vast and often quite successful social and pedagogic project to change our very understanding of the key concepts that guide our sense of self and others and that we use to evaluate our institutions—with "democracy" being a key signifier (Foner, 1998). Furthermore, these movements and this project are increasingly global and have to be thought about that way. Carlson, Luke, and Torres very nicely illuminate this, for example, in their chapters in this book.

Concepts such as "movements" and "global" have a benefit of pointing to motion, to a world that is constantly being transformed (for good and bad) and to social actors who are anything but passive. As Fine so clearly recognizes, assumptions based on passivity are empirically and historically incorrect, something that she herself has documented repeatedly in her own work and in her work with Lois Weis (Fine & Weis, 1998; Weis, 2005) and something that is ever present as well in Cameron McCarthy's and Greg Dimitriadis's ongoing individual and collective work (see, e.g., Dimitriadis & McCarthy, 2001). This is a theme I have repeatedly stressed over the years, partly stimulated by Paul Willis's germinal efforts (Willis, 1977; see also Apple, 1995), but also partly based on my own continuing political actions both here and abroad.

The word "abroad" again reminds us of the global contexts in which we all operate. Indeed, even such simple acts as "eating cheap French fries" connect us in powerful ways to the global relations of capitalist expansion and rapaciousness and to the realities of (mis)education in other parts of the world (Apple, 1996). As a number of chapters here indicate, critical analyses of globalization are crucial; but we need to be very cautious not to assume either that there is only one form that globalization takes or that all forms and effects of globalization are necessarily bad (Apple & Buras, 2006; Apple, Kenway, & Singh, 2005). Not only is this reductive, but it naturalizes the relations of dominance and subordination that have existed at the local, regional, and national levels.

Thus, one can envision a situation in which new technologies such as cell phones and global positioning devices are given to women in rural areas of, say, Brazil, where the rates of violence against women are quite high. Such "global" technologies and the connections they make possible may allow for greater safety for women than before. My use of the example of Brazil is not accidental. As Gandin indicates in his very honest portrayal of the reception of and my ongoing work there, I have had a good deal of experience in Brazil and remain deeply committed to supporting the efforts of critical educators and social movements in that nation and a number of others. While I hope I have had an effect there, there can be no doubt that these Brazilian experiences, like so many other international and national ones, have taught me an immense amount—and I continue to learn and be transformed by these international experiences. At the very least, this makes it much more likely that I will see the world through the eyes of those people who must suffer so that we can eat our cheap french fries and drive our SUVs and Hummers.

HAVING AN EFFECT

Any author, and certainly myself, should be pleased when her or his ideas are recognized and have a lasting intergenerational effect. Effects can be shown in a variety of ways in which people choose to respond. One way is through ideological stereotyping and dismissal. In my own case, this has been visible in the response by some "vulgar" postmodernists who seem to have never read anything I wrote after *Ideology and Curriculum* and who see me as an uncritical defender of reductive forms of structuralist Marxism. The fact that many of these people may not have done all of their homework—nor unfortunately have some of them ever read sufficiently widely within the Marxist and neo-Marxist traditions (the plural is crucial here)—is more than unfortunate.

A second way in which effects can be shown is rather more cute, but also dismissive. This is more than a little evident in rightist attacks on the progressive ideas that I and others, including many of the authors included in this book, represent. In my case, this has gotten a bit personal as in the case of the attacks on me and on my patriotism by both the *Wall Street Journal* and the Fordham Foundation. However, if one is known by one's enemies, these are enemies I am glad to have.

These points aside, in my mind the best way of showing an effect—and the sincerest form of respect—is to treat an author's work seriously enough to use it, criticize it, and go beyond it when this is necessary. The chapters in this volume do all of this and each of the authors recognizes the collective nature of what needs to be done in order for all of us to go further. Since I am not in the business of creating or wanting "clones," all the editors and contributors have my profound thanks for this.

CONCLUSION

There is so much more that needs to be said. But let me close these comments with a return to one of my originating themes in *Ideology and Curriculum*, a theme that resonates throughout all of my books and plays such an important part in the newest material on understanding and interrupting the Right—the critical interrogation of what counts as "commonsense." For the Right, such critical analysis has become tantamount to being unpatriotic and wanting to "leave children behind." One of the functions of a vibrant and committed Left (and yes, even with the complexities and contradictions of these terms, I do think they still are more than a little useful) has been and remains to hold a mirror up to this society and its antagonisms and inequalities and ask that they be taken seriously as matters of life and death. What Bourdieu would call "symbolic violence" and the economic and bodily violence all around us are deeply connected.

Sometimes this requires that the broad Left also holds a mirror up to itself, as many politically committed scholars within the feminist, gay, disabled, postcolonial, and environmental communities have done. As long as it does not require that we fully *substitute* a politics of recognition for a politics of redistribution (Fraser, 1997), this should be welcomed. Yet, for some parts of the Left, openness to new approaches and to a more complex politics amounts to something like treason, as if Marxism and other critical approaches were frozen in time. Much of what is commonsense in education—and unfortunately in some critical educational circles part of what we have simply taken for granted has reduced itself to nice sounding political slogans that may be good for mobilizing sentiments, but not so useful in actually tactically analyzing the realities of power, how the Right employs it, and what we can actually do to challenge its use—acts as an invitation to shut down thought. We need constant self-criticism and renovation, at the very same time as we defend key concepts, traditions, and politics from the trendy and the seemingly radical that again takes no risks. This is clearly a hard path. The editors and authors represented in this volume are parts of an emerging tradition that takes this responsibility seriously.

I do not want to be misunderstood here. This does not mean that I think that "anything goes," that we should somehow throw away traditions that continue to be immensely productive. The politics of official knowledge is not guided by a relativistic position, by a forever shifting assemblage of wants and needs in which there is no firm grounding. Indeed, I believe that there are powerful arguments that can be and have been made to justify the grounds on which our work and our economic, political, and cultural claims rest (see, e.g., Fraser 1989, 1997). Certainly, my own position has never been that of vulgar relativism. For me, the resort to relativism is something of a slight of hand in that it simply becomes a convenient way of explaining away serious conflict (Eagleton, 2003, p. 109).

As I point out in *Ideology and Curriculum*, such conflict should be welcomed. Building counter-hegemonic movements that push such conflicts further and that can occupy the spaces that these conflicts create has been a driving force for educational transformation in the past. Obviously, I believe that we must not simply analyze them but should join them. But in the meantime, there is also work to be done in those places we call schools and communities. Getting our hands a little more dirty might not be a bad idea.

But there are a lot of places where we can get our hands dirty and a lot of movements that can use our help and that can help us. This is a very real problem. I have tried to answer this by suggesting that we need to think more rigorously about what might be called "nonreformist reforms." Of all of those things that need to be done, choose those that have the greatest probability of opening up further spaces for substantive and lasting political/educational gains (Apple, 1995). This requires a greater tactical and strategic sensibility than some of us are used to. But it is exactly what the Right has done. It may be unfortunate, but perhaps we have something to learn from them—something I have argued at much greater length in *Educating the "Right" Way*.

Like all of the others involved in this book, there is a political edge at the forefront of our actions, a critical sensibility that both denies the all-too-often repeated claim by the powerful that "There is no alternative" and affirms both the possibility of and the right to build such an alternative. It might be useful to remember something that Terry Eagleton also said. "Capitalism needs a human being who has never yet existed—one who is prudently restrained in the office and wildly anarchic in the shopping mall" (2003, p. 28). As every contributor to this book recognizes, our task as critical educators is not to assist a system that produces such human beings. Even with our differences (and I do mean this play on words), this is something that binds all of us together. The struggles continue inside and outside our schools and communities. The question remains: What roles can and do people such as ourselves play in these movements?

REFERENCES

Anyon, J. (2005). *Radical possibilities: Public policy, urban education, and a new social movement.* New York: Routledge.

Apple, M. W. (1995). *Education and power* (2nd ed.). New York: Routledge.

Apple, M. W. (1996). *Cultural politics and education.* New York: Teachers College Press.

Apple, M. W. (1999). *Power, meaning, and identity.* New York: Peter Lang.

Apple, M. W. (2000). *Official knowledge: Democratic education in a conservative age* (2nd ed.). New York: Routledge.

Apple, M. W. (2001). *Educating the "right" way: Markets, standards, God, and inequality.* New York: RoutledgeFalmer.

Apple, M. W. (2004). *Ideology and curriculum* (3rd ed.). New York: RoutledgeFalmer.

Apple, M. W. (2006). *Educating the "right" way: Markets, standards, God, and inequality* (2nd ed.). New York: Routledge.

Apple, M. W. et al. (2003). *The state and the politics of knowledge.* New York: RoutledgeFalmer.

Apple, M. W., & Beane, J. (Eds.). (1995). *Democratic schools.* Alexandria, VA: Association for Supervision and Curriculum Development.

Apple, M. W., & Buras, K. L. (Eds.). (2006). *The subaltern speak: Curriculum, power, and educational struggles.* New York: Routledge.

Apple, M. W., Kenway, J., & Singh, M. (Eds.). (2005). *Globalizing education: Policies, pedagogies, and politics.* New York: Peter Lang.

Apple, M. W., & Weis, L. (Eds.). (1983). *Ideology and practice in schooling.* Philadelphia: Temple University Press.

Dimitriadis, G., & McCarthy, C. (2001). *Reading and teaching the postcolonial.* New York: Teachers College Press.

Eagleton, T. (2003). *After theory.* New York: Basic Books.

Fine, M., & Weis, L. (1998). *The unknown city.* Boston: Beacon Press.

Foner, E. (1998). *The story of American freedom.* New York: W. W. Norton.

Fraser, N. (1989). *Unruly practices.* Minneapolis: University of Minnesota Press.

Fraser, N. (1997). *Justice interruptus.* New York: Routledge.

Morley, D., & Chen, K.-H. (Eds.). (1996). *Stuart Hall: Critical dialogues in cultural studies.* New York: Routledge.

Smith, L. T. (1999). *Decolonizing methodologies.* New York: Zed Books.

Weis, Lois. (2005). *Class reunion: The remaking of the American white working class.* New York: Routledge.

Weis, L., & Fine, M. (2004). *Working method: Research and social justice.* New York: Routledge.

Whitty, G. (1985). *Sociology and school knowledge*. London: Methuen.
Williams, R. (1977). *Marxism and literature*. New York: Oxford University Press.
Willis, P. (1977). *Learning to labour*. Farnborough, England: Saxon House.
Young, M. (Ed.). (1971). *Knowledge and control*. London: Collier-Macmillan.

APPENDIX

Interviews with Michael W. Apple

The following interview material is culled from two sources—Carlos Alberto Torres' *Education, Power, and Personal Biography: Dialogues with Critical Educators* (1998) and Michael Apple's *Ideology and Curriculum, Third Edition.* (2004). The interview with Torres highlights the connections between Apple's personal biography and his political and academic commitments. Among other things, it offers insight into his generous (and generative) critical disposition—in particular, his willingness continually to challenge theoretical and political orthodoxies inside and outside the classroom. As this interview demonstrates, Apple's commitments are always in productive dialogue with the "gritty materiality" of his life as well as the lives of others in the U.S. and around the world. As he tells Torres, "I am always in transition."

Indeed, much has changed on and along the political landscape in the years since this interview was first published. Not surprisingly, Apple's critical framework has changed with the times. We have therefore included a portion of an interview published more recently, in the third edition of Ideology & Curriculum (2004). In this relatively brief selection, we see Apple responding to and thinking through the contemporary challenges of the neo-conservative and neo-liberal movements—what he has aptly termed the "conservative restoration." These are themes taken up in his recent volumes, The State and the Politics of Knowledge (2003) and Educating the "Right" Way, 2nd ed. (2006).

219

Taken together, these interviews reveal Apple's mind "at work" in particularly telling and provocative ways.

> Q: Back in 1988, Raymond Morrow and I interviewed you to try to place your work in perspective. What has happened in your life and research agenda since then?
>
> A: On a personal level, having lived through five more years of the rapaciousness of the Right has had a profound impact. It's had a profound impact in increasing my sense of the utter import of coming to grips with the liberal tradition and of rethinking the difficult questions of social democracy. And living under the Right has also made me think about the gains that have been made under the social democratic accord—that even though there were compromises, there also were successful struggles.
>
> I have an older son who is African American and who is mentally ill. In the time of the conservative restoration, all of the things that were built into the social institutions as a safety net for people who have mental illness were being withdrawn: things such as medical care, health care, and social workers to deal with people who are dumped from institutions and placed on the streets. This has caused me to rethink certain things at a very personal level, which, as you would imagine, has a major impact at the level of theory.
>
> My older son was institutionalized. He became quite violent because of the chemical imbalance in his brain that showed up over time. Because of this, he signed himself into a hospital. We were faced with $90,000 in medical bills not covered by the increasing destruction of the mental health apparatus under Reagan/Bush. It enabled me to see at a personal level what it meant for the Right to be in power. We found out, for instance, that our insurance policy didn't cover mental illness for more than thirty days. So the embodiment of rightist programs was literally that: an embodiment through my son's body that massively increased his risk of death.
>
> Now, I mention the personal here because the arguments, even originally in *Education and Power*—of changing our ideas about who is on the bottom, blaming them rather than blaming a structural crisis of the economy—became even more powerful for me, and not just at the theoretical level of

"I understand this better." If I did not have a decent salary, my son would be dead. That created a very different way of looking at the state. Thus, even though my intuitions were changing—that is, I was beginning to see that the state was a site of contradictory struggles—these personal experiences made some of this even more vivid. It became even clearer to me that there are both progressive and retrogressive elements within the state; that the state is a site of victories, not only defeats; and that the social democratic accord was, in fact, a partial victory, as well as a hegemonic alliance and compromise. What it meant was that my intuitions were made even more certain. Here we have an instance where hidden discourses of race that were profoundly affecting the state meant black poor people, or any poor person—but in this case, an African American child who is my son—are faced with a situation, where the social supports that were there, the safety net that was won through decades of struggle, were simply gone.

There you have an example, lived out, of my intuitions— that for all of our arguments about the state apparatus being a tool of capital and my arguments against that—here we have an instance where we see that when the state is withdrawn, when it's purged of its gains, when the Right says privatize everything, you see what really happens, even to people within the middle class. So we spent $90,000, and the only institution that would take him—there were no spaces in state institutions—was the "Cadillac" of mental institutions, at $1,000 a day, not covered by insurance. If my wife and I had not been able to raise this money, I am certain that my son would be dead. Think about the thousands of parents who would *not* be able to do this. I don't mean to use this example egotistically. But it does mean that personal experiences are crucial for critical work. If all one does is write about things critically and never puts oneself in a position of real struggle, I must admit that I mistrust their writing.

As I mentioned in the previous interview, I've always sought for this combination of theoretical elaboration and personal struggles. That's what we mean by praxis. It's constant reflexivity, and reflexivity is brought about by political struggles at many levels: the cultural level, the economic, and political, the struggle over the body and sexuality. Thus, I don't want to reduce everything only to class struggles. All of this revivified in practice my understandings and made them clearer. Gains in the state were withering. They were being destroyed for many people. The last five years have made this crystal clear to me.

Q: What kind of theoretical challenge did you take up in the past years?

A: The past five years have increased my struggle to come to grips with postmodernism. At the same time as it was influencing me, I wanted to critically question some of the core assumptions some postmodernists were uncritically accepting. As you know, I was one of the people, certainly not the only one, in this large collective endeavor who argued against the reductive and class analytic tendencies within the neo-Marxist tradition. But in the United States, the neo-Marxist traditions were not grand narratives. That is, they were always the results of struggles. There's never one narrative within the Marxist traditions. It's a mistake, it's a misreading of history, and it's a loss of collective memory, to assume there was one, that all of them were reductive.

Simply because one called oneself a neo-Marxist, which was a handy title, it's a historical concept and didn't mean that you agreed with all this stuff. It was a contested arena, and it was struggled out. My intuitions were that discourses and practices of class, of race, of gender, were parallel. They formed each other, as well as having partly separate histories. They were relatively autonomous, but you couldn't talk about class without talking about gender and race, since they were formative dynamics in it. That led to some difficult and real issues of how many dimensions of power should one consider. If things are not seen as always coming from "above to below" all the time, then the distinction between micro and macro becomes much less useful, and that opens the door to a position that recognizes multiple discourses, multiple sites, etc. It makes Foucault seem attractive, and I hope I have taken that seriously.

Even though I want to be open to new theories and politics, over the last few years I've begun to get quite nervous about

certain tendencies within postmodernism. Now anyone reading my recent books, *Official Knowledge* and *Cultural Politics
and Education*, can see the influence that postmodernism had
on them. When I talk about the politics of pleasure, when
I talk about discursive practices, or about Channel One as
an example, when I show the way the state at many levels
has multiple relations of power, how hegemonic alliances
are built, not simply on class terms but in racial and gender
terms, and the politics of sexuality and religion, all of those
working together and in opposition to each other: that shows
the influence of some critical postmodern theory on my work.

The keyword here is critical. I am very worried that much
of critical "post" work has lost some of what we gained
through neo-Marxist work and has created a false history of
"neo" work. Not everybody agreed that you should deal with
class only structurally, me being one of them. Just because
class is called now (through what I think is a misreading of
history) a "grand narrative," one that takes a reductive form,
this doesn't mean that class has gone away. I think that that is
a very dangerous tendency within some aspects of postmodernism. Too often the idea that class analysis was "reductive"
has meant that people feel free to ignore it. This is disastrous
theoretically and politically. To purge class does a disservice
to the women and men whose shoulders we all stand on, not
just to their theory but even more importantly to their lived
struggles. In order for people like us to be at institutions of
higher education and to have the ability to even have a job
where we can write about these things, we have to understand
that someone labored. These institutions are the embodiment of the past, not just of intellectual labor, but of the paid
and unpaid labor of women and men. So we live off of their
lives. That's a basic structural point, and I think we ought to
remember that.

I've spent years arguing against reductive analyses of political economy, such as Bowles and Gintis's earlier work, which
was a major intervention and one that still deserves to be
respected even though I still disagree with 60% of the book.
But there is this tendency in too much current and supposedly critical work simply to evacuate questions of political

economy as if they're no longer important. That is about as dangerous as you can get.

Take as an example the deconstruction of the idea of the nation-state. No doubt, one of the reasons we no longer talk as easily about the nation is not simply because of the discourse of the state and the discourse of nation, but because capital is internationalizing. It is not simply a text, although we may make texts about it. There's a gritty reality of people starving. There's a gritty reality to imperialism, in postcolonial situations, to what happens when people's land is taken from them by international capital. And there's a gritty reality to the consumption practices of the United States. You don't have to look at what some people arrogantly call the "Third World" in order to find this. To assume that the politics of consumption totally has eaten the politics of production is to have this fictitious vision that somehow this is all a postmodern economy. Well, manufacturing is still done. Production is still done. We need to ask who does it, what the social relations of production are, who gets to consume what, etc. I think that we're in great danger of forgetting the insights that were generated and that still provide meaningful political activity for close to a majority of the world's population. Recognition of this has led me to struggle with positive and negative moments of different kinds of theories and politics. That kind of struggle, and those tensions, are seen in *Official Knowledge* and my newest book *Cultural Politics and Education,* which is my attempt to, again, write as clearly as possible without sacrificing theoretical elements or political commitment, and at the same time to work through, in public, where I see postmodern forms helping, where I find them less helpful, and where I want to retain, still critically, aspects of the neo-Marxist traditions that I think have been too easily moved away from.

Q: Let me go back to one of your last books, *Official Knowledge.* At the same time, you embedded in the text theory and some research. You are not known as an empirical researcher, but yet you feel the tension of going back to produce or review data. But what I found in this book is that every time you moved from a narrative into a more political analysis, you are apologetic. Was that a rhetorical strategy or was that part of these tensions of going back and forth between the demands of politics and actions?

A: It's both. I struggle very hard at making books approachable. I work hard to rewrite, to make certain that the crucial points can be understood at many levels. I think it's very important, and also hard work. So part of it is my commitment to a readership. This is where I reject the negative arguments about the politics of clarity that we are attempting to deskill an audience. People in their daily lives who are not privileged to be at universities having the privilege to spend time doing stuff like this, who have to struggle throughout their daily lives, do not need to be spoken to in our all-too-usual mystified neologistic ways. We need to meet them halfway. However, some critical scholars may be a bit too arrogant when they say that this implies that I am arguing that "ordinary people are not smart enough to get it," or that "we prevent them from learning serious theory." This is not my point at all. Reality is complicated, and we must not damage that complicated quality. I do not ever want to write simply, because I think that is, in fact, a deskilling process. But, and I argued this as strongly as I possibly could in *Teachers and Texts*, I think that the reader is not the only person who has to struggle over this process of understanding. Trying to be clear is part of a political commitment on the part of those of us who, again, have the luxury of time to help people think about this. Otherwise, I do believe we are being arrogant. There is a very real politics of writing and of how we treat our audience.

Q: This is very much Marx's suggestion when he was criticized for his style in the 1844 *Philosophical-Economic Manuscripts* of being unclear. He argued, "This is the process of research." But then you have to think about the process of exposition of the research. It's a very different attempt.

A: That's what I attempt to do. I write, and then I ask for criticism from all kinds of people. Part of it is an attempt to make certain I am taking seriously those commitments I believe in. I do the research, and then write the first draft, second and third and fourth drafts of a book. I give it to people to look at. That's why there is this long list of acknowledgments in my books. I say, "Look at this. What do you think?" This enables me to learn from multiple groups of people—scholars, activists, etc.—not just conceptually but learning how to put my ideas down on paper so that they can be engaging. I don't think we should learn to write simply, but I think it is part of our past, pedagogically, to engage people in a way that provides the door for people to struggle with us, but the door must be provided by all of us.

Then there's the rhetorical theme. I do want people, when they're reading my material, to feel as if I'm talking to them. I do not want to be just some author talking to some invisible reader. Because of this, I do employ some rhetorical strategies. I do sometimes say, "If you are a little worried about the theory, you can skip the next three sections and go on." I do that in a historical chapter in *Official Knowledge*, knowing full well that there are multiple kinds of readers of my books.

I am still a teacher, and all of us, no matter what we are in the academy, are teachers, first and foremost. No matter how much we write, we're teachers. That's our profession. So whether you're in a nursing school, or in a law school, or in cultural studies, or in sociology, or in education, you're a teacher. At the same time, we are writers and we do have the luxury of stepping back. There ought to be some worry about that. It is very seductive to define ourselves only as "writers of theory" and to forget about the grittiness of reality. It's that tension that is the most productive part of what keeps me going. I must always act with the realization that there are real schools, real children, real teachers. We have to find ways of dealing with the tension of wanting to make a difference in real people's lives and needing to step back to make sense out of it. That is a tension I feel all the time. When I stop feeling that tension, I think I may be in danger of losing my commitments as a critical educator.

Q: I see my own writing as a very strange combination of pleasure and agony. Pleasure because you try to disentangle your understanding of the complexities of reality. And the agony of it comes, first of all, from whether you get that understanding or not. But there's another aspect that's involved there, which is whether what you are saying is going to make a difference. If someone approached me now and said, "Give me one paragraph that impacted you from Apple's book, *Official Knowledge*," I could cite many, but the following one is particularly telling:

> The very idea that there is one set of values that must guide the "selective tradition" can be a great danger, especially in contexts of differential power. Take, as one example, a famous line that was printed on an equally famous public building. It read, "There is one road to freedom. Its milestones are obedience, diligence, honesty, order, cleanliness, temperance, truth, sacrifice, and love of country." Many people may perhaps agree with much of the sentiment represented by these words. It may be of some interest that the building on which they appeared was in the administration block of the concentration camp at Dachau. (Apple, 1993: 63)

I had to put the book down, think about it, my own feelings in relation to your writing, and how the rhetorical strategy was one that really had impacted me.

A: I want people to understand that these are life and death issues, and when we are writing it is torture to get it right, although I don't ever think that I do get it totally right. Every book is a sequel. Writing is self-formative. I think that we have to understand that writing is a way in which you form yourself as well as, hopefully, help other people form themselves. When a book is done, and it is always a torture and a pleasure (I think those are lovely metaphors for this constant turmoil), I already know as much as any author can that there may be holes in my arguments large enough for a truck to go through. Thus the task of the next book is to say, "Okay. The arguments in that book were until further notice. Here is my further understanding."

Sometimes we need to use metaphors to shock. This helps us understand contradictions, as I try to show in *Teachers and Texts* and *Official Knowledge*. In my recent work, I am trying to use some postmodern traditions as well as political economy, class analysis, analyses of ideology. I want to blend those together, to let them rub against each other, so that contradictions are visible. Bourdieu has a brilliant phrase that simply says, "Progress is made from trespassing." As I mentioned in the earlier talk with you, I'm not in a church. I'm not worried about heresy. What I'm worried about is getting it right and helping myself and other people keep this vast river of democracy flowing; knowing that there are multiple streams in it, and it's not my task to judge which of these streams is always right; but given this vast river, to make certain that the pieces that I'm deeply involved in continue. I want people to remember, when I'm talking theoretically about the nature of texts, that some of these points can be quite paradoxical and contradictory. Thus, I want to say, "Remember Dachau, where some of these sentiments were expressed." Now that's a slightly posty position. It implies that one should say, "Wait a minute, even your best intentions can work against progressive things."

An example would be in *Education and Power*, where I talk about contradictory ideological moments in all of this. Those more "neo" traditions said exactly the same thing, and I think many times they actually said them better and with more political efficacy than some of this stuff that comes out of newer traditions. That's again one of my worries, that we have found new ways of saying old things but in the process have depoliticized what is going on. But I still want to take seriously the fact, and I want it to jar, that we need to stop and examine contradictions in what we assume is the case.

There are many colleagues of mine throughout the world who have now turned to Foucault. Yet they have simply turned him into a more elegant theory of social control. Their position is more Nietzsche, not Foucault, but they combine the two. Foucault becomes no longer a form of serious self-reflexivity in which you stop and think about what your "political" grounds are, and this is the most positive moment in Foucault. In many ways, it's an excuse to move back to something like the theories employed by Bowles and Gintis. There's no agency; discourse is simply structuring you; the world is a vast radio set with a lot of stations coming in at the same time; you can't turn them off. Even turning them off is another discourse. That's silliness. That's self-refuting. So I want to find a style that enables people to stay self-reflexive,

and sometimes that requires the shock, the paradox. That is
something that I need. Whether other people need it, I don't
know. But obviously from your reaction it works.

Q: Education is, above all, a process to persuade others about
the strength of an argument or how compelling an ethical
imperative can be. In politics there is an instrumental element involved that is really to win one position or idea over
another. It is really to succeed, and to succeed in a way that
someone fails. I mean, in politics, really, the notion of zero
sum is a reality whether we like it or not. But you cannot say
that in politics everybody wins or everybody loses. I have
argued that, at some point, we should look into the politics
of educating for tolerance and the notion of oppression and
hegemony. In response, I have been accused of using an
instrumentalist view of politics. That is a very postmodern
criticism. How would you react to that?

A: It's a very complicated issue. There are some feminists for
whom I have great respect, who have argued that any construction of a zero sum game, anything that makes it seem
like win-loss, is the ultimate embodiment of masculinist
reasoning. It is simply one more way in which dominance
is reconstructed in society. I have some sympathy with that
position. On the other hand, there are, objectively, winners
and losers right now. As one example, the rightist coalition
that is currently so powerful has created conditions, material
and ideological, in which people starve on the streets. This
must be taken very seriously. We cannot simply say that we
should engage in educational activity to dialogue over these
beliefs, that we can't construct this as a war or battle, because
those are masculine forces. There is a danger in my taking this position. What gives me the right to say that they're
wrong? Well, I'm sorry, but I don't find myself paralyzed
by relativism. I think that there are ways of justifying, on
an intellectual and political level, particular concerns with
politics, ethics and morality. We want to use tolerance in two
ways. We want to talk about tolerance as a search in which
we will not become Stalinists or we will not be so secure in
our own reasoning that we no longer listen to the discourses
of people we may call "the rightist other." On the other hand,

that can be quite paralyzing unless we take seriously the collective struggles for transforming material conditions that create ways in which we are in identifiable groups: African Americans, poor people, Latinos and Latinas, etc. Unless we take seriously the fact that this will be a struggle in which there will be winners and losers, we're engaging in mystification. I don't want simply to impose a solution. I want a democratic solution to evolve, but I think it's very important that we understand what oppression looks like and what the struggles are against it. The solution is not simply establishing discussion groups, since the material conditions limit the voices who will be heard. So a lot depends on who is issuing the discourse of tolerance and what its uses are socially.

Q: Early on you were very critical of the new social policy that has been advanced by the Clinton administration. Have you changed your perceptions?

A: In *Official Knowledge* and *Cultural Politics and Education*, I argue that the rightist coalition is very broad. It has economic modernizers, old Tories, members of the new middle class, education efficiency experts, authoritarian populists of the New Right religious groups, etc. It actually is very tense, fracturing all the time and having to be rebuilt. It has changed the way we think about social policy in education. I'm "horribly pleased," that is, I'm pleased that I was right and horrified by the fact that most of the predictions in *Official Knowledge* are coming true, that the Right has transformed the terrain on which we are dealing. We have in fact transformed the meaning of democracy, so now it's almost all about consumption practices. We have de-classed, de-raced, and de-gendered people, de-sexed them, de-territorialized them in some ways, so that we're all individuals. What's public is bad, and what's private is good, by and large. There are, of course, contradictory things happening. As we look at what is going on in class, race, gender, and other kinds of terms, the state is still an arena of struggle. But the discussion almost always now occurs on the terrain of the Right.

One of the first things that Clinton did was to promote the right to abortion. That's quite interesting. Out of this politics, there are certain gains that are now institutionalized within the state over women's right to choice. While this was progressive on many other kinds of things, the state is still profoundly a racial state. Clinton has tried to build some moderate policies in reaction to Reagan/Bush, who aggressively used the state to support attacks on gains that people of color made. That will be mediated now, so over some racial politics there will not be a radical transformation but a moderating influence. Yet, in terms of economic form, it will still be based on the rapaciousness of the commodification system. We are also seeing a rapid growth of rightist nativism, which says protect our borders, kick out the immigrants. I think Clinton's intuitions economically are slightly right of center, but in a time when the center has moved remarkably to the right, this makes Clinton seem liberal. I don't want to be too negative, however. I think, as well, there will be some gains, continual gains, over the politics of bodies. That is, I think it will be harder for there to be utter murderous discrimination against gays and lesbians, people with HIV/AIDS, as an example. There will be some transformations, and I don't want to say that those are not major ones, because people's lives are at stake here. Yet, in general, by and large in the economy, in the role of the state in supporting capitalist social relations, there will be basically a continuation of "moderate" yet increasingly rightist policies that would have been considered quite conservative thirty years ago.

In education, Clinton gets support from many people who are "progressive," because of the great fear of privatization and the great fear of the racial terrain that is being established. He will use the bully pulpit of the federal government to argue against total privatization and that's had some effect. I think Clinton will slow the movement toward voucher plans and total privatization. But I think privatization and choice programs will grow massively at a state level. We'll have poor schools with declining budgets for the poor inner-city kids and rural kids, largely made up of kids of color and poor whites, and we'll have the relatively affluent in schools in other areas. And one of the reasons is that Clinton has not taken a strong position. He hasn't effectively used the power of the state. Because he has not taken a strong stance in educating the public about what the outcomes would probably be (by and large, I think his intuitions are relatively conservative), what we'll have is a partly failed presidency that, under the aegis of "we want to keep the far Right out," cements much of the discourse and practices of a more slightly moderate rightist principle in the economy and social welfare, etc.

Take, for instance, his proposal that says after a few years someone must be off welfare. Well, there's no money to create state jobs, so all you're doing is saying, "You're out of here." The effect is to export the blame onto the backs of people by saying they don't want to work. Given the economic crisis that I think will get even more severe for those on the bottom, even if someone is ultimately elected in the next decade under a slightly more moderate but partly progressive regime, there's not much that can be done since not only will money not be available but rightist policies will be even more dominant in government. So I'm quite pessimistic about what can happen. But I do want to support Clinton where he has made gains. I think he should be given some credit on the politics of people's bodies and certain parts of a moderate women's agenda, etc.

It will be imperative for multiple progressive groups to form alliances to keep pressure on him, and on Congress in general. He has some intuitions that aren't more progressive, and pressure must be placed by educators, by women's groups, by people of color, in combination, to make certain that some sort of united movement keeps them moving in a direction that moderates the rightist tendencies that are incredibly well funded. If anything, what his victory did was to make the Right redouble its efforts at the local, state, and regional levels.

Often, the Right has contested through "stealth" politics. That is, generally, they keep their real politics and real agenda from the public. They have won many elections this way. The Right is building an ideological infrastructure on sewer commissions, on planning boards, on school boards, that will mean that it may make little difference what Clinton does, by and large. The Right is building the infrastructure from below. Those of us who call ourselves progressives have a lot to learn from them. They have learned how to mobilize successfully at many levels. Thus, we've got to focus on Clinton and push that administration in a progressive direction, but in the meantime we've got to redouble our efforts at the local level.

Q: Some people argue that you have become a cultural and educational icon of the Left in the United States and internationally. Some argue that you are not a token leftist in Madison because Madison has a tradition of progressive thought. Others may argue that, despite your transformation, you still work from a critical neo-Marxist ideology that enables but also constrains some of your options. It could be argued, I think wrongly, that to endorse a neo-Marxist agenda in academia now is to remain isolated, because there is no social movement to back you up. If what you are saying cannot be grounded in the experience of people who are exploited and are trying to change it, then you could become a crier in the desert. How do you relate these criticisms to your own trajectory? Also, what have you done to enhance the presence of this kind of critical thought?

A: Yes, I do have an endowed chair. I'm quite proud of having gotten that, and that has to do with my autobiography. I'm a kid from the working-class inner city who went to night school and made good in the midst of an institution that is filled with people who never had to experience poverty. Yet, when I look back on my life, I owe deep debts to many people for what I have become. However, of all the people I went to high school with, most of them never got the opportunity to become this. So, in a paradoxical way, it reminds me of my grounding. On the other hand, there's a sense of victory. That is, whatever mobility exists in the United States, none of it was a gift. It all came about through struggle, social movements pushing the state, pushing civil society to say you can no longer do this to us. There's a recognition of collective victory in the fact that somebody like Michael Apple can get to have a distinguished professorship.

I don't think about the distinguished professorship. It's almost beside the point. I'm still doing what I have to do. There is a certain sense of personal pride and gratification in gaining it without making political compromises. As you know, I come from a long family of printers: my grandfather was a printer; my father was a printer; I worked my way through undergraduate school as a printer.

Both my father and my mother were political activists who struggled against oppression and for a better life for their children. In their mind, now they're justified, not just socially but personally, when they look and say, "That's our son." I think there's a certain amount of pride that goes with that. But by and large, I don't think that the recognition has changed me at all. I would hope not. I don't think about it, but it's nice to have it, and it would be a lie to say it's not nice, not just for me, but for the people whose shoulders I stand on.

Now what does it mean in terms of institutions? Well, Madison is a very special place. Wisconsin has a very long history of progressive activity. The fact that someone who is not quiet about his political position, is ratified by an institution where there are very limited numbers of endowed chairs, says something about the institution. I've worked in an institution where you are not alone about these kinds of things. There's a very different tradition in Wisconsin than in many other institutions. The assumption is that everyone is doing serious work, and that serious work is empirical, historical, conceptual, critical. It says that there are multiple kinds of such work and that there's respect for all of it. That says something not about how easy it is here but about, again, successful struggles that have been waged over time. Thus, we need a sense of history. This place was not just there; it was built by real people with real political commitments. I don't want to romanticize it. I don't think this place is perfect at all. But it has enabled me, and not just me but many others, to do very interesting and important work in teaching, and especially in research.

While "I" think I've been relatively effective here, a better word that should be used is "we." This institution sought me out. They seek out many other people. The School of Education here is known for that. It's a center of critical work, with the stress on the word *critical*. Over the last seven or eight years in Educational Policy Studies and in Curriculum and Instruction, let's say ten people have been hired. Seven have been women, a number have been gay and lesbian activists, and a number are activists in antiracist struggles and scholarship. Thus, you've got an institution that has been a site of progressive movements. While I was relatively alone in terms of overtly political kinds of research when I got here in 1970, that's always been highly respected, and this is now a center for such work. Thus, I don't want to say it's all Michael Apple. That is, there are institutional conditions for doing this. This kind of critical work is done in the subject-matter and teaching-methods areas as well. For example, we have people in mathematics education who do mathematics and critical race theory. That's quite remarkable. The institutional climate, hence, has an effect not just in the "normal" sort of general areas, sociology, curriculum studies, etc., but in what are called the "content fields," including teacher education. While I think I may have had some hand in that, certainly I would never want to claim that Michael Apple is either the stimulus or the cause of any of this. Again, the best metaphor is that there's a vast river of democracy, and this place is one of the places that's in that river. This is not to say it has been easy. There are ideological battles. There are disagreements. There are debates over what counts as critical work, and there are debates—ones that are quite serious—over particular forms of postmodernism, over particular antiracist theories, over particular neo-Marxist constructions.

Wisconsin is not unitary. For example, there are cultural conservatives on the faculty here who do not always agree with their students' politics, but who do object to professorial arrogance and bad teaching. Yet alliances among the conservative faculty are formed, even though as educators pursuing good teaching, they may dislike those colleagues who seem quite unresponsive to students. There's an ethical quality to Wisconsin that I have tried to keep on track by forming such alliances around responsive and responsible teaching. I've played a serious role, but I think that certainly it's been a collective struggle, with me being one among many.

The danger in human beings is arrogance, that you think you have a lock on reality. This is especially a danger for people who call themselves critical. One of the things that I do not want is clones as doctoral students. As you know, I've had many highly talented students who went on to become quite well-known folks. I meet with my students every Friday afternoon. If I don't get reconstructed every time I walk into the Friday seminar ...

Q: ...you're dead.

A: That's right. My task is to let people stand on my shoulders, and that requires that they look back occasionally and say to me, "You were wrong." Not just then, but constantly, and that's what I want of my colleagues as well. I don't want people who only agree with my politics. Of course, I want people around me who are progressive, and I will fight for that. But broadly progressive, and that includes the politics of differently-abled folks and class and gender and race and sexuality. I want these things talked about and argued about. I want them integrated within daily discourse in education and research. But if everybody agrees with me, that's quite a bad situation, not just for them but for me as well.

There are multiple movements here, and there are people whom I respect, who respect me, and yet who disagree quite strongly with my politics, but who are progressive as well.

I don't find labels always useful. The fact that I've labeled myself, and was labeled by others, as a neo-Marxist pointed to something that I avow, which is the utter centrality of material analyses. But culture has its own materiality. It's not possible or desirable to always merge it back into the politics of political economy. Such an analysis pointed to the centrality of class relations, but that was not the only thing that was at its center. Yet, you couldn't do an analysis without considering it. It was one building block. Just as when you're building a house, you need more than one block. Class was one block. There are other blocks, and building a house out of one material means that when a hurricane comes it may fall apart. Speaking metaphorically, there are different kinds of hurricanes. There are hurricanes over the racial state, there are hurricanes over patriarchal relations. They all tend to intersect in real life. Power relations and dynamics are very complex.

Thus, I am always in transition. That is one of the reasons I worry a bit about identity politics movements. The self is always becoming, and I think that there is an essentializing quality to some of those movements that say "I am defined only by the fact that I am working class, or only by the fact that I am gay or lesbian." Of course, there's no unanimity within the gay or lesbian multiple and working-class communities about this, so I do not wish to create stereotypes. Yet I do worry that there are essentializing moments in this. We are all multiply subjective, we are multiply interpolated. I am always trying to figure out where I stand on these multiple movements. Clearly, *Official Knowledge* and *Cultural Politics and Education* are attempts by me to come to grips with this, with one foot in "newer" analyses and one foot remaining in structural and cultural analyses within a tradition that recognizes its roots in neo-Marxist analysis. I don't think that this tradition is passé at all. In fact, I think it is a linguistic sleight of hand to assume that it is. People making such claims are also in institutions that are supported by capitalist social relations, as well as racial relations and gender relations and other relations of power. It's simply a linguistic sleight of hand not to look at your own structural position and ask, "Who's paying my salary in order for me to make the claims that class is passé?" I think that asking such a question about one's own (dare I say) class position is absolutely essential. Without doing that, under the guise of total "postmodern" reflexivity, there ain't much reflexivity about one's other subjectivities at work here. I am always in the process of finding out who I am. It's quite existential, but I have nothing against that.

But there is great danger in forgetfulness. The democratic socialist tradition is constantly being rebuilt and placed in practice again. In the United States, I don't see that the decline of state bureaucratic socialism has had any effect whatsoever in my own position on what counted as socialism, and whether it's a good idea or not. We are always asked, "Can you find one example?" It was very difficult to find one model of already existing socialism that didn't have state bureaucratic elements that I and many others disagreed with. There are positive examples of it—Cuba, for a while, certainly Nicaragua before the incredible attacks on it, parts of the Yugoslavian experiences, etc. There are parts of many things that I still believe in very strongly; but I think that state bureaucratic socialism is a perversion of a particular philosophical, political, and economic idea. We need to have some of the gains that were made in the idea of democratic economic planning to be put together with political deliberation "from below," with autogestion as much as possible. I'm a socialist populist, and populism (not in its current rightist articulations) is important to me. That's in my mind a particular kind of radical democracy with an economy that is democratically deliberated over. There are strong elements of socialism within that, and I will avow that. I think it's very important.

Is there a social movement to create this? Certainly, the Right has built a movement that might be called a popular front. It will promise certain things about the economy that simply cannot be delivered because the nation-state no longer controls its own economy. The Right has been able to build an alliance by trying in a fictitious, as well as real way, to take seriously people's worries that some things are out of control. I think it's quite possible to take such populist sentiments and organize people now moving in an ultraconservative direction around a more progressive agenda, and to have them participate in forming that agenda at the same time. So I am actually optimistic about the failure of many aspects of the current rightist resurgence. But, that doesn't mean that politics will automatically move in a progressive direction. However, I think that there are spaces to act. Part of my task is to help form them and to be formed by them.

Personally, I am deeply involved in building a coalition of activists in education, in keeping a democratic socialist agenda alive in the United States, at the level of policy and at the level of practice. I want this agenda to be constantly reformed by similar agendas, by the multiple agendas about race, class, sexuality, disability, and so on. I want to help form, when possible, what I call in *Official Knowledge*, a decentered unity. Such a social movement is not unitary, it is decentered. But I still think we have a right to call it progressive. Part of my task is the restoration of collective memory. That's partly an educational issue. It also means not simply standing above the intellectual and ideological fray, but constantly reminding people who move too rapidly toward uncritical acceptance of some forms of postmodernist and poststructuralist theories. I want to maintain critical discussions over this so that people who I think have genuinely political interests don't become depoliticized under the guise of a new metanarrative. Of course, I benefit from these debates as well.

I don't think I'm crying in the desert at all. As a matter of fact, the Right could not have articulated people to a rightist agenda if there wasn't a real sense among so many people that things are truly destructively out of whack. People's intuitions, more and more, are that there is something seriously wrong with our economy. The Right has been able to export that blame onto racial and gender forms. The most interesting and massive political and educational project has been the rightist alliance and its ability to use these worries to suture people into their conservative project. That's very interesting. This has been an educational project, one that recognized the ferment that's in this society. It's not a desert. There's all kinds of things growing.

My task as a pedagogue is to try to help people grow in ways that I think are more productive. Many people do know that something is very wrong. And so I never feel alone. I certainly don't feel alone here, and I don't feel alone in terms of friendships and solidarity with groups throughout the world. I don't feel alone in terms of political ferment. This is a time when this society is up for grabs. While the Right has a huge amount of power and money, there's a lot of activism happening in schools and in other institutions. That's one of the reasons why I wanted to be connected closely with movements in schools, for example. As Jim Beane and I show in *Democratic Schools*, there's some remarkable stuff going on in schools around social justice and critical literacy. The Right would love to tell us, "It's a desert out there, you're alone." Well that's not true. There are real and vital social movements going on right now. The task is to have those movements begin to speak to each other. Not only do I not feel alone at all, but I will not give to the Right what they haven't won. If the group of people who are sisters and brothers in the larger movement of what I call the river of democracy have anything to say about it, we will show that while the Right has been powerful before, that doesn't mean that it always wins. That's where a sense of history is useful.

Q: Gramsci notes the pessimism of the intelligence and optimism of the will.

A: That's exactly the case. I say in my new books that anger is one of the things that keeps me going. If we return to the beginning of our conversation, the importance of that anger was made very clear to me by my older son's situation. This is a society where luckily my wife and I had economic and emotional resources to save his life.

Other people don't have the luxury of those resources. But having to fight the state apparatuses, the insurance companies, etc., seeing how power really does work, how this kind of economy makes it impossible for some kids to survive bodily, as well as in other ways, makes you angry. And you have a right to be. The anger that my younger son has about the injustices that pervade this society has led him toward political activism as well. I'm very pleased with that. While there's undoubtedly some intergenerational teaching going on here, there's evidence of genuine concern over the way people are treated. The task is to make that anger collective, and not to let it lead to arrogance. Anger is a very, very productive thing. It's one of the reasons again why I wanted to call on us not to be simply theorists, why we need to be grounded in the lives of students and teachers and community activists. Not to be engaged in a political practice is to make the anger simply rhetorical, and that's a bad thing. That's fake anger, not real anger, and if you'll forgive me for establishing categories here, I think that fake anger is not very productive.

Q: You have two new books?

A: Both are now published. One is a very different kind of book. The ASCD, the Association for Supervision of Curriculum Development, approached me, and said, "You've criticized, you've given principles and suggestions for how education could be transformed. But so far there's been no detailed description and analysis of what you think ought to go on." So I've finished a book called *Democratic Schools* with Jim Beane. ASCD has published over 100,000 copies of this book. It's one of their books that goes to all the members. In this book, I act not as an analyst but as a secretary. I am the amanuensis for four democratic schools that are educationally progressive and committed to social justice. Of course, democracy is a sliding signifier. It has multiple meanings. But I think there are ways of justifying particular definitions of it. I think that the book is a serious political and practical intervention. It is meant to show that there are real alternatives to rightist efforts to marketize and privatize schools.

The other is based on the John Dewey lecture that I gave on the politics of national curriculum and national testing. As I noted, that book is called *Cultural Politics and Education*. It goes further than even *Official Knowledge* in analyzing the Right and its agenda and in showing what's possible and what's not possible. Again, it is meant to be an intervention at the levels of policy and theory. When I began the book, I wanted to interrogate the proposals for national curriculum and to show how they were ultimately a stalking-horse for national testing and restratification, and are the first step, paradoxically, toward voucher plans and marketization. One of the reasons you have a national curriculum is so you can have national tests. Once a national test is put in place, it undoubtedly will be of the usual paper and pencil kind, largely because we can't afford anything else. That will ultimately lead to voucher plans. Once a test is in place, national tests will be a way of putting price tags on schools. Once you have choice plans for the private and public schools, you will provide a mechanism through which "consumers" can say, "That's a bad school. This is a good school." With this kind of mechanism, the market can be set loose, with predictable effects such as an actual increase in educational apartheid. Further, a national curriculum will reduce what counts as official knowledge to largely the knowledge respected by the conservative alliance. Kids with the gift of cultural capital from their parents, from elite and middle-class groups will do well on it, as usual; but this will be covered by the rhetoric of choice, standards, and accountability. Thus, I see my task as twofold: to interrogate critically the conservative restoration in education and the larger society; and to help make public the daily struggles to form an education in which democracy, caring, and social justice are not simply empty slogans.

The following is excerpted from "On Analyzing New Hegemonic Relations: An Interview," first published in Apple's *Ideology and Curriculum, Third Edition* (2004).

Q: What current political and sociological issues are now affecting education?

A: Right now there are major transformations going on. As an example, we are changing education into a commodity to be purchased. The very meaning of democracy now is consumption practices. What was once a political concept and practice, one based on collective dialogue and negotiation, is now a wholly *economic* concept. Under the influence of neo-liberalism now, the very meaning of citizenship is being radically transformed. The citizen is now simply the consumer in all too many countries. The world is seen as a vast supermarket. Schools and even our students (as in the case of Channel One in the United States where children are sold as a captive audience for commercial advertisers who market their products in schools) become commodities that are bought and sold in the same way everything else is bought and sold.

That is a major transformation in the way we think of ourselves. Thinking about citizenship as a political concept meant that to be a citizen was to participate in building and restructuring your institutions. To be a consumer is to be a possessive individual who is known by her or his products. You are defined by what you buy, not by what you do. Thus, the general sociological and economic movement that redefines democracy and citizenship into being a set of consumptive practices, and in which the world is seen as a vast supermarket, is having a major effect on education.

There is another movement, or rather movements, that I think are having a major effect as well. These movements are what some postmodern and poststructural theories are trying to represent. These movements are aimed more and more toward what we might call decentered unities—that is, political movements that are no longer centered only around class, labor unions, and our traditional assumptions about who the "real" historical actors are. Yet, these do not assume that a simple additive model is sufficient. Thus, they do not assume that adding race and then simply adding gender is enough. We are no longer centered around only race lines; we are no longer centered around only class lines; or we are not only centered around lines of sex/gender.

This partly responds to the partial fragmentation of social movements. There are black lesbian social movements; there are gay Hispanic and Latino social movements; there are movements based upon environmental destruction that combine race and class in complex ways. Therefore, there are large-scale collective movements, ones that most of us would associate with needed progressive transformation in society and education, but which our accepted theories may not recognize as major actors. This sense of fragmentation of "the" emancipatory project is unsettling for many critical educators. What were once certain as the defining issues (class, the economy, the state) have been added to. Issues of sexuality and the body, disability, postcolonialism, and many more have been not simply added but have been taken up as substitutes for struggles that many people have given their entire lives to. This situation has created a real crisis because the rightist movements are relatively coherent and the politics of the Left now are extremely fragmented.

In a number of recent books, I've argued that I am not in a church so I am not worried about heresy. But, I do have some reservations about some aspects of both postmodern politics and postmodern theories, especially when they lead us, as I said earlier, to ignore class and political economy and treat the world as a text. These forms of "romantic possibilitarianism" are worrisome to me. My own position is that I would hope for what I call a decentered unity—groups and movements that work together on a number of broad fronts. This has some similarity to past "popular front" politics that enabled people to join together rather than fighting against each other.

But I would broaden the range of politics and issues that are seen as important. The politics of the body around AIDS, for example, combines international economic struggles, the dominance of profit in the pharmaceutical and medical industries, the exploitation of Third World peoples, neo-liberal policies, masculinities and cultural struggles for women's rights, gay and lesbian rights, the control of the media and of the politics of representation, education in sexuality and its suppression by conservative movements, to name but some of the issues and movements that must be jointly involved if progress is to be made.

HIV/AIDS is not a "minor" issue. It is having a truly devastating effect on entire continents and is one of the areas in which class, race, gender, sexuality, anti-imperialism, colonial and postcolonial realities, and religion intersect. Economic, political, cultural, and educational struggles are all joined together here. It is no more and no less important than class and labor struggles or other battles over school policies and practices. It is not a replacement for other crucial issues, but one example of how certain issues require the building of coalitions across difference in order to effectively create counter-hegemonic alternatives. This is why the work of writers such as Nancy Fraser, Judith Butler, bell hooks, and others becomes so important. They are trying to chart an intellectually/politically/culturally defensible path that provides ways of understanding and acting on what are dynamics that now too often divide people who need to come together to deal with a range of oppressions nationally and internationally.

Let us be honest. This will be very hard to do, as will be the maintenance of equally important class, race, and sex/gender movements inside and outside of education. One of the major reasons for this is because of the increasing power of the new hegemonic movements that I talked about at the beginning of this interview. Ideological transformations that redefine citizenship, that redefine democracy, have as one of their effects that declassing, deracing, and degendering of people. That is, to define everyone as a consumer and democracy as individual consumer choice is a radically individuating project with a radically individuating set of identities attached to it. A politics of the left or multiple politics of the Left then become even more difficult.

Q: In what other ways does the resurgence or the strength of the current political right affect education?

A: I would like to talk here more proximally, more practically, closer to the realities of classrooms. Let's take textbooks as an example. More and more as the right gains power, especially the religious Right as well as the neo-conservative and neo-liberal Right, what we all too often find is the following at the level of the curriculum.

In the United States, even though there is no official rule that states this should be the case, the curriculum *is* the textbook in a large number of classes. Even though we don't have a national curriculum in the U.S. and we don't have a national Ministry of Education that says that all teachers must use textbooks, it is quite clear that, whether we like it or not, most teachers use textbooks. While they can choose among many texts, nearly all the textbooks look basically the same. This has to do with the political economy of textbook publishing. Textbooks are sold on a market and written to the specifications of what the most populous states want. Because of this market, any content that is politically or culturally critical or can cause a negative reaction by powerful groups is avoided.

Thus, at the level of the textbook we are witnessing a growing movement away from any kind of provocative material. Anything that can jeopardize sales is to be avoided. This has created a situation of what has been called "dumbing down" (meaning trying to make the textbooks quite simple and bland). Another effect of the increasing power of the Right is the movement toward quite conservative positions or away from many social democratic or certainly any radical position that might have been found in the core of the curriculum in earlier periods. Since the American curriculum was always a result of compromises over what and whose knowledge should be declared legitimate, it always had some progressive elements in it. Partially progressive discussions of race, gender, and class dynamics and histories had found their way into the curriculum after decades of efforts. While these elements are not now removed, they are made much "safer" and are integrated under much more conservative themes and perspectives.

These are important points because, in order for the dominant group to maintain their leadership, they had to compromise. They had to have some content about unions, about women, about the lamentable past (and even present) of racial dynamics in their history. Currently, we are seeing a movement away from that. But, we are also seeing a movement towards certain other kinds of things. For example, for the neo-conservative Right, the notion of tight control over schools becomes crucial as a way to make certain that the appropriate values and knowledge are taught to everyone.

Of course, their definition of "appropriate" is very different than, say, an antiracist perspective or one that assumes that knowledge is constructed through action, not pregiven and simply taught in such a way that the role of the student is only to master whatever content is given. Neo-conservatives are pressing for "a curriculum of facts." They want a national or state curriculum and national or state testing, and these in turn should be centered around the "accepted" facts that make up "real" knowledge and on the measurement of outcomes in which students and teachers are to be held strictly accountable for such mastery.

But facts are not alone as an emphasis. Accompanying this is a neo-conservative emphasis on reinstilling values in the curriculum of a conservative kind, and also having these values emphasized in the curriculum, in our teaching practices, and on the tests. All of this is indicative of the fact that, while some of the latest reform rhetoric stresses decentralization, just as often in reality control is just as likely to be going more and more toward the center.

Neo-conservatives are not alone here, as I said. At the same time, the most powerful element within the new alliance surrounding conservative modernization—neo-liberals—want a closer connection between schools, and the (paid) economy. (This again demonstrates that underpinning neo-liberal positions are patriarchal assumptions—and racial ones as well, a fact that is documented at much greater length in *Educating the "Right" Way* and *The State and the Politics of Knowledge*.)

One of the effects of this has been the growth of "school to work" programs.

Such things are contradictory. They have elements of good sense and bad sense within them. They involve positive possibilities in some ways, since many curricula are aimed toward university-bound students and the majority of poor students and/or even working-class students will never go beyond secondary school. (Whether or not you feel that it essential for all students to go beyond secondary is not the issue here.) This provides an opening for a discussion of a focus on a polytechnic education as something that is probably wise for *everyone*, not just the working class. There is a long history of such discussions, including the work of John Dewey and others. Thus, oddly enough, neo-liberal positions can provide space for a different kind of debate about the ends of education.

But the way this discussion has been defined is exactly the opposite. Neo-liberals are critical of existing definitions of important knowledge, especially that knowledge that has no connections to what are seen as economic goals and needs. They want creative and enterprising (but still obedient) workers. Flexibility and obedience go hand in hand here. Due to this, a creative and critical polytechnic education that combines "head, heart, and hand" is not sponsored by neo-liberals. The possible space for that discussion is closed down by an emphasis on an education whose role is primarily (and sometimes only) economic.

The movements associated with this aspect of the Right are having a profound effect at the level of textbooks, at the level of testing, and at the level of curriculum. To give another example, one of the mandatory courses that all teachers had to take in my own home state, Wisconsin, in order to become licensed or certified as a teacher was "Education for Employment." The legislation that mandated this also mandated that every curriculum unit in every subject from kindergarten to secondary school must have identifiable elements concerned [with] education for employment. Wisconsin has historically been one of the most progressive states in the entire nation. The fact that it has such legislation speaks to the growing power of the hegemonic discourse of neo-liberalism. One can see, again, that movement towards the Right is having a profound effect.

Finally, there is the authoritarian populist Right. They are making their position known quite strongly and are increasingly influential in conflicts over texts, over teaching and evaluation, and over the place of religion in the schools. (They want a "return" to fundamentalist and conservative evangelical religious emphases in the curriculum and/or a de-emphasis on secular perspectives in schooling.)

State-sponsored prayer in schools is illegal in the U.S. (In some states, you have moments of silence or the prohibition of state-sponsored school prayers is simply ignored.) The re-emphasis of conservative religious impulses by authoritarian populists is making teachers quite fearful of being attacked. In many schools' districts, teachers are increasingly cautious about what they teach and how they teach it, since they are deeply worried that the curriculum has become subject to severe criticism by religious conservatives, many of whom want to radically alter the curriculum to bring it into line with their own theological and moral positions.

So, with the rapid growth of such rightist populism, there is a growing feeling right now of mistrust of teachers, mistrust of the curriculum, and mistrust of the very idea of public schools among such conservative advocates. Not only do teachers throughout the U.S. feel that they are under attack from these various groups, but there has also been a rapid increase in the number of conservative parents who are now engaged in "home schooling." It is estimated that between 1.5 and 2 million children are now being schooled at home to "protect" them from the supposed ideological, spiritual, and moral dangers of public schooling. This number is many more than children in, say, charter schools—schools that get much more publicity but may be considerably less important than the growth of home schooling.

To this we need to add the repressive forms of compulsory patriotism that have now surfaced and the attacks on dissent in education, the media, and other institutions, and the hidden effects that this movement has had. As I've stated time and again, criticism is the sincerest form of patriotism.

It means that "this is our country as well" and we expect, demand, that it live up to the ideals for which it supposedly stands.

Obviously, I've only been able to give a bare outline of what is a very complicated, contradictory, and tense situation here. But I've discussed this in a much greater depth in *Cultural Politics and Education* and, especially, in *Educating the "Right" Way.*

CONTRIBUTORS

Jean Anyon is one of very few educational scholars whose work investigates the political economy of cities and schools. Her book, *Ghetto Schooling: A Political Economy of Urban Education*, was reviewed in the *New York Times* and is widely used and cited. She has written many scholarly pieces on the confluence of social class, race, and education, several of which are classics, and have been reprinted in over 40 edited collections. Her latest book is titled, *Radical Possibilities: Public Policy, Urban Education, and A New Social Movement*. On January 1, 2004, Jean and colleagues were awarded a $10 million grant from the National Science Foundation to set up a Center for Learning and Teaching Urban Mathematics. She teaches social and educational policy at the Graduate Center, Doctoral Program in Urban Education, City University of New York.

Michael Apple is the John Bascom Professor of Curriculum and Instruction and Educational Policy Studies at the University of Wisconsin, Madison. Among his recent books are the 25th anniversary third edition of *Ideology and Curriculum*, *The State and the Politics of Knowledge*, and the new second edition of his award-winning book, *Educating the "Right" Way*. The recipient of a Lifetime Achievement Award by AERA and of the UCLA

Medal, he has worked with educators, unions, governments, and dissident groups to democratize educational research, policy, and practice throughout the world.

Madeleine Arnot is Professor of Sociology of Education, Fellow of Jesus College, Cambridge University and a Fellow of the Academy of Social Sciences. She is an internationally recognized expert on gender, social class, and race equality issues in education, equality policies, and citizenship education. Her recent publications include *Reproducing Gender? Selected Essays on Educational Theory and Feminist Politics* (Routledge, 2002), *Challenging Democracy: International Perspectives on Gender, Education and Citizenship* (with J. Dillabough, Routledge, 2000), and *Consultation in the Classroom* (with D. McIntyre, D. Peddar, and D. Reay, Pearson, 2004).

Dennis Carlson is a Professor of Curriculum and Cultural Studies in the Department of Educational Leadership and a member of the Center for Education and Cultural Studies at Miami University, Oxford, Ohio. He is the author of *Leaving Safe Harbors: Toward a New Progressivism in American Education and Public Life* (2002), *Making Progress: Education and Culture in New Times* (1997), and *Teachers and Crisis: Urban School Reform and Teachers Work Culture* (1992). He is also the editor or coeditor of several books in education, including (with Michael Apple) *Power/Knowledge/Pedagogy: The Meaning of Democratic Education in New Times* (1998), and has published in major educational journals. He is president-elect of the American Educational Studies Association.

Greg Dimitriadis is Associate Professor in the Department of Educational Leadership and Policy at the University at Buffalo, The State University of New York. Dimitriadis is the author of *Performing Identity/Performing Culture: Hip Hop as Text, Pedagogy, and Lived Practice* (Peter Lang) and *Friendship, Cliques, and Gangs: Young Black Men Coming of Age in Urban America* (Teachers College Press, Columbia University). He is coauthor of *Reading and Teaching the Postcolonial: From Baldwin to Basquiat and Beyond* (Teachers College Press, Columbia University), *On Qualitative Inquiry* (Teachers College Press, Columbia University), and *Theory for Education* (Routledge). He is coeditor of *Promises to Keep: Cultural Studies, Democratic Education,* *and Public Life* (Routledge), *Learning to Labor in New Times* (Routledge), and *Race, Identity, and Representation in Education* (2nd ed.) (Routledge). He edits the book series "Critical Youth Studies" for Routledge.

Michelle Fine is a distinguished Professor of Psychology, Urban Education, and Women's Studies at The Graduate Center of the City University of New York. Her recent books include *Echoes of Brown: Youth Documenting and Performing the Legacy of Brown v. Board of Education* (with Rosemarie Roberts, Maria Elena Torre, Janice Bloom, April Burns, Lori Chajet, Monique Guishard, and Yasser Payne, Teachers College Press); *Working Methods* (with Lois Weis, Routledge); *Off White: Essays on Power, Privilege and Contestation* (with Lois Weis, Linda Powell Pruitt, and April Burns, Routledge); and *Changing Minds: The Impact of College in a Women's Maximum Security Prison* (with Maria Elena Torre, Kathy Boudin, Iris Bowen, Judith Clark, Donna Hylton, Migdalia Martinez, Missy, Melissa Rivera, Rosemarie Roberts, Pamela Smart, and Debora Upegui, (www.changingminds.ws).

Luís Armando Gandin is a Professor of Sociology of Education at the School of Education of the Federal University of Rio Grande do Sul in Porto Alegre, Brazil. He has earned his Master's degree in Sociology at the Federal University of Rio Grande do Sul and his Ph.D. in Education at the University of Wisconsin–Madison. He is the editor of the Journal *Currículo sem Fronteiras* (*Curriculum Without Borders*, http://www.curriculosemfronteiras.org), has published four books in Brazil and Portugal, and several book chapters and articles in peer-reviewed journals in Brazil, the United States, Australia and the United Kingdom. Professor Gandin's research interests are in the areas of sociology of education, educational policy, curriculum theory, and progressive educational reforms.

Andrew Gitlin is Professor of Elementary and Social Studies Education at the University of Georgia. His previous books include *Educational Poetics: Inquiry, Freedom, and Innovative Necessity*; *Becoming a Student of Teaching: Methodologies for Exploring Self and School Context*; *Power and Method: Political Activism and Educational Research*; *Teachers' Voices for School*

Change: An Introduction to Educative Research; and *Teacher Evaluation: Educative Alternatives.*

Allan Luke teaches educational sociology, discourse analysis, and literacy education at Nanyang Technological University, Singapore. His current work is on cultural and economic reproduction in Singapore schools and on the development of distinctive "new Asian pedagogies" in the contexts of political change, institutional and cultural practice, and economic globalization.

Cameron McCarthy teaches mass communications theory and cultural studies at the University of Illinois at Urbana-Champaign, Illinois. He is Research Professor, Communications Scholar, and University Scholar at the Institute of Communication Research. He has published widely on topics related to postcolonialism, problems with neo-Marxist writings on race and education, institutional support for teaching, and school ritual and adolescent identities in journals such as *Harvard Educational Review, Oxford Review of Education, British Journal of the Sociology of Education, Studies in the Linguistic Sciences,* and *International Studies in Qualitative Research.* Cameron has authored or coauthored the following books: *Race and Curriculum* (Falmer Press, 1990), *Race Identity and Representation in Education* (Routledge, 1993), *Racismo y Curriculum* (Morata, Madrid, 1994), *The Uses of Culture: Education and the Limits of Ethnic Affiliation* (Routledge, 1998), *Sound Identities: Youth Music and the Cultural Politics of Education* (Peter Lang, 1999), *Multicultural Curriculum: New Directions for Social Theory, Practice and Policy* (Routledge, 2000), *Reading and Teaching the Postcolonial: From Baldwin to Basquiat and Beyond* (Teachers College Press, Columbia University, 2001), *Foucault, Cultural Studies and Governmentality* (SUNY Press, 2003), and *Race, Identity and Representation, Volume Two* (Routledge, 2005).

Yoshiko Nozaki is Assistant Professor at the Department of Educational Leadership and Policy, State University of New York at Buffalo. She earned her Ph.D. at the University of Wisconsin-Madison, where she studied curriculum history, educational anthropology, cultural studies, and critical and feminist theories. She was a social studies teacher in Japan in the 1980s, and has also had teaching experience in the United States, Australia, and New Zealand.

Carlos Alberto Torres, a political sociologist of education, is Professor of Social Sciences and Comparative Education at the Graduate School of Education and Information Studies, University of California, Los Angeles. He is jointly with Paulo Freire the founding Director of the Paulo Freire Institute in São Paulo, Brazil (1991), founding Director of the Paulo Freire Institute, UCLA (2002), and founding Director of the Paulo Freire Institute, Argentina (2003). Past President of the Comparative International Education Society (CIES) he has been Director of the Latin American Center at UCLA (1995–2005) and he is currently the President of the Research Committee of Sociology of Education, International Sociological Association. Author of more than 50 books and 175 research articles and chapters in books and encyclopedias, his most recent publication is a novel, in Portuguese, *The Manuscript of Sir Charles* (Lisbon, Dom Quixote, 2005).

Lois Weis is Distinguished Rrofessor of Sociology of Education at the University at Buffalo, The State University of New York. She is the author or coauthor of numerous books and articles pertaining to social class, race, gender, and schooling in the United States. Her most recent books include *Class Reunion: The Remaking of the American White Working Class* (Routledge, 2004); *Working Method: Research and Social Justice* (with Michelle Fine, Routledge, 2004); *Silenced Voices and Extraordinary Conversations: Re-Imagining Schools* (with Michelle Fine, Teachers College Press, 2003); and *Beyond Black and White: New Faces and Voices in U.S. Schools* (with Maxine Seller, State University of New York Press, 1997). She sits on numerous editorial boards and is the editor of the "Power, Social Identity and Education" book series with SUNY Press.

Geoff Whitty has been Director of the Institute of Education, University of London, since September 2000. He was previously the Karl Mannheim Professor of Sociology of Education. His main areas of teaching and research are the sociology of education, education policy, and teacher education. His recent publications include *Making Sense of Education Policy* (Sage, 2002) and *Education and the Middle Class* (with Sally Power, Tony Edwards, and Valerie Wigfall; Open University Press, 2003).

INDEX

A

Abortion, 230
Abu El-Haj, Thea, 161
Achievement testing, standardized, 129
Acker, Sandra, 31
Activism, political, anger and, 239–240
Acton, Lord, 49
Advanced Placement (AP), 148
Advocacy research, 24
Affirmative culture, 174–175
A Framework for Understanding Poverty,
      105
African Americans, language and, 105,
      107
"Aha! Process," 105–107
AIDS, social issues, 243–244
Althusser, Louis, 71, 86n4, 193–194
American Educational Research
      Association, viii, x
A Nation at Risk, 95
Antiessentialism, 82–84
Antiscience, 74, 75, 87n8
Anyon, Jean, viii, 2, 10, 26, 37–44, 211
Appadurai, Arjun, 162
Appalachian youth, language and, 105
Apple, Michael W.
      anger and political activism,
         239–240

Brazil and, 185–200
Citizen School Project, 158–159,
      190
on Clinton administration, 230–232
commonsense, 171
conservative modernization,
      211–213
contesting research, 163
critical studies, 160
culture and politics, 209–211
on current social movements,
      235–239, 241–248
curricular reform, 100–101
dominance in education, 148
early influences on, 204–207
effects of, 213–214
Geoff Whitty on, vii–x
hegemony defined, 58, 195
ideology and neo-Marxism, 193
impact of Right on, 220–222
influence of, 1–2
interview with Carlos Torres,
      219–241
on knowledge, 69, 167–168, 181–182
on Madison, Wisconsin, 232–235
on neo-Marxism, 185–186, 193,
      222–224
neo and post traditions, 207–209